PRAISE FOR TONY LEON'S PR

Future Tense

'From the vantage point of years in active politics, Tony Leon provides a lucid analytical balance sheet of SA Ltd 2021. Eschewing political correctness, Leon tells it as he sees it.'
– Judge Dennis Davis

'Anyone who wants to understand South Africa today – a country so beautiful, yet so broken – simply has to read this book.'
– Niall Ferguson, author of
The Ascent of Money and Civilization: The West and the Rest

Opposite Mandela

'In the confiding, winningly self-deprecatory style that defines Leon's authorial voice, he offers us a unique personal insight into Nelson Mandela and guides us, engagingly and provocatively, through the most turbulent and exciting times in contemporary South African politics.'
– John Carlin, author of *Playing the Enemy*

'A frank, fair-minded memoir of the Mandela years by a political opponent whom Mandela himself clearly liked and respected.'
– JM Coetzee

The Accidental Ambassador

'As a fellow accidental ambassador, reading Tony Leon's adventures in the land of the original Evita and the gauchos reminded me there are reasons to be grateful we live in South Africa after all.'
– Evita Bezuidenhout

On the Contrary

'Magisterial ... Written with effortless authority and with unique access.'
– Peter Godwin, author of *Exit Wounds*

ALSO BY TONY LEON

Hope and Fear:
Reflections of a Democrat (1998)

On the Contrary:
Leading the Opposition in a Democratic South Africa (2008)

The Accidental Ambassador:
From Parliament to Patagonia (2013)

Opposite Mandela:
Encounters with South Africa's Icon (2014)

Future Tense:
Reflections on My Troubled Land (2021)

Being There
Backstories from the political front

TONY LEON

JONATHAN BALL PUBLISHERS
JOHANNESBURG • CAPE TOWN

All rights reserved.
No part of this publication may be reproduced or transmitted,
in any form or by any means, without prior permission
from the publisher or copyright holder.

© Text Tony Leon 2025
© Cover image 2025 by Nardus Engelbrecht
© Published edition 2025 Jonathan Ball Publishers

Published in South Africa in 2025 by
JONATHAN BALL PUBLISHERS
A division of Media24 (Pty) Ltd
PO Box 33977
Jeppestown
2043

ISBN 978-1-77619-381-3
ebook ISBN 978-1-77619-382-0

Every effort has been made to trace the copyright holders and to obtain their permission for the use of copyright material. The publishers apologise for any errors or omissions and would be grateful to be notified of any corrections that should be incorporated in future editions of this book.

jonathanball.co.za
X.com/JonathanBallPub
facebook.com/JonathanBallPublishers

Cover by Sean Robertson
Design and typesetting by Martine Barker
Printed and bound by CTP Printers, Cape Town
Set in Garamond Premier Pro

*'Time present and time past
Are both perhaps present in time future,
And time future contained in time past.'*
– TS Eliot, 'Burnt Norton', from *Four Quartets*

*Dedicated to the memory of three patriots who
helped build democracy in South Africa:*

*Dene Smuts (1949–2016)
James Selfe (1955–2024)
Greg Krumbock (1960–2024)*

CONTENTS

I   THE IDEA

Introduction   3

II THE JOURNEY

1. Lunch with Arafat   9
2. Counting Jews with Sharon   20
3. Winning Lessons from 'Loser' Peres   28
4. Leadership Matters   34

III THE MONEY

5. The Art of the Ask   43
6. The Patrician and the Boytjie   48
7. Ronnie to the Rescue   58

IV THE NEGOTIATION

8. Creation   65
9. Endgame   102
10. Aftermath   129
11. Fractures and Finesses   149

V   THE EXPERIMENT

12. A Quiet Death, A Loud Aftermath   161
13. The Interview   165
14. Two Weeks Hate   169

VI THE REAPPRAISAL

    15 What If?   175
    16 FW de Klerk's Needle-threading   178
    17 Nelson Mandela's Mask   186
    18 Mangosuthu Buthelezi's Need   195

VII THE *NOSTOS*

    19 'Nostalgia Isn't What it Used to Be'   207
    20 A Personal Pentimento: Fresh Paint on Old Signs   213
          1. Twenty Votes   213
          2. Durban Days   217
          3. Hit Parade Nights   221
          4. Pampas Years   225
          5. On Da Nang Beach   231
          6. A Bar in Berlin, A Garden in Kanazawa   236

VIII THE RETURN

    21 Return to Parliament   245

Acknowledgements   251
Notes   252
Index   257

I
THE IDEA

'One doesn't recognise the most important moments of your life until it's too late.'

– Agatha Christie

Introduction

One of my favourite philosophers, Marx (Groucho), apparently said: 'I have inner beauty, but no camera has yet been invented to capture it.' The other, entirely humourless Marx (Karl) offered more profound thoughts, but since millions were killed in pursuit of his 'scientific' philosophy, all things considered I'd choose Groucho over Karl.

Being There was written to capture several often-elusive aspects from my life to date, both from a very public career and from earlier years before it commenced. It is my own camera into what happened at certain times and who starred on the stages described, and, entirely subjectively, I try to capture both personalities and places.

The idea behind this book, suggested by Jeremy Boraine, publisher-at-large for Jonathan Ball Publishers, is to tell the backstories and provide some colour on interesting, even dramatic events beyond the sepia-tinged mythology that encrusts many of them now.

In the stories I recount, I go back to personal events and some major political dramas in which I was involved to explore purpose and even a hidden meaning or two, hopefully without too heavy a touch. Some of them illuminate present and, perhaps, future times too.

In some cases, recent information offers new light on some famous personalities since I last wrote about them in earlier books (for example, my reappraisal of presidents FW de Klerk and Nelson Mandela). I also explore more mundane singular experiences to excavate contemporary meaning from past times. For example, returning to my boarding school 50 years after matriculating conjured memories not entirely congenial about obedience to authority but also showed the adaptiveness of old institutions.

Sitting on a beach in Vietnam allowed contemplation of how one small nation, which was the graveyard of empires and poster child for left-wing anti-Americanism at the height of its war with the US, managed years later to embrace both an aggressive capitalism and admiration for Donald Trump. A visit to Japan and a political gathering in Berlin provided reminders of how two aggressor nations that engulfed the world in the greatest conflagration in human history later carved out very different peaceful futures after their near extinction in the world war they started.

Argentina, situated on the other side of the South Atlantic, provides this book with another lens for home thoughts from faraway. My work and life there were vastly different from anything I had experienced before. Yet political pathologies and siren songs, including the 'hate as hope' brand of populism, whether sung in Spanish by Evita Perón or in isiZulu by Jacob Zuma, are eerily similar.

In today's 'cancel culture' world (also explored in this book) it is probably incautious to quote Woody Allen. But he offered the best one-line explanation of how timing, chance, circumstance and career can affect your life and the direction it takes – and not least the people you meet on the journey. He said: 'Most of success in life is just showing up.'

I had a lot of encounters that happened when I 'showed up'. One of these relates to journeys to the Middle East, where I met some of the leaders embroiled in the region's never-ending conflicts. On one occasion, more authentic meaning was gleaned from the humble driver of the official car than from a president or prime minister whose private conversations mirrored the same clichés as their appearances provided on television. However, not every political leader is cut from this cloth and, as some of the pages following offer, there are those who inspire and innovate.

Politics has been memorably defined as 'show business for ugly

INTRODUCTION

people'. And, looks aside, there are a lot of rum characters in the political world, some of whom – together with their enablers and funders – you will meet in these pages.

Although I left parliamentary politics and the leadership of my party in South Africa back in 2009, it was the unexpected call from the current leader of the Democratic Alliance (DA) that led me back into the ring in June 2024. I retell here in some (necessary) detail precisely what happened when South Africa underwent the novel, often hair-raising experience of forming a coalition government, necessitated when, for the first time in 30 years, the mighty African National Congress (ANC) tumbled at the polls. I also explore how likely (or not) is the endurance of its second government of national unity (GNU) and the chokepoints on its fragile progress to date.

I have had five different, often intersecting careers: I was at different times, briefly, an attorney, an academic and a diplomat; for far longer I was a politician; and latterly I have been in business, chairing a strategic communications company.

For most of this time I have also been an inveterate scribbler of notes, diaries, journals and many newspaper columns and – to date – have published five books. This is the sixth.

Writing is a daunting, even haunting undertaking, whether it is each Tuesday morning facing a blank computer screen and a looming deadline for my newspaper column or setting out the first lines of this book and the long journey to its final chapter.

A few years ago, I hosted a lunch in Cape Town for a writer I greatly admire. Roger Cohen is the Paris bureau chief of *The New York Times* and the author of many fine books and erudite columns. His parents were South African, and he was partly raised in this country. Recently, he inscribed to me his latest work, *An Affirming Flame: Meditations on Life and Politics*. Its subtitle well describes this book. Then there is the wisdom he offers on the creative process:

> A column needs a voice, or it is nothing. It requires an idea, and they do not fall to order from trees. The best columns

write themselves. They come, all of a piece, a gift from some deep place. They enfold the subject just so, like a halter on a horse's face.

Such inspiration is rare. Most columns resemble exquisite torture ... but also live or die on their ability to establish an emotional bond with the reader.[1]

This book is not a series of columns, although Cohen's testament to the process of writing fully resonates. I hope that *Being There* also establishes 'an emotional bond with the reader'. But that, of course, is for you to judge.

Tony Leon
Cape Town
March 2025

II
THE JOURNEY

*'Men and nations behave wisely when they have
exhausted all other resources.'*

– Abba Eban, Israeli statesman

1
Lunch with Arafat

My late mother, Sheila, of imperishable memory, totalled three husbands in her 72 years of life. She noted waspishly, 'If you get married three times, you choose each husband for a different reason.' My father, Ray Leon, was followed in line by Dick Prior and then Paul Schulz. This led a friend to accurately pun her 'Mrs Leon Prior to Schulz'.

Neither Dick nor Paul was Jewish – in contrast to my parents – and when, many years ago, Dick was asked by someone, 'What is your opinion of Zionism?' he responded, 'I can't really say, but I do embrace it every night!'

I had no such uncertainties, even though I was brought up in a very secular Durban home and attended Christian schools, and beyond the obligatory rituals of the faith – circumcision and a bar mitzvah – had only the vaguest knowledge about my religion. But Israel and its right and need to exist, and the price paid in blood and treasure for its existence, was hard-wired into my earliest memories. Even so, I was hardly an uncritical supporter of the expansionist aims of its right-wing governments, which dominated its polity from the 1990s onwards.

And then, of course, my own practical, as opposed to ideological, embrace of Israel came in 1996 when I commenced a relationship – soon to be consecrated by marriage – with an Israeli, Michal Even Zahav, my wife now for 24 years. (Incidentally our first meeting at a conference she organised in Jerusalem for an NGO, the Israel Forum, which she led, proved, in our case at least, that not every political jamboree is a waste of time, and this one had a happy real-life consequence.)

So, both matters of the heart and the swirl of political storms in the Middle East were a constant background to some immersive political journeys.

❏

The American Colony Hotel in East Jerusalem optimistically describes itself as 'an oasis of tranquillity in the Palestine-Israel conflict'. Certainly, its Ottoman architecture – it commenced its existence in the late nineteenth century as home to a grand pasha's harem – and distinguished guest list, which included TE Lawrence and Winston Churchill, give latter-day visitors wandering under its cool porticos and in its fragrant gardens the feeling of living history.

One day in early October 2002, it was the rendezvous point for my journey to meet the president of the Palestinian Authority, Yasser Arafat.

That trip gave me a closer understanding of Israel's existential angst and the human misery behind its occupation, since 1967, of the West Bank. It also offered insight into how South Africa then saw itself as some sort of mediator in the intractable struggle of Jew and Palestinian for the disputed sliver of territory between the Mediterranean Sea and the River Jordan. This would explode again 20-plus years later, on 7 October 2023, when Hamas insurgents invaded Israel from Gaza, slaughtering and raping 1 200 Israelis and kidnapping some 240 others, unleashing a furious and predictably violent and deadly response from Israel.

Going to meet Arafat in his compound at Ramallah – I had briefly met him when he visited South Africa a few years before – comported with the adage of one of my favourite writers, John le Carré, who wisely advised, 'a desk is a dangerous place from which to watch the world.'

But, beyond obtaining a first-hand view, there was a backstory to that visit, which centred on how South Africa's governing party, the ANC, would weaponise this conflict for cynical electoral gain and also, into the bargain, burnish its very tattered and extremely one-eyed credentials as champion of oppressed peoples and enemy of Western colonialism and white oppression (the very inexact, historically questionable template it applied to Israel as overlord of the suffering Palestinians).

As the ANC ceaselessly reminded voters, I was a white South African. When President Thabo Mbeki took umbrage at my critique of his disastrous, in fact deadly, Aids denialism (an estimated 350 000 South Africans needlessly died of HIV/Aids owing to his decision to ban antiretrovirals from state hospitals, according to an authoritative study[1]), he branded me 'the white politician [who] makes bold to speak openly of his contempt for African solutions'. This was in response to my jibe that his health minister's suggestion that an industrial solvent, Virodene, was a miracle cure for Aids (it was later banned as unsafe for human use) amounted to 'snake oil cures and quackery'.[2]

But the ANC got what is termed a 'twofer' (two for the price of one) by the fact that, added to my whiteness, I was of the Jewish faith (the first and to date only Jew to become leader of the official opposition) and – to cement a conspiracy of international dimensions – married to an Israeli.

This played itself out, a few months after Mbeki's 'white politician' sneer, in the December 2000 local government elections when I led the DA to victory in Cape Town. During that campaign, a series of posters had appeared in the heavily Muslim area of Athlone proclaiming, 'A vote for the DA is a vote for Israel,' against a background of the Israeli flag dripping with blood and barbed wire. The posters were allegedly distributed in the name of the 'Friends of Palestine'. While the ANC officially denied involvement, my party quickly found out that the printers responsible employed two brothers of ANC Western Cape leader Ebrahim Rasool, leading our strategist, Ryan Coetzee, to brand the ANC denial a lie.

I thus thought it both interesting and politically useful to meet Arafat in person and on home ground, reckoning that beyond going to see matters first hand, as Le Carré advised, it would rebut the stereotype of my alleged blind support for Israel and dismissal of any rights for Palestinians in this contested terrain.

The easiest part of the visit was to arrange it. My parliamentary office in Cape Town couldn't believe how quickly and efficiently the Palestinian embassy in Pretoria both obtained the go-ahead from Arafat's office for the meeting and then proceeded to interact with the South African diplomatic mission in Ramallah to fine-tune the logistics. I imagined that the prospect, and photo opportunity, of Palestine's leader meeting the Jewish leader of the South African opposition was an opportunity too good to miss.

From my point of view, the October get-together was ideal as I would be visiting Israel for my sister-in-law's wedding. But from the more vexed dateline of conflict in the Middle East, and between Israel and Palestine, getting to the rendezvous at that time was nothing if not hazardous.

The distance between East Jerusalem and Ramallah is barely more than 20 km, approximately the same as between Constantia and Sea Point – in normal times no more than a 30-minute drive in traffic.

But October 2002 was hardly a normal time in Ramallah and surrounds. There was something depressingly familiar about the cycle of violence and its endless doom loop. Earlier that year, Palestinian suicide bombers had concentrated attacks inside Israel, targeting civilians – including a gory Passover special when 30 Israelis were massacred during a celebratory dinner in Netanya. Israel responded by unleashing Operation Defensive Shield, something of a titular euphemism given that an estimated 500 Palestinians were killed and three times that number injured during the campaign in the West Bank.

By the time of my visit, Israel had banned Palestinian travel in much of the territory then under the notional control of Arafat's regime. Just weeks before I arrived at his headquarters, Israeli forces besieged the building and smashed many of the surrounding structures with bulldozers, demanding that the Palestinian Authority hand over terror suspects. A few days before my meeting, Israel ended its siege of Arafat's HQ after intense American pressure.

Surprised as I was that our meeting would proceed as scheduled, more surprises awaited me after my pick-up at the American Colony Hotel.

The first of these was meeting the young South African diplomat who headed the mission in Ramallah. She was around 30 years old and seemed both earnest and enthusiastic. Although like me a white South African, she had clearly 'gone native' – in the argot of British diplomacy – and shed the objective, even cynical detachment of the diplomat and was all-in on the Palestinian cause. She wore a *keffiyeh* – a scarf symbolising Palestinian resistance.

On meeting me, she gushed, 'What an honour you have received to be meeting the President' (Arafat). I had other ideas about it but kept my counsel.

After the Hamas attack on Israel on 7 October 2023, the *keffiyeh* became a mandatory item of dress for President Cyril Ramaphosa, ANC secretary-general Fikile Mbalula and sundry cabinet members. But by then both party and government – essentially indistinguishable – had given up all pretence at even-handedness in a conflict that had both curdled and massified in the intervening decades.

But it was the journey and the narrative provided by the embassy driver, an amiable middle-aged gentleman who advised me that he was a Palestinian-Armenian – an interesting ethnic combination imbued on both sides by decades of exclusion, marginalisation and worse – that was the most illuminating, arguably more so than the meeting itself.

The journey took about 90 minutes each way, with our progress – a generous description – at times glacial. Israeli checkpoints populated the route with ever-increasing frequency the closer we inched towards Ramallah. The South African pennant on the bonnet of the bullet-proof car and the diplomatic number plates front and back had little impact on the young Israeli soldiers who interrogated our driver closely and held us up for some time at each stop. This allowed the driver to give a full and frank account of – for him – the horrors of living under Israeli occupation.

He no doubt assumed that, since I was both from South Africa (one of Palestine's staunchest backers) and en route to an appointment with the hero of Palestinian liberation, I must be a strong sympathiser with the cause. He had no idea that I was in Israel to attend the wedding of my Israeli sister-in-law.

Many years before this drive, I received a useful tip from Michael Holman, the great journalist who was the Africa editor of the *Financial Times*. He advised, 'I always get my most useful intel from taxi drivers; they know the local buzz best.'

Or, in this case, the embassy driver. Unbidden by me, he catalogued the daily difficulties and humiliations which the Israeli occupation caused the locals, ranging from hours spent at checkpoints and difficulty in accessing employment opportunities or even hospital visits in Israel to the disdain of the occupation forces for the elderly and the infirm. Of any culpability borne by the notoriously corrupt, and arguably feckless, Palestinian Authority, he said nothing.

Just two years before this visit, Arafat had spurned the Camp David negotiations, which would have seen around 73 per cent of Palestinian land returned in the West Bank and 100 per cent of the Gaza Strip, and the right to administration, though not sovereignty, of East Jerusalem. But that would be, imperfect in design perhaps, at least the two-state solution. US President Bill Clinton, who brokered the talks, heaped blame on Arafat for their failure, pointing out that he simply walked away and made no counteroffer. And in the aftermath of this failure, the unleashing by Arafat of the so-called second intifada in part accounted for the stringent nature of the Israeli conduct the driver was complaining about. Still, on the Michael Holman principle of listening to the buzz from the driver, I took careful note. It was also clear that his views were sincerely held and deeply felt.

In many ways, his views were far more useful than the self-serving justifications that were soon to be offered by Arafat. The driver had the ring of unvarnished authenticity.

LUNCH WITH ARAFAT

The scene round Arafat's compound, when we finally arrived, was extraordinary. I advised a journalist I briefed afterwards that it resembled in real time the photographs I had seen of the rubble in Berlin at the end of World War II. Only Arafat's building had been spared bombardment or destruction, and the area around it was a wasteland, with even the Israeli bulldozers left in place outside.

After a very cursory security check by plainclothes Palestinian guards outside, I was led upstairs to the chairman's office, where the world-famous figure, dressed in military fatigues and *keffiyeh* and sporting his familiar (if scratchy on embrace) facial stubble, warmly kissed me and gestured for me to take a seat, which I duly did.

I noted that his desk was covered with papers and files spread in towering quantity. He was accompanied by a senior Palestinian figure whom I had met on previous occasions, Saeb Erekat, whose volubility and fluency in English compensated for the quieter ways of his boss.

Nevertheless, after some opening pleasantries, I commended Arafat for managing an appearance of normalcy inside the building given the scenes of destruction outside. He countered that he had not left the building once during the Israeli siege, no doubt an explanation for the Israelis' sparing it from the destruction visited on all the surrounding edifices. I was later advised that Prime Minister Ariel Sharon of Israel had given an undertaking to US President George W Bush that Arafat would not be harmed during the blockade.

I did venture to ask Arafat if he felt he bore any personal or political responsibility for the events in the immediate past – of which the wrenching scene outside bore grim testimony. He literally waved away the question, and any culpability, by airily stating that with the assassination of Israeli Prime Minister Yitzhak Rabin some seven years before (in November 1995), 'I lost both my friend and my partner for peace.' On hearing this I couldn't help but recall when Bill Clinton basically forced the monosyllabic Rabin to shake hands with Arafat on the White House lawn back in 1993: the expression on the face of Arafat's 'friend' was less a smile than a rictus.

I quickly realised that I would not glean much more from this encounter than I could see on CNN – it would be performative boilerplate – and there was no prospect that the Palestinian leader would unburden himself to a visitor such as me. His political lieutenant, the ever-mellifluous Erekat, then provided a drum roll of Israel's malfeasance and double-dealing.

An interrogation of the failures at Camp David two years back, when Arafat and Erekat were facing a far more moderate Israeli prime minister (Ehud Barak) than Ariel Sharon, proved equally barren territory for any meaningful insights or acknowledgements. There was merely a recitation of how 'you cannot compromise on an existing compromise' (a reference, I imagined, to the idea that ceding more territory was off limits for the Palestinian leadership, despite it being the best offer yet received or seen since).

I kept thinking, but diplomatically not uttering, the famous remark of Israel's long-time foreign minister Abba Eban that the 'Palestinians never miss an opportunity to miss an opportunity'.

There was one topic, when we reached it after more unrewarding back and forth on Israel and Palestine, which would soon loom large across the world and where Arafat's warning that morning proved prescient. I asked the Palestinian leader how he viewed the ratcheting tempo of the American demand for Iraq's Saddam Hussein to surrender his 'weapons of mass destruction' and the evidentiary value of British Prime Minister Tony Blair's dossier of evidence on this score.

Arafat said two things that morning which events just a few months later fully justified, although I tended at the time to dismiss them given his close affinity with the dreadful Saddam Hussein, whom he held in high esteem. He said he knew first hand that Saddam possessed no such weapons and then added words to this effect: 'If America and its allies invade Iraq, make no mistake, it will be like taking a stick to a hornet's nest. It will provoke local furies and sectarian enmities that Saddam Hussein has kept in check.' Events soon enough would prove Arafat correct at least on this.

Before conversation could continue, the Palestinian leader advised,

'You are in the Middle East, and you must eat.'

I had always enjoyed Arab cuisine – the hummus, felafels, lamb skewers and salads. And the feast of such delicacies, extraordinary given the siege conditions under which his headquarters operated, that Arafat's aides laid out for us in the boardroom adjoining his office was an epicurean delight.

And so we continued over the mezze, with the Palestinian leader – seated directly opposite me – insisting that his servers pile more delicacies on my rapidly emptying plate.

The distinguished *New York Times* Middle East correspondent Thomas Friedman, in his magisterial book *From Beirut to Jerusalem*, described Arafat as a political thespian playing a role in a tragicomedy of violent absurdity. This was at the time of Israel's 1982 invasion of southern Lebanon: 'Beirut was a theater and Arafat thought he could star in it forever.' The operation was masterminded by Arafat's nemesis, Ariel Sharon, who was described by Friedman as 'a big man, a fat man, and he did not understand the logic of the play ... Sharon did not play games with his enemies. He killed them.'[3] More on the 'big man, a fat man' anon.

I was to witness, that day in Ramallah, Arafat in full theatrical mode. I could scarcely believe my eyes when, just after the plates were cleared, ushered into our presence was a tall, black-frocked figure, complete with wide-brimmed hat and full beard, in all appearances with the bearing of a rabbi, which indeed he was. Arafat proudly announced him as 'my dear Jewish friend'.

I discovered later that the rabbi was in fact a leading member of an extremist anti-Zionist sect, the Neturei Karta, a tiny group of ultra-Orthodox Jews who actively opposed both the principles of Zionism and the existence of Israel, on the basis that neither could exist until the Messiah arrived.

Absent any sighting of the Holy One during the long lunch (I was amazed that Arafat seemed to have all the time in the world for our get-together), said rabbi, with a strong North London accent, offered us several blessings as the meal concluded.

His presence added, in the same way as the old apartheid government used to trot out various obscure Black figures to endorse their own subjugation to visiting foreigners, a surreal endpoint to my Ramallah sojourn. As per Friedman's remark about Arafat starring in 'a theatre', it also suggested that the stage for our encounter was tinged, like a play by Harold Pinter or Samuel Beckett, with the absurd.

After warm farewells before a bevy of media, which the Palestinians had thoughtfully arranged, the return journey to Jerusalem was even longer than the morning trip, and the checkpoints seemingly multiplied – or each of them simply took longer to pass through.

The evening of my return to the safer climes of Tel Aviv, and in a modern high-rise apartment in one of its plush suburbs, I had a get-together with former Israeli minister of education Amnon Rubinstein. At the time, we were fellow vice presidents of Liberal International (a rather grand title for an umbrella body of minority parties worldwide, which I cruelly dubbed 'the club of losers', an accurate indicator of the limited electoral appeal of liberal parties in most places).

Amnon and his wife, Roni, offered warm hospitality. After my long journey to Ramallah, I rather hoped that, at 6 pm, a stiff libation would be on offer. (My late dad, a nightly whisky-and-water man, always announced, 'The bar opens at six.') But, as befitted Israelis of an older generation, such as my hosts, this was coffee, not drinks, time.

I recounted to Amnon, both a staunch liberal (in a polity where the creed was in danger of extinction) and a thoughtful jurist, a summary of my day with Arafat. 'That man is a liar – he even lies in his sleep,' Rubinstein exclaimed. But when I shared with him the remarks of the Palestinian chauffeur, he offered me perhaps the best one-line description of the moral compromises, or worse, embedded in the decades-long occupation of the West Bank: 'The only way to occupy a people against their will is with brutality.'

The hideous mass slaughter of 1 200 Jews and Israelis on 7 October 2023 lay long in the future, and the terror there was unleashed from Gaza by Hamas, the implacable enemies of Arafat's Fatah organisation. But on the dilemma confronting Israel, coarsening its society, threatening its long-term security and later nearly splitting it apart, the unresolved occupation remained at its core.

The incomparable Israeli author Amos Oz once described the tragedy of the Israel-Palestine conflict as one where, as Howard Jacobson puts it, 'both parties could be said to be in the right, and when the situation worsened, both parties could be said to be in the wrong.'½

2
Counting Jews with Sharon

For some time after my Arafat luncheon – both to balance the political books and out of a deep sense of personal curiosity – I wanted to meet with Israel's prime minister, Ariel Sharon, who was elected to the top post in February 2001.

But while one phone call from my office to the Palestinian embassy secured the Arafat confab, repeated attempts to obtain an audience with the Israeli strongman via the country's embassy in Pretoria produced a nil return.

Enter Cyril Kern.

Kern, a wealthy British businessman, settled for the past few years in Cape Town, had become friendly with Michal and me. He was a passionate Zionist, and his long-time friendship with Sharon was the defining feature of his life. Kern had fought as a 19-year-old volunteer in Israel's 1948 War of Independence, and during that conflict had forged an adamantine bond with the Israeli statesman, then at the dawn of his career as one of Israel's most famous and daring soldiers.

Sharon was also famously disobedient of his superiors' orders and developed a reputation both for dissembling on some matters and for being opaque when it came to the sources of his wealth.

Kern achieved his own slice of notoriety in his entanglement in the weeds of Sharon's finances, when the so-called Kern Affair burst across the media in both South Africa and Israel.

At the heart of the scandal – if that is what it was – were funds Kern had apparently lent to Sharon's son Gilad, to the tune of around $1.5 million. But Israeli authorities, and a huge media storm, were suspicious that Kern was simply fronting for European businessmen who had illegally donated to Sharon's campaign to become leader of the Likud party, which had secured his premiership. Sharon denied any knowledge of the funding and claimed to have no idea that Kern had loaned such a vast amount of money to his son.

It was also a matter of imaginative contemplation how Sharon – a career soldier turned professional politician – had accumulated sufficient funds to own the largest private ranch in the country.

Despite acres of media space and a series of criminal investigations, neither Sharon nor Kern was charged with any offence. But the affair proved just how closely the two men were tied to each other, even if its detail stretched the bounds of credulity.

Thus, one night at a dinner with Kern, when I expressed some frustration at the inability of the Israeli embassy to arrange a meet-and-greet with his friend, Kern responded, 'Leave it with me. I speak to Arik [the universal nickname for Sharon] every Saturday and I will arrange it.'

Sharon had long held a fascination for me, and not just for his daring exploits on the battlefield. Most famously, during the 1973 Yom Kippur War, he had changed the course of the conflict by crossing the Suez Canal, against orders, encircling the Egyptian Third Army and occupying huge swathes of territory west of the Suez Canal and within 100 km of Cairo.

His bulldozer tactics in war were matched by his approach to politics too. Sharon was the political architect of the right-wing Likud party, a modernist project which in 1973 melded the so-called revisionist strands of Zionism, embracing an expansive version of the founding of the State of Israel. However, he was no party loyalist. When he found his pragmatic decisions as prime minister thwarted by hard-right Likud colleagues, he simply abandoned the party in 2005 and created another political home, Kadima (Going Forward). This related to his unilateral decision to end Israel's occupation of Gaza, a decision that would reverberate with terrifying consequences when Hamas launched its brutal and barbaric attack on Israel on 7 October 2023, some eighteen years later.

Kern succeeded where formal diplomatic channels failed. And on a visit to Israel in 2004, accompanied by my wife and my speechwriter Joel Pollak, an impassioned Zionist, I found myself outside the rather modest offices of the Israeli prime minister in Jerusalem awaiting an audience with the big man.

On entering his office, the difference between the hard-edged Sharon and his nemesis Arafat could be discerned in the expansiveness of the latter's welcome and long lunch and Sharon's briefer, less effusive and more direct approach to matters. With his mountainous frame sprawled behind his efficiently neat mahogany desk, we commenced the talks, or rather he gave a one-way lecture.

Sharon did not engage in niceties much, beyond a perfunctory enquiry about his friend Kern, and proceeded to deliver to us, an audience of three, a 30-minute monologue on how he saw his role as prime minister of Israel and the challenges confronting the country. Again, it was familiar stuff that could have been downloaded from the internet. I rather had the impression that when the prime minister granted audiences to political tourists, such as our trio, he would, like a tape recorder with the repeat button pressed, provide each with the same spiel.

But there was one line in his remarks that did surprise me, coming as it did from a famous Israeli nationalist and Sabra (Israeli-born Jew) who, like me, did not have much interest in religious observance or ritual. He told us, 'I see my essential task as the guardian of the Jewish people in this corner of the world.'

Many years later, I had the opportunity to interview, via video link, the famous British Jewish comedian and commentator David Baddiel at a community fundraiser in Cape Town. He had written an influential polemic titled *Jews Don't Count*. During our exchange, he highlighted a comment in the book on the difference between Israelis and the rest of the Jewish tribe: 'Israelis aren't very Jewish anyway … They're too macho, too ripped and aggressive and confident. [Israelis are] Jews without angst, without guilt. So not really Jews at all.'[1]

Yet here was the macho supreme Israeli prioritising his task as safeguarding all Jews, not just Israelis.

I did manage to probe Sharon on one issue not in his script. But first, recall that our encounter took place in a far-off time when South Africa still held pretensions to being an honest broker and promoter of a two-state solution between Palestine and Israel. To this end, perhaps rather pretentiously given our lack of heft in the region, President Thabo Mbeki had initiated the Spier Initiative (named after the Stellenbosch wine farm where meetings were held), in which his government would arrange meetings for delegations from Israel and the Palestinian Authority to discuss using the template of the vaunted 'South African miracle democratic transition' as a basis for consideration in the Middle East cauldron.

I was intensely sceptical of the exercise of trying to panel-beat the vastly different circumstances of South Africa's democratic transition and the Israel-Palestine model of conflict.

For Mbeki and his successors, it provided an opportunity for much posturing. I remembered well the judgment of statesman Abba Eban on 'the perils of analogy', warning that 'history is baroque' and does not admit of replication in most circumstances. In a lecture he used the example of a red rubber ball and a shiny red apple: 'This apple is round, red, shiny, and good to eat. This rubber ball is round, red, and shiny. Therefore, there is at least a strong probability that it will be good to eat.'[2]

I imagined, correctly, that Sharon would have had no truck with red apples and red rubber balls. So, when I asked him if he saw any role for South Africa in peacemaking in the Middle East, he dismissed the question: 'Your government is completely pro-Palestinian. It has no role to play here.' Long after this, some 16 years after Mbeki had been ejected from office, and a decade after Sharon's death, South Africa's infamous decision to place Israel in the genocide dock before the International Court of Justice would provide posthumous vindication for Sharon's view.

After an official entered the prime minister's office to indicate that our audience was at an end, Sharon bustled up from behind his desk to warmly shake hands and pose for the obligatory photos, and then off the cuff (and off script) he asked me how the South African Jewish community was getting along. And how sizeable it was. I responded then (but would certainly give a different and far more negative answer today) that the community was fine, though reduced in number (from a high in my youth of around 120 000 to a 2004 estimate of half that number). I added that while there were only around 60 000 Jews in the country, 'many assume there are at least a million of us given the influence the community appears to have.'

Sharon stopped, eyes a-twinkle, and, half smiling, told us a story from his time on an officers' course in England in the 1950s: 'At the mess one day, I was asked by one of the British officers, "How many of you chaps live here in England?" (meaning Jews).' Sharon said he responded, 'I think about 200 000.' 'Good heavens,' the officer remarked, 'I thought there were millions of you here.'

'You see,' the Israeli prime minister intoned as we made our way to the door, 'everywhere in the world, they assume we are far larger and more influential than is the case.' A classic antisemitic trope, in other words.

That subtle form of antisemitic profiling would give way to a far more overt Jew hatred, in both South Africa and the United Kingdom and across much of the world, after Israel launched its ground offensive against Hamas in Gaza and the body count mounted in that densely inhabited territory in the wake of the 7 October massacre.

The difference, of course, was that while most Western governments allied themselves with Israel, despite the strong feelings of many protesting citizens, in South Africa the government implicitly backed Hamas. This included refusing to label Hamas as a 'terror organisation' and welcoming its leaders to the country, while the pompous and preening international relations minister, Naledi Pandor, engaged in diplomatic initiatives with its chief backer, Iran. And demanded that Israel abandon any attempt to defend itself.

Does the South African government hate Jews? Is the ANC funded by Hamas sponsors Iran and Qatar? Is South Africa attempting to replace the existing international order? These were three of several questions that percolated through the local discourse on why the otherwise rights-delinquent South African government placed Israel on the rack of international justice and condemnation and managed to filter out far worse violators of regional and international peace, from Sudan and Syria to Russia and many centres of despotism in between.

I thought the best single explanation for South Africa's moral blindness in conciliating Hamas and condemning Israel, a sort of grotesque inversion of both morality and cause and effect, came from the British columnist Daniel Finkelstein, writing in *The Times* of London. He located exactly where the ANC placed itself, the blind spot or several of them that created the one-eyed approach of the 'progressive left'. This, in his view, derived from 'the left's idea that it should ally with anti-colonial resistance movements, whatever the broader politics'. All, from Castro's Cuba to Chávez's Venezuela and Khomeini's Iran – a triptych of ANC favourites – 'were at the front line of the battle against global capital. And this is the only battle that really matters, the one from which all freedoms derive.'[3]

'Bingo,' I thought on reading this, and the plus factors for the ANC demonisation would be that they viewed Israel through the lens of being a white, Western, pro-American outpost in a sea of Araby. Never mind the details of history and the inaptness of the colonialist template. Israel was shoehorned into an antique world view that hadn't advanced much since the founding of the Non-Aligned Movement in 1961, or since the end of the Cold War 30 years later.

And if Hamas and the rulers of its sponsor Iran, or indeed the government of Cuba, are among the most repressive, barbaric and murderous regimes in the world? Finkelstein's explanation was on the money here as well: 'So it doesn't matter if a group jails opponents or rapes women or throws gay people from buildings [Hamas being affirmative on all of these]. As long as they help bring down capitalism – which, as anti-imperialists, they do – they are liberating forces and their other faults will dissolve once capitalism dissolves.'[4]

Doubtless the ANC, which also viewed itself – 30 years after being installed in government – as a revolutionary liberation movement, also saw an identity of interest with the Hamas leadership, which enjoyed luxurious lifestyles (in the safety of Qatar) while its subjects lived in Gaza in conditions of immiserating poverty.

This too had a local resonance: ANC ministers walled themselves off from the sufferings of ordinary people with taxpayer-funded homes, blue-light police escorts to stop traffic and generators to obviate electricity blackouts. Lavish top-ups accrued to personal bank accounts via an army of state contractors and middlemen, often closely related to this or that cabinet minister.

Two years after my meeting with Sharon he was felled by a massive stroke and remained in a vegetative state until his death eight years later, in 2014.

The enigma that Sharon took to his grave was this: he gave no clue whether his brilliant and brutal military tactics and political iconoclasm were part of an overall strategy for peace in the region or the limits of it. And viewed through the depressing and clouded lens of today, under the leadership of Benjamin Netanyahu – once Sharon's ally and later his great foe – we can only speculate whether Sharon would have altered the trajectory on which his country now seems set.

And of Arafat, beyond his rejection of the Camp David plan for a sovereign independent Palestine – was he simply holding out for a time when, 'from the river to the sea', a Palestinian state would occupy and engulf the current state of Israel? Did he have the imaginative courage, or would circumstances have conspired to force him, to compromise on a maximalist approach and obtain the three-quarters of the loaf that was on offer from the US and – for a time at least – the government of Israel?

This riddle, too, was unanswered at the time of his death in 2004, just months after my meeting with Sharon. But the two, as Thomas Friedman noted in 1989, certainly loathed each other. Unto death in their case. Indeed, and without evidence, many in the Arab world, including the Palestinian's widow, suggested that Sharon had ordered the poisoning of Arafat, leading to his death. (The Arab Middle East is awash with conspiracy theories, especially those implicating Jews.) Sharon, by contrast with Yitzhak Rabin and Shimon Peres – two of his predecessors in office – never once met Arafat face to face.

3
Winning Lessons from 'Loser' Peres

Shimon Peres, the Israeli politician who died in 2016, aged 93 (fully healthy until the very end), left behind no unfinished business. On many encounters, over three decades, he offered up no end of personal and political paradoxes and some of the most compelling thoughts. These were delivered in such memorable metaphors and imaginative phrasing that, but for his heavy accent, it was easy to forget that English was only one of at least six languages he spoke after his native Polish, alongside Hebrew, French, Russian and Yiddish. In his storied career, Peres held every important office of state – prime minister, foreign minister, defence minister and president.

To me, Peres offers a leadership portrait etched by resilience, imagination and vast amounts of creative eloquence, and humanised by petty-minded low politics and scheming, all inspanned to the service of nation and self. Very often, the two sides were intertwined and indistinguishable. Benjamin Netanyahu, his great contemporary rival and the man who beat him in elections for the highest office, observed on the morning of Peres's death: 'Today is the first day of the State of Israel without Shimon Peres.'

I first met Peres in 1991, when I was a 34-year-old backbench MP, and many engagements followed over the next decades. That first occasion was during a visit arranged by my (future) wife Michal's NGO, the Israel Forum.

Meeting international politicians is the price tag attached to an all-expenses paid overseas jolly, which usually has the add-on of what Paul Keating, the former Australian prime minister, called the 'colonial cringe'. This meant that, for a thrusting, ambitious politician as I once was, any article or speech datelined from an exotic locale such as Jerusalem was more than likely to get placement in a local rag, not because of the merits of the remarks but because of the place of delivery or the photo op with the meeting's famous host. Offer similar remarks in plain Johannesburg and coverage would be less likely.

Encounters with Peres, though, went beyond this ritualistic trope. And unlike others of his tribe, each remark was weighted with unusual gravity and thoughtfulness, entirely unaided by a script or even cue cards.

At our first meeting back then, with a group of fellow international political tourists, Peres, his height and slim frame outlined to advantage in his impeccably tailored suit and silk tie – no rough-and-tumble, open-necked Israeli politician of popular mythology was he – drew a distinction that has aged well. This was the rhetorical dividing line between successful and failed states, even before the popularisation of the latter term.

He told us, 'To be a winning nation is hard. The price of admission to the front row of leading nations is steep, where the view of the world stage is close up. Far away from the stage is the overcrowded balcony of the also-ran countries. There the price of admission is cheap, but the view of the stage is poor.'

Recounting this meeting now, decades later, is to be reminded that South Africa, for example, paid a steep price for its admission to the international front row back in 1994 when it surprised itself and the world by overcoming centuries of enmity, division and conflict. For a golden moment, it was one of the most admired members of the international community. But, 30 years on, the view is far less hopeful and a reminder that opportunities not seized, and legacies left unattended to, squander fleeting advantage – as our drift from the front of the hall of nations to the overcrowded balcony reflects.

I was blown away by both the profundity and eloquence of Peres and enthused about the encounter to my Israeli political minder, the witty but obscure right-wing Member of Knesset Ruvi Rivlin. He waspishly told me, 'That's the problem with Peres; he impresses everyone from overseas, and few at home.'

There was a double irony in that remark: in 2014, Rivlin would end up as Peres's successor as president of Israel, and in 2015 gave an impassioned speech on the 'four tribes of Israel' in which he included Israeli Arabs. He also forged a close friendship with Peres in later years. And, of course, it was Rivlin who, in his first attempt to win the presidency of Israel, in 2007, lost out to the so-called loser Peres, who won on his second try.

But of the 'political loser' label he gave to Peres there was much truth. Peres, with his foreign accent, reputation for double talk, lack of a military fighting record and deep intellectual bent, was not a vote-winner in a macho land. Indeed, in seven elections for the leadership of the Labour Party he lost four (thrice to his great internal rival, Rabin), and his attempts to win direct election as prime minister foundered at the polls in 1996. (He obtained the post twice, first courtesy of a grand coalition rotation with Likud in 1984 and then finally after the assassination of Rabin in 1996.) Yet his persistence in politics, often in the face of humiliating defeat, was characteristic. And a helpful model for wannabe politicos everywhere.

In 2003, twelve years after that first encounter, I was present at the Mann Auditorium, Tel Aviv, as a guest at Peres's 80th birthday celebration. It was a glittering event attended by such eminences as Bill Clinton, Mikhail Gorbachev, FW de Klerk, Barbra Streisand and Ariel Sharon, at the time on the opposite side of the political aisle from the guest of honour. In truth, though, it appeared to be a celebration of past accomplishment, not future achievement, a gilded epitaph to a storied career. Yet, just four years later, at the age of 84, Peres was elected – on his second attempt – as president of Israel.

WINNING LESSONS FROM 'LOSER' PERES

Beyond his extraordinary comeback persistence, in my 2003 encounter with him he expressed views that at the time I dismissed as over-sophisticated and unrealistic. Peres invited me after the event to a meeting at the office he maintained at his nanotechnology institute. It is a field of which I was (and remain) woefully ignorant.

After an exchange of pleasantries and mutual salutations, Peres asked me for an update on the situation in South Africa and the African continent, about which, among many areas of interest, he had a keen curiosity. After I finished my spiel, he said something along these lines: 'You know, Africa, with all its problems, has great potential. Because of its sunshine, wind and vast waterfalls and riverine systems, it simply needs technologies to harness these natural attributes to provide alternative and much cleaner energy. Your continent has the supply side; it just needs the delivery mechanisms and, believe me, in a few years they will be to hand.' Bear in mind that this conversation occurred more than 20 years ago. My scepticism was wrong; his vision was right. Wind, solar and clean energy and the transition from fossil fuels are now front and centre in the world, with technologies adapted for them. Peres foresaw this change decades ago. And Africa's abundance of critical minerals for the green transition places it at ground zero for the new technologies needed to save the planet.

Peres was criticised by many as a party-hopping opportunist. He, like Sharon (and Churchill come to think of it), discarded his political homes when opportunity beckoned elsewhere. His primal political loyalty, though, was not to a party but to a person: David Ben Gurion, his mentor, first prime minister of Israel and the key advancer of his career. Peres once described himself as a 'Ben Gurionite'.

In fact, beyond personal loyalty, there was another aspect of the Ben Gurion character infused in Peres. The latter liked to quote the former, who observed, 'All the experts are experts on what was. There is no expert on what will be.'[1] Peres suggested that to become an 'expert' on the future, vision must replace experience and nostalgia must give way to a forward-looking orientation. As he wrote, 'People prefer remembering to imagining. Memory deals with familiar things;

imagination deals with the unknown. Imagination can be frightening – it requires risking a departure from the familiar.'[2] I am reminded that former German chancellor Helmut Schmidt advised that 'people with visions should go to the doctor'. But it is precisely Peres's ability, until the end of his life, as a nonagenarian, to dream the future that explains, beyond raw ambition, his persistence.

Once again, there is a decidedly South African echo to this observation. Our country's often depressing and backward-looking politics, premised on 'vote for a better yesterday', is captured by the past – ancient conflicts, old loyalties and outdated policies. And our regression at home and in the world is the result.

Peres, like Mandela and De Klerk, was awarded a Nobel Prize for Peace, in his case for his imaginative endeavours to settle the intractable conflict with the Palestinians. By some measure, and viewed from today, this could be added to the list of his heroic failures and a case of his imagination trumping hard reality.

It is beyond the scope of this book to outline why the Peres-inspired Oslo Accords essentially failed or remain today beyond realistic attainment. But in considering the theme of leadership against the grain, Peres's attempts to help create what he called 'the new Middle East' offer some lessons. Here are just two of them.

First, Peres allowed circumstance to evolve his thinking and strategy. He was a young man in his twenties when Ben Gurion entrusted him with building the Israel Defense Forces into one of the best equipped and most capable militaries in the world. In the 1950s, he was front and centre at the birth of Israel's initially secret nuclear weapons programme at Dimona. As minister of defence, he was the leading political force behind the Entebbe Raid of 1976; in 1975, in contrast, he allowed the first group of Israeli settlers to stay on in the West Bank. He then greenlit other settlements that, in the view of his critics, simply laid the first obstacles to the two-state solution.

Yet, paradoxically, he was the architect of an enduring peace agreement with Jordan, and of the Oslo Accords of 1993 – the very agreement that attempted to square the occupation/security conundrum. Some critics complain that the compromises embedded in the Oslo Accords were all of a piece with his equivocal personality and politically hedging style. Tom Segev, a well-known Israeli journalist and historian of my acquaintance, wrote, in Peres's obituary, on the controversy over Oslo: 'The right called Mr Peres a defeatist for ceding some control of the West Bank, the left called him an expansionist because the agreement didn't end the occupation. Both sides were not entirely wrong. In fact, Mr Peres was trying to please everyone, settlers and peace activists alike. That was the storyline of his political life.'[3]

But not the entirety of it. There is evidence in his five decades of political struggle to support the notion of Peres as an inveterate, principle-splitting schemer. But then there is the quality of his imagination and his unshakeable optimism, surely key items in the leadership survival kit for which he was Exhibit A in Israel and the wider world. Peres was, in other words, a complex paradox. And in both paradox and complexity true leaders confront great events. That would be the second lesson from his career.

I do not doubt that Peres's defence of the Oslo Accords and the now-disappearing consensus on a two-state solution is also a sort of last will and testament to his own political endeavours and an offer to the future. He said: 'There was no alternative. We had to do it. An ancient Greek philosopher was asked what is the difference between war and peace. "In war," he replied, "the old bury the young. In peace, the young bury the old." I felt that if I could make the world better for the young, that would be the greatest thing we can do.'[4]

He never lived to see the prophecy realised. It remains beyond reach, years later. But the acclaim after his death, from across the bitter divides of his country, does suggest that endurance, flexibility, optimistic leadership and, most of all, the quality of imagination can make a profound and lasting impact. And offer a light to the future.

4

Leadership Matters

Where are the leaders?

It is a predictable and wearying complaint to excoriate the quality of political leadership in South Africa, Israel and indeed the world. Cyril Ramaphosa is neither a Nelson Mandela nor an FW de Klerk. Benjamin Netanyahu, beyond his extraordinary political longevity, bears no resemblance to David Ben Gurion, Shimon Peres or Ariel Sharon. And while Rishi Sunak was a vast improvement on his fellow conservative Liz Truss, he pales by comparison with Margaret Thatcher, for example. Ditto for Keir Starmer and Tony Blair. And Donald Trump is far removed from the optimistic Republican internationalism of Ronald Reagan.

One of the reasons for this is that circumstances today are so fraught and complex, and politics is a far less appealing career for talented people than it was in yesteryear.

Then there is the generational component. Most of the leaders in South Africa certainly and even in Israel and Britain today have known no career outside politics, and only very few, if any, did anything of real consequence before entering the political fray. Paul Johnson, the historian and journalist, once described the 'great human scourge' of the 20th century as being 'the professional politician'. Or at least those 'without a hinterland', to quote British statesman Denis Healey, who had a rich interior life beyond politics.

In the South African cabinet in 2023, for example, there were perhaps two or three members of this gargantuan body of 28 ministers and 32 deputies (one of the largest in the world and in 2024 to expand further) who had known any occupation apart from party or trade union activist. And very few of them could find a senior position in a well-run business outside government.

Still, there are elsewhere, such as in war-ravaged Ukraine, exemplars of real and courageous and against-the-odds leadership to inspire us. And there is always the hope that a better alternative might emerge.

Dr Kissinger's prescription

Dr Henry Kissinger, the American statesman extraordinaire, had long since left public office when he visited Cape Town in 1996. His close South African friend, and my political funder, the business titan Harry Oppenheimer, arranged a lunch for the two of us at the stately Mount Nelson Hotel.

I was suitably awestruck but alas remember little (and kept no notes) of the encounter beyond Kissinger's humour, friendliness and acute observations on the state of American politics. (President Bill Clinton was facing a re-election contest against Republican Senator Bob Dole.) It seems now like a golden age, more assured than today. And he thoughtfully inscribed the *Years of Upheaval*, the 1982 volume of his memoirs (the second volume of three), with some affirming words above his spidery signature.

I thought meeting Kissinger was an encounter with 'living history' – lunch with an American 'Lion in Winter'. I had little idea that he would live another 27 years and provide an object lesson in how to live a purposeful and long life. He died in 2023 at the age of 100. In 'retirement' he wrote many magisterial tomes and provided counsel to every US president from Clinton to Trump. His sagacity was sought at the international summits that mattered and by a slew of world leaders, many of whom had been at primary school when he exited the White House as US Secretary of State in 1977, my first year at university.

In 2022, at the age of 99, and a year before he died, Kissinger published another lucid and learned door stopper of a book, *Leadership: Six Studies in World Strategy*. Like Shimon Peres, Kissinger was no slouch on the metaphor front either. He writes how the present age is 'unmoored' because it lacks 'a moral and strategic vision' and the leaders to steer the ship of state: 'The vastness of our future as yet defies comprehension. The increasingly acute and disorienting steepness of the crests, the depths of the troughs, the dangers of the shoals – all these demand navigators with the creativity and fortitude to guide societies to as yet unknown, but more hopeful, destinations.'[1]

Israel, the Middle East, South Africa and a world in conflict need such navigators today.

New-age problems

There are several problems, though, that daunt even the most visionary political shapeshifters. Populism and 'cakeism' are two of the most potent. For example, a critic of Donald Trump's brand of ethnonationalist populism suggested that his support and tribe of supporters were woven in 'a tapestry of resentment and victimhood'. But how to unstitch this is no easy task unless the basis for their rage is understood.

Reading a slew of newspapers and journals each morning is how, plus coffee, I start each day. While I am ecumenical in whom I read, skip over or glance through, I am a close reader of *Financial Times* journalist Martin Wolf, the newspaper's chief economics editor. I bypassed economics at university and I'm a dud at maths and statistics, so Wolf and a clutch of other specialists have provided me with a later-life understanding of 'the dismal science', as Scottish historian Thomas Carlyle described the discipline of economics in 1849.

Wolf does not just write up economic trends and their implications. He deeply understands many of the entropic forces driving politics in the world, and the close connection between them. Some of these have washed over our southern shores as well.

In July 2016, just weeks after the consequential Brexit referendum and at a time when Trump seemed an unlikely winner of the US presidential election in November, Wolf penned a prescient analysis. It appeared under the warning headline, 'Global elites must heed the warning of populist rage'.[2] Contrary to swathes of other expert opinion, his article still rings both immediate and true some nine years later.

Wolf quoted HL Mencken's observation, 'For every complex problem, there is an answer that is clear, simple and wrong.' The 'aspirants to power' (such as Trump, or Marine Le Pen in France) 'offer clear, simple and wrong solutions – notably, nationalism, nativism and protectionism'. Such aspirants, one could add, also dish up a set of identifiable 'villains' to blame for the problem. The range is vast: George Soros, Muslims or Jews depending on the audience, but also 'foreigners', 'white monopoly capital', wokeists, racists, and so on.

This he then qualified: 'The remedies they offer are bogus. But the illnesses are real. If governing elites continue to fail to offer convincing cures, they might soon be swept away and, with them, the effort to marry democratic self-government with an open and co-operative world order.'

The diagnosis of the discontent and alienation afflicting electorates across the world is both connected and varied: stagnant or declining household incomes; financial crises that 'destroyed popular confidence in the competence and probity of business, administrative and political elites'; resentment of outsiders (immigrants); and cultural upheavals.

Trump and other populist politicians might offer quack and chauvinistic responses, but those who stand against these politicians and their appeal to base instincts must re-establish the balance 'between democratic legitimacy and global order'. In Wolf's view, this needs 'imaginative and ambitious ideas'. Of course, there is no shortage of these, from the gauzy and generalised idea of 'stakeholder capitalism' to the specifics embedded in a 'universal basic income'. (In South Africa, this is termed BIG, or basic income grant.)

And protectionism, correctly dismissed until recently as the progenitor of both trade wars and consumer inflation, is making a storming comeback from both left and right. Shoring up the home worker via tariffs and barriers – regardless of cost – is seen as key to retaining or reviving political support. However, this addresses one set of challenges identified by Wolf (democratic legitimacy) at the cost of the other, namely, liberalising and advancing 'the global order', as embedded in the architecture of post-World War II arrangements such as the World Bank and NATO.

Cakeism

On challenging and confronting voters with some hard choices and a few dollops of short-term pain for longer-term sustainability, there are few, if any, brave leaders prepared to have a serious adult conversation with their supporters.

Jean-Claude Juncker, long-serving president of the European Commission, famously and cynically said of much-needed structural reforms in the states of the European Union (EU), 'We all know what we have to do, but we don't know how to get re-elected once we have done it.' This became known as the 'Juncker Curse', where the cost of necessary reform imperils electoral success, and vice versa.

Boris Johnson was, politically, the nemesis of Juncker, since the tousle-haired UK politician led the successful campaign to eject Britain (then the second-largest economy in Europe) from Juncker's beloved EU. Which in turn propelled Johnson to the leadership of the Conservative Party and a tumultuous, ill-starred and relatively brief three-year premiership ending in 2022.

Back in time, Johnson's power base was no larger than the scruffy offices of *The Spectator* magazine. Through mutual friends, I had been introduced to Johnson, whom I found witty and frantic and sharply intelligent. He was much taken with and warmly supportive of the opposition project I then headed in South Africa. On one of my visits to London, he invited me to join an editorial conference at the magazine. I was amazed – as a regular reader – how such a sleek weekly could emerge from the hectic, freewheeling chaos of the editorial meeting. We remained in touch for a while, but after I retired from politics, Johnson was not yet in the ascendant.

Johnson might have been the antithesis of Juncker on the EU, but he splendidly – arguably dishonestly – proved anew the 'Juncker Curse' and added a twist of his own, which was dubbed 'cakeism'.

In the referendum campaign of 2016, Johnson offered a basic bargain to voters before he unravelled later, namely, 'My policy on cake is pro having it and pro eating it.' So, on the one hand, he offered the Tory faithful the red-meat promises of low US-style tax rates; on the other, to entice Labour voters in the North of England to switch their support, he promised Scandinavian-style high levels of social benefits.

It was other aspects of dissembling and dishonesty that did in his leadership, but as columnist Nick Cohen wrote – in *The Spectator* nogal – cakeism 'shows how Boris Johnson degraded public life, and will carry on degrading it long after his overdue departure from Downing Street.'[3]

There is no shortage of cakeists in the South African body politic today either, although most of them lack Johnson's presentational skills and affability. On the one hand, the government solemnly promises the restive financial markets that it will control the runaway national debt (which costs around R1 billion every day simply to service), interest charges on which crowd out a swathe of government expenditure. Yet, the same government pushes ahead with an uncosted National Health Insurance (NHI) scheme. When challenged on its exorbitant burden on both the fiscus and the taxpayer, the health minister dismisses the enquiry, in measured words, as 'mathematical hooliganism'.[4] Then, based on near zero per cent economic growth (0.6 per cent in 2023), the same government pays out social grants to over 25 million people at a cost of more than R250 billion per year.

There is no serious conversation or levelling with people that this is completely unsustainable and that some other beloved policy shibboleths will have to give.

Dual empathy

A final thought on conflict resolution. What is essential, beyond bold and imaginative leaders but usually exhibited by the best of them, is moral clarity and an ability to define the core issue at stake. I witnessed this too in Israel some years ago, at one of the political conferences I attended there, although the speaker was not an Israeli but an American (of British origin). And a very ancient one as well, I thought, as a frail white-haired person I had until then never heard of (in fact he was one of the most acclaimed Orientalists of his time) approached the podium.

Yet when Bernard Lewis spoke on that occasion, he identified with crystalline clarity and originality the existential conflict.

He put the question crisply: 'What is this conflict about? Is it about the size of Israel or about its existence?'

He suggested that if the issue, which had run like a stake through the Middle East and now engulfed the world, was about the size or the borders of Israel, then 'it is not easy but is possible to solve in the long run, and to live with in the meantime'.

And then he added the crucial caveat: 'But if the issue is the existence of Israel, then clearly it is insoluble by negotiation. There is no compromise between existing and not existing. And no government of Israel is going to negotiate on whether the country should exist or not exist.'

This, in my experience, applies beyond the borders he mentioned that day. It is the essence of intelligent leadership and problem-solving: empathy for both sides and an understanding of 'the other'. Asking the right question often leads to moral and strategic clarity. Even if the question is not easily answered.

III
THE MONEY

'Money is the mother's milk of politics.'

– Jesse M Unruh,
Californian political power broker

5
The Art of the Ask

'Let me tell you about the very rich. They are different from you and me,' F Scott Fitzgerald famously wrote in 1926.[1] Seventy-plus years later, I would find this out for myself.

A core aspect of my job as leader of the opposition in South Africa was to raise funds for my party. This was no easy task back in the 1990s and 2000s when ANC hegemony was at its height and business cowered before its rapacious juggernaut and bent its collective knee to the demands of the ruling party.

I thought the best single-line description of the role of fundraising in politics came from a long-forgotten and unsuccessful US Senate candidate who described it as 'like chemotherapy, unpleasant but necessary for the health of the body politic'. He was a Democrat tilling the stony political soil of South Carolina, a little akin, I thought, to pushing the plough for the DA on the rough terrain of South Africa.

Back then I had dinner with Alec Broers, vice chancellor of Cambridge University. He was visiting South Africa as part of a global effort to raise £1 billion for his university, which he duly accomplished. He breezily advised me that 'fundraising is easy. There are a lot of rich people in the world who are looking for a good reason to part with some of their loot, and I place before them a compelling case to do so.'

This no doubt was true for Cambridge University and its many thousands of well-heeled alumni, especially those whose quids could be exchanged for the quos of naming rights to buildings and academic centres. Funding for the opposition cause in one-party-dominant South Africa was more unrewarding and certainly less forthcoming.

In the refulgent glow of the final year of the Mandela presidency, there was less fear and loathing in business and political circles than during the dark era that would follow his exit from office, together with his essentially optimistic view of how South Africa and South Africans could work together while maintaining a critical discourse.

In 1999, when the Democratic Party (DP) was advised by highly paid US political consultants on our audacious bid to wrest official opposition status from the foundering New National Party (NNP), then more than ten times our parliamentary size, they offered an expensive campaign plan centred on the slogan 'Fight Back'. The question, though, was how to fund it.

After a great amount of hoop-jumping, my indefatigable personal assistant, Sandy Slack, confirmed the most difficult-to-obtain appointment with the largest of the Stellenbosch big-business beasts, a man of enormous wealth and weighty opinions. The doyen of what would later be termed the 'Stellenbosch Mafia' regaled Douglas Gibson (on whom more anon) and me with a lengthy (around four hours beyond the 30 minutes scheduled) series of views of what was right and wrong with South Africa in 1999. But he delighted in the 'Fight Back' idea. I was often told by my mother that I was too talkative – 'a chatterbox'. But that morning my host's volubility reduced me to unaccustomed muteness. And I wasn't going to blow this rare opportunity by going much beyond a nod and a muttered 'yes'.

When the fateful moment of the quantum arose, he offered an extraordinary $250 000 to fund our effort. As we departed, Douglas reminded our host, 'That amount is dollars, not rand, right?' To which came the immortal rejoinder, 'Douglas, I might not know too much, but one thing I do know is the difference between a rand and a dollar.' And he delivered on his pledge.

After that hugely successful election, which toppled the NNP, we still had no porticos on which to slap our donors' names. Most of the DA funders of my time gave their funding behind hidden hand and shuffling foot, fearful of any public association with the democratic opposition project, whose legitimacy and patriotism was relentlessly questioned by the all-powerful new president, Thabo Mbeki. Little wonder, then, that the chapter in my 2008 memoirs dealing with this era of tangling with the ANC at the height of its dominance was titled 'Against Goliath'.[2]

Decades later, and after Mbeki was ousted and successor Jacob Zuma had pillaged the state and its institutions, business became more public and visible in its opposition to the ANC. Also, by then public disclosure of donations had normalised the concept and reality of political giving. But during my time at the helm, it was pretty much hand-to-mouth when it came to keeping the show on the road and the party creditors at bay. And, in my case, on the money side, David's slingshot was not much to take on Goliath.

On the eve of the 2006 local election, when again I was chief debt collector for the opposition, the pervasive fear of the ANC felt by business was brought home to me one crisp March morning in Morningside, Johannesburg.

My fundraising appointment was at the home of a person who required no persuasion on the merits of the case. Tony Trahar, chief executive of mining and resources behemoth Anglo American plc, was a long-time sympathiser with the party cause, and his company had, over the decades, been its most important funder (which didn't prevent former leader Van Zyl Slabbert grumbling that Anglo could have done much more in this area).

Normally, a visit to the chief executive of the mighty Anglo (today a much-reduced entity in the mining and resources world) would have involved a sumptuous lunch in a wood-panelled boardroom at the company's monumental stone headquarters in Main Street, Johannesburg. That this fundraiser was at the chairman's home was an indication that something was off.

Again, I was accompanied to this event by Douglas Gibson, our estimable chief whip and a remarkable optimist – in contrast to my often Spenglerian gloom. I once referred to our enduring political partnership as the essence of a manic-depressive duo. However, even his cheer lessened when Tony Trahar advised us, as we sat sipping coffee in his lounge, that 'Anglo will not be making a donation to the party this time.' But he immediately scribbled on his notepad, 'Let's go into the garden.'

Outside, under the trees, Trahar informed us that 'they bug my office and even my home' before making a significant funding pledge.

If Henry Kissinger was right that 'even paranoids have real enemies', it is worth a line in the context of those times. In an earlier observation, Trahar had, in contrast to the obeisance to government which at the time was deemed obligatory by most business leaders, offered an unremarkable and entirely objective assessment. He told an interviewer, 'I think the South African risk issue is starting to diminish – although I am not saying it has gone.' Mbeki's response was furious: 'Was Anglo now saying that democratic South Africa presents the business world ... with a higher political risk than did apartheid South Africa?'[3] While I termed this vintage presidential tirade 'angry, resentful and intemperate', not a single business leader came to his defence.

While political fundraising amid such atmospherics was not for the faint-hearted, it continued apace. I would enter any social situation with my internal radar on high alert as to who was a potential candidate – in terms of wealth or office – for a future shakedown. Perhaps the best part of leaving politics was to enjoy conversations and encounters without having to mentally filter who was the next candidate for a fundraising visit, as indeed did my well-heeled friends and acquaintances, liberated on my retirement of any such obligation.

Of course, there is an essential difference between prising donations for a cause greater than yourself and self-enrichment. Since I viewed my job as ensuring the prospects of multiparty democracy and a viable opposition party able to contest elections effectively, I felt far less constrained than if I was doing it for my own account. And, as I trudged through rejections or widow's mites offered by those who could well afford to give generously but found myriad reasons not to, I reminded myself of the distinction between the personal and the political – often to lessen the sting from the brush-off.

6

The Patrician and the Boytjie

Anglo American Corporation, which Tony Trahar led early in the 21st century, had for most of the previous century, since its founding in 1917, dominated the South African economy, first in minerals and then across practically all its sectors.

By the time of this writing (early 2025), Anglo was a fraction of its former size and wealth and was in the process of either being dismembered or disappearing into the folds of one of its competitors. In this there was no end of ironies, for each of these competitors was once a fraction of the size of Anglo or came into existence long after the South African miner's heyday. But by 2024, in fact decades before, Anglo had ceased to be a South African-based entity, and its few local assets were seen – in the words of the *Financial Times* – as a 'poison pill' in any takeover or merger transaction. The ANC government had, in the words of another local miner, made mining in this country 'uninvestible'.

But in Anglo's heyday, in the late 1980s and early 1990s, at the time of my entry into South African politics, it was the biggest behemoth – by far. Anglo controlled much of the market cap of the JSE, the local stock exchange, and was at one time, through its Minorco entity, the largest foreign investor in the United States.

THE PATRICIAN AND THE BOYTJIE

I had many encounters with Harry Oppenheimer, whose father, Sir Ernest, had established the company during World War I in Kimberley. HFO – as he was ubiquitously called – was an amalgam of contrasting parts: a man of refined sensibility and culture, with a sharp eye for a business deal. He was politically progressive in the context of his times and a staunch opponent of the apartheid system, and yet intrinsically conservative. His company also profited from the essential conditions put in place by the National Party (NP) and its predecessors – the pass laws, an exploitative migrant labour system and the closing of the local economy to foreign competition. On a personal level, too, there was a contradiction: HFO was born Jewish and converted at some stage with his father to Anglicanism, but to all appearances he looked remarkably like my great-uncle 'Chookie' Herman. Yet he was the top WASP in the country and not a single Jew sat in the apex leadership of Anglo.

As the chief funder of the progressive opposition (in the form of the Progressive Party and its successors), HFO was essential to the survival of the liberal opposition project. In May 1994, when I became leader of the DP – at the time the current iteration of the original Progressive Party – I thought I would have more difficulty establishing a rapport with the great man than had my forerunners. After all, I was 50 years younger than him and did not enjoy the same political and personal connections as did my predecessors Colin Eglin, Helen Suzman and Zach de Beer, who had all served alongside him in Parliament in the 1950s.

It was in fact Zach who provided the clue on how to approach Oppenheimer: 'HFO – although exquisitely polite – bores easily. Try to tell him something he doesn't know. He will enjoy political anecdotes and a bit of gossip, in addition to your plans for the party.'

I had met and dined with Oppenheimer a few times before a crunch meeting with him at the Anglo headquarters shortly after my election as party leader. Although officially retired, HFO maintained a corner office – and huge influence – on the first floor.

On entering his impressively but discreetly furnished lair (English period pieces, soft pile carpets, the office dominated by an oil portrait of his father, Sir Ernest, and, aptly, gold nuggets displayed in a glass cabinet), I was struck by his diminutive frame and his frailty – he was 86 at the time. But there was nothing faltering about his emphatic grasp of the new South Africa, its potential and its pitfalls. Forewarned by Zach, I recounted to him such titbits as I could muster. He was most engaging and gently probed our prospects, although he was unwavering about his continued support. We ended the meeting with a firm handshake and the promise of future funding.

A year or two after this meeting, I had dinner with Oppenheimer and his warm but very opinionated wife, Bridget, at the home of my father and stepmother, Jacqueline, in Durban. They were social and bridge-playing acquaintances. I thought the event was purely social and enjoyed regaling the table with some stories from Parliament while Bridget, far more outspoken than HFO, described a 'dinner party from hell' at their London home. Apparently, then South African High Commissioner Mendi Msimang had become so drunk at the table 'that he slipped right under it', on Bridget's version, before being bundled out of the apartment entirely.

After our less liquid Durban dinner, HFO – to my surprise – directly asked me, 'How much money would help the party right now?' Since we were running at the time on proverbial fumes, I plucked entirely randomly what I thought to be a very generous sum (R600 000). Oppenheimer nodded and smiled, and we moved on to other topics. A few days later, via intermediaries, that precise sum dropped into the modest coffers of the DP.

In 2021, Mike Cardo interviewed me for his fine biography of Oppenheimer.[1] When I was recounting this story of Oppenheimer's unsolicited funding question, I speculated in reply, 'I wonder what would have happened if I had asked for ten times that amount?' Indeed.

To be invited to the sprawling Oppenheimer estate, Brenthurst, in Parktown, Johannesburg, or to their palatial Durban beachside compound, Milkwood, in La Lucia, was, I guess, a little like a dinner invitation to Buckingham Palace. The Oppenheimer family flew in the stratosphere while other business and social leaders floated far below in the cumulus clouds.

On one such occasion, in Durban, Bridget announced to the table, 'I have decided we will, in honour of Tony, have a bottle of Petrus this evening' (a rare and exquisite French Bordeaux and one of the most expensive wines in the world). But then she added, 'Tony, you are not so important that we will open more than one bottle!'

In fact, my last meeting with Harry Oppenheimer was just weeks before his death. On 25 July 2000, the night the Concorde crashed shortly after taking off from Charles de Gaulle Airport, Paris, I was back at Milkwood at a dinner *à trois* with HFO and Bridget.

The purpose of the dinner was to explain to one of our major donors the recently announced merger of the liberal DP with its historical nemesis, the NNP. A political take-off of a different sort to help unify the opposition, which also had an early crash.

I approached the evening with a mixture of anticipation and anxiety: HFO always gave wise counsel and support, and Bridget combined warmth and grand hosting together with a vivid view of the world shorn of any political correctness.

My nervousness was occasioned by the deep antipathy with which Oppenheimer – during his near decade in Parliament in the 1950s and after – had been treated by the Nats. And his long-voiced opposition to them. After all, Jan Smuts had proposed the toast at Oppenheimer's 21st. Following the defeat of Smuts's United Party at the hands of the NP in 1948, Oppenheimer, by word and financial deed, became a leading member of the parliamentary opposition. Even after his retirement from Parliament, he remained an outspoken critic of the NP government's policies. In the 1970 general election, the NP minister of mines even threatened to revoke Anglo American's mining licences owing to Oppenheimer's opposition to government policy. 'Hoggenheimer', the agent of British-Jewish capital, was the NP's cartoonish vilification of Oppenheimer and his father.

Oppenheimer listened carefully as I spluttered out the proposal for the Democratic Alliance to tackle the hegemony of the mighty

ANC. After I concluded, he cocked his ear to one side and said in his measured manner, 'I might not understand this fully [in reality, he got the point immediately], but it seems to me what you are saying is that after this merger is completed, we will be much bigger than before ... a jolly good thing too, I think.'

He died just weeks later, on 19 August 2000.

❏

In South African and even in global terms, the Anglo American Corporation built by Oppenheimer *père et fils* bore some resemblance to the graphic description offered of Goldman Sachs, the international investment banking giant: 'A great vampire squid wrapped around the face of humanity, relentlessly jamming its blood funnel into anything that smells like money.'[2]

One of the corporations into which Anglo had jammed its 'blood funnel' was South African Breweries (SAB), in which it held a big stake. Doubtless, SAB CEO (and later chairman) Meyer Kahn often met with Oppenheimer, and they both inhabited the small ecosystem of Johannesburg's business elite. Yet, in almost every other respect, the two offered a study of deep contrasts.

On Kahn's death in June 2022, he was described by a close friend and business colleague as 'an ordinary man possessed of quite extraordinary abilities'. Indeed, under his stewardship, he and Graham Mackay piloted Breweries (later SABMiller and now merged into AB InBev) to global heights. In Kahn's time, SAB ranked as one of the last industrial giants in South Africa and across the world.

By contrast to Oppenheimer's gilded upbringing, much of it spent at top private schools in England and then at Oxford, Kahn grew up in the hardscrabble Transvaal town of Brits (today part of North West province), northwest of Pretoria. From here came the appellation, which Kahn relished, 'the boytjie from Brits'.

He had no dynasty to inherit or expand, but instead, with business acuity, earthy wit and sheer ability, he propelled himself from a junior management post at OK Bazaars (in its day the country's leading retailer) eventually to the top positions at SAB.

In the mid-1990s I visited Kahn, then chairman of SAB, at the group's iconic headquarters at 2 Jan Smuts Avenue, Braamfontein. Aside from providing some much-needed cash (a pittance by the demands of today and the amounts solicited and spent) for my political cause, Kahn would invariably impart some wisdom, offered with a warm slap on the back and peppered with a string of expletives. He was splendidly politically incorrect to boot. The first visit was the start of a series of get-togethers, usually held outside the main building in the forecourt, allowing Kahn to puff away on his ubiquitous Benson & Hedges cigarettes.

Several of his vignettes are worth reprising.

Kahn, who was outspoken in the demand for both more economic freedom and greater law and order, said then: 'You know, Tony, the Nats did their best to fuck up our economy and they failed; the ANC seems equally determined, and they will fail too.'

However, decades later, I never asked Kahn if he still held that opinion. Not on the earnest attempts of both parties (and governments) to blow up their economies, but whether in fact the ANC had not in fact outperformed the Nats not in moral terms, but in toppling over what was once the industrial powerhouse of Africa and emerging markets everywhere.

There is a wonderful phrase that describes the 'tyranny of hindsight' as a 'lordly perspective that reduces a complex, contingent sequence of events to an irreversible progression'.[3] The destruction and deindustrialisation of the South African economy during three decades of ANC (mis)rule was something to behold and certainly would have been beyond the imagination of someone like Kahn, who essentially was an optimist tempered by a realistic outlook.

In the 1990s, it was by no means foreseeable that the basically sound economics of the early years of ANC governance – until 2007, when Jacob Zuma took the reins – would give way to the populism and bad public finances that long outlived Zuma's presidency, the regression accelerating, at pace, under the allegedly 'business-friendly' Cyril Ramaphosa.

On the eve of the 2024 general election, an old friend, Alec Russell, who had been a young foreign correspondent based in Johannesburg when Nelson Mandela ascended the presidency, returned here as foreign editor of the *Financial Times*. Russell wrote a penetrating long report describing Ramaphosa as South Africa's 'lost leader'.

In two crisp paragraphs, Russell summarised the deep malaise of the South African economy and its continued regression:

> When he became president in 2018 there was hope that Ramaphosa would draw on his experience in the private sector to revitalise the economy after the radical anti-capitalist lurch of his predecessor. Opting for hope over experience, many in the business sector chose to forget that he had kept silent for many of his years serving [as deputy president] under Zuma. Today, the business leaders and former policymakers who were among his most vocal backers are deeply frustrated by his government's record.
>
> 'Out of 10, I'd give his economic performance a two,' says a former official, who is sympathetic to the president's political predicament but not his economic record. 'He inherited a very bad situation but he's done almost nothing to fix it.'[4]

Indeed, my former colleague from the faraway days of our time on the Wits University SRC, Hilary Joffe, in her capacity as editor-at-large for *Business Day*, put some numbers on the vertiginous decline caused by Ramaphosa's do-nothingness: 'The failure narrative tends to be compelling,' she wrote in the week before the 2024 poll. 'Load shedding [electricity blackouts] went to stage 6 [meaning up to 12 hours of no electricity per day] in the first year of his presidency and then went up to record levels five years later.

'The trains went off the rails, the ports staggered, unemployment picked up to 33% and the government's debt burden jumped from 53%

to 72% of GDP. Economic growth averaged just 0.5% over six years. Even excluding the 2020 Covid-19 crash, average economic growth was hardly higher than the 1.5% of the nine years of the Jacob Zuma presidency.'[5]

South Africa lost its investment-grade status, in the view of the international rating agencies, having been relegated to 'junk' status in 2020, and went several notches below that in subsequent years, which exacerbated the costs of government borrowing. While some reforms were in the works by 2024, the facts on the ground were grim: more than R280 billion had been pumped into failing and often corrupted state-owned companies, and the faltering economy generated less than one job for every four entrants into the labour market. This led analyst Ann Bernstein to observe: 'There is no country in the world in which a smaller proportion of the total population is engaged in income-generating work than South Africa.'[6]

Ironically, though, it was Meyer Kahn who, in 1997, hand-picked Cyril Ramaphosa for a seat on SAB's main board. For more than a dozen years, his director's fees, share allocations and flow of dividends made Ramaphosa a very rich man. As Russell noted in his report, 'As companies run by, and for, white people sought black partners to meet new regulations on racial equity and management, a number of senior ANC figures, including Ramaphosa, were given stakes in consortia ... Ramaphosa became a popular pick for corporate boards in London and Johannesburg.'[7]

In the run-up to the 2004 election, I again answered a summons from Kahn to present myself for receipt of the election contribution from SAB, approved by the board on which, of course, Ramaphosa sat.

Kahn had a brilliant way of rationalising the unpalatable. The board, doubtless nudged by Ramaphosa and other ANC sympathisers on it (it was conspicuous that no opposition figure bar Van Zyl Slabbert was appointed to a corporate board in South Africa after 1994), had decided on a rationale for funding political parties. It would be on the basis of a formula 'aligned to the levels of support enjoyed by the party at the last election'.

This meant that, of the total SAB pot, the DP/DA (around ten per cent in the 1999 election) would get R1 million, while the ANC (66 per cent) would receive around R5 million. Lesser amounts would be doled out to all the other parties, provided they supported the Constitution.

While welcoming the donation, I pointed out to Kahn that this simply froze the status quo, and in any event the smaller parties needed the most resources.

'Ha,' he responded, 'but the difference is that I know that when I give you this cheque, the full amount will be deposited into your party's bank account, and it will be properly spent for election expenses.

'But with the ANC, when they come around to get the cheque, if they actually pitch at all, some of the amount will either be stolen or pissed against the wall, so their apparent funding advantage will disappear!'

For all his cynicism, Kahn was also a deep patriot. In 1997, he put his hand up and accepted the request of President Nelson Mandela to serve as the chief executive of the South African Police Service (SAPS). It was in so many ways an extraordinary time. Cadre deployment and racial profiling were not yet chiselled into the government edifice. Mandela was always on the lookout for people outside the ranks of his party hacks to set South Africa to rights. Kahn joined others from the private sector, such as Nedbank chief Chris Liebenberg, who served as finance minister, and Dirk Ackerman (disclosure: we are business colleagues), who was sent to run the Airports Company of South Africa. National service meant a willingness to lend a hand to a government that was, in those times, willing to extend it. And there were many others who crossed the borders from the boardroom to help build a new democracy.

Kahn did not find entering the belly of the beast of state a very satisfactory experience, stymied as he was by an ingrained bureaucratic culture indifferent to the top person. As he ruefully pointed out afterwards, 'You can't just hire good cops and fire nonperformers.' He even had difficulty making the SAPS printing operation more efficient and cost-conscious.

While crime was on a steep rise in the late 1990s, at the time when Kahn was trying to right-size the police, twenty-five years later it is a veritable tidal wave of rampant violence. Figures for the first quarter of 2023 indicated, for example, that 'living in South Africa is twice as dangerous as living in a war zone' such as Ukraine.[8]

7

Ronnie to the Rescue

In the early 2000s, around the time the ANC held an iron grip over the country and its financiers, I was on holiday in London, and perhaps the most unusual source for funding my political cause appeared. Shirley Eskapa, a mutual friend who was keen to promote and support my political career, arranged a meeting with Abe Jaffe, whom I had heard a great deal about but had never met before.

Jaffe was a legend in the motorcar business in South Africa and later in the UK and US. In all three countries he had built and operated Currie Motors and established a business empire based on property as much as on cars. In the UK, Jaffe was well placed on the *Sunday Times* Rich List (of the wealthiest Britons). Currie Motors' tag line, 'nice people to do business with', was clearly aimed at reassuring new owners, especially of used cars, that they were trustworthy; car salesmen, alongside politicians and estate agents, 'enjoy' low trust measurements among both consumers and voters.

However, I was advised that Jaffe's interest in meeting me was not because he necessarily wanted to have drinks with the leader of the opposition in South Africa. Rather, it was the result of his infuriation with his brother-in-law, Ronnie Kasrils, the brother of Jaffe's wife, Hilary.

A few nights later, I presented myself for our get-together. Jaffe was slightly built, quietly spoken and very sharp. Hilary was more ebullient and warmer. In short order, Jaffe cut right to the chase. He said that during Kasrils's long years in exile from South Africa, 'I kept him in comfort, sending money to him every month, whether in Moscow, Angola or here in London. Believe me he did not starve, far from it.' As an Umkhonto we Sizwe (MK) and South African Communist Party (SACP) commander in Durban, Kasrils had been involved in sabotage and was arrested before he fled the country. Jaffe also marvelled how Kasrils, a committed communist and revolutionary, 'had no problem in accepting funding from an arch-capitalist like me!'

I had first met Kasrils in the early 1990s at the Codesa (Convention for a Democratic South Africa) constitutional negotiations and got to know him better after we were both elected to the first democratic Parliament in 1994. He was, on election, immediately appointed deputy minister of defence and would later hold various cabinet positions until Thabo Mbeki was ousted from the presidency in 2008.

Kasrils had a big and very mixed reputation and record, although none of it reflected his relationship with his multi-millionaire brother-in-law.

At a personal level, Kasrils exuded a sort of blokeish charm. He enjoyed relating tales from his youth in Yeoville, Johannesburg, where, on his own recounting, he had been something of a juvenile delinquent. And he would regale any drinks sessions after Parliament rose for the evening with his feats of derring-do in the cause of struggle, at home and abroad.

Kasrils's schtick was fomenting revolution and insurrection. He had made his name in the ANC and SACP (and indeed was rewarded with a high eighth place on the ANC's parliamentary list in 1994) by directing the movement's underground struggles and had ended up as 'MK regional commissar' in Angola. But it was after the unbanning of the movement and his subsequent return to South Africa that events, and his direction of them, cast him in a darker light.

In September 1992, while the negotiations process was stalled, he was fingered as the person responsible for what became known as the 'Bisho Massacre', an attempt by the ANC to topple the Bantustan government of Ciskei. When the smoke cleared from this unsuccessful attempt, 28 people lay dead. The Goldstone Commission, an independent investigative body, duly investigated the events and concluded that Kasrils was primarily responsible for the fiasco and the loss of lives. It called on the ANC to 'publicly censure' Kasrils and others, noting that they had 'knowingly or negligently [exposed] marchers to the danger of death or injury'.[1]

The ANC ignored the finding.

In our conversations long after the dust of Bisho had settled and the dead and injured had been consigned to oblivion, Kasrils assumed that our common Jewish faith (though he was an avowed atheist) gave us, across a chasm of conflicting ideologies and party loyalties, a basis for common understanding. He would often intersperse his conversation with words or phrases in Yiddish, which I did not understand or speak.

Not that Kasrils's Jewish origins would go unheralded by the local community leadership. After 1994, the South African Jewish Board of Deputies and certainly the chief rabbi, Cyril Harris, did their best to claim the revolutionary Jews who had fronted the white struggle against apartheid, such as Kasrils, as 'our own'. It was a misjudged effort to ingratiate the community with the new political order.

Its apogee (aside from senior members of the lay leadership offering prayers at ANC rallies) was reached when, in December 2000, I attended the opening of the new South African Jewish Museum in Cape Town, officiated by Nelson Mandela himself.

But the really toe-curling aspect of that evening came after the opening ceremony, when the audience shuffled into the auditorium to watch a new documentary, *A Righteous Man: Nelson Mandela and the Jews of South Africa*,[2] starring the 'usual suspects' – Kasrils, Albie Sachs, Joe Slovo, Denis Goldberg, Ben Turok, and several other ANC luminaries. I was seated next to a friend, Mervyn Smith, a leading local attorney and staunch liberal, and no admirer of the ANC or the attempts by some in the community to claim some vicarious validation from people who, in the words of the Marxist writer Isaac Deutscher, were at best 'non-Jewish Jews'.

Smith whispered in my ear, 'These people on the screen have as much in common with the average South African Jew as the man in the moon!'

The co-opting of Kasrils to the local Jewish cause would come back to bite the community leadership with a vengeance. Before that, however, Abe Jaffe made his own determination on the role of his brother-in-law.

Jaffe's long support for, and presumably patience with, his errant brother-in-law finally snapped, he recounted to me, when Ronnie wrote a polemic in 2001, under the headline 'Declaration of Conscience by South Africans of Jewish Descent', targeting Israel's policies in the occupied territories. I noted cynically at the time that 'Ronnie is like an old rooster seeking a new perch. Now that he thinks his cabinet post might be in danger, he cranks up the volume on Israel to renew his relevance.' This declaration would prove, over time, to be weak tea compared to his ever more envenomed outpourings against the Jewish state.

But it was quite enough for Jaffe and his wife, Kasrils's sister. That night, he told me that he'd had enough and had not only cut off all funding to Kasrils but now intended – hence the reason for our meeting – to provide funds for the DA, assuming we were the staunchest domestic opponents of the ANC.

What particularly angered the Jaffes was the fact that their son, Ian, had migrated to live in Israel some years back. For the family, Ronnie's attack on Ian's new homeland, an attack that would shortly ratchet up in intensity, was seen as the ultimate betrayal.

Ever the tough businessman, Jaffe informed me there would be no one-off donation: 'Rather, I will provide your party with a quarterly stop order and will keep it going, even increase it, unless there are things you do I don't agree with.' For quite some time he provided handsome amounts via his preferred method of giving.

I would subsequently meet up on occasion with Abe and Hilary when they visited South Africa and stayed in their exceptionally modest cottage in Muizenberg. I recall vaguely, but not now why, that Jaffe terminated his DA debit order shortly before I left the party leadership in 2007. However, I have often marvelled at how Ronnie Kasrils inadvertently became a fundraiser for the DA!

But it was less marvellous in November 2023, following the Hamas massacres inside Israel. Kasrils, long since retired and deeply disillusioned with the ANC, found his voice in public in support of Hamas. His dislike of Israel had by now curdled into a bilious stew of unrestrained hatred.

At an event hosted by Africa4Palestine – a local NGO that specialised in targeting stores with Jewish ownership or that stocked Israeli products – and filmed for posterity, he was in overdrive. He rejoiced in the slaughter of 7 October, the single worst attack on Jews anywhere in the world since 1945, describing it as 'a brilliant, spectacular guerilla warfare attack. They swept on them, and they killed them and damn good. I was so pleased.'[3]

Kasrils, by then 85 years old, had no political career left to advance. But he breathed new life into Harold Wilson's put-down of his cabinet colleague, Tony Benn, of whom Wilson said, 'he only immatures with age.' The ANC, with Kasrils tagging along, used the 7 October Hamas attack and massacre in Israel to intensify its pro-Palestinian, anti-Israeli credentials, singling out the Jewish state alone in the world for condemnation on human rights violations, 'genocide' and the whole nine yards.

The days when the local Jewish community screened such panegyrics as *A Righteous Man* are long forgotten, never to be revived.

IV
THE NEGOTIATION

'All fixed, fast-frozen relations, with their train of ancient and venerable prejudices and opinions, are swept away, all new-formed ones become antiquated before they can ossify. All that is solid melts into air, all that is holy is profaned.'

– Karl Marx

8
Creation

'Living big history'

On Sunday 2 June 2024, I received a phone call that propelled me again into the swirl of a political drama, with plenty of subplots and prima donnas and lesser villains. In just four weeks, it changed the course of the country.

John Steenhuisen, leader of the DA, was on the line. He requested me to come to Johannesburg to join a negotiations team he was about to announce, charged with talks leading to the party, potentially, entering the national government. This remarkable turn of events was triggered by the outcome of the election just four days earlier.

Peggy Noonan, a wordsmith I admire, was speechwriter for presidents Ronald Reagan and George HW Bush during the 1980s. In 1988, Bush, whose intelligence and dutifulness were not matched by eloquence (he famously said once he had a problem with 'the vision thing'), had Noonan to thank for crafting one of the most inspirational nomination speeches ever delivered at a Republican convention. He described civil society and volunteers as 'a brilliant diversity spread like stars, like a thousand points of light in a broad and peaceful sky'.

More than 30 years later, in July 2024, from her perch as a columnist with *The Wall Street Journal*, Noonan wrote of current times: 'We are living big history. We do that so often we don't always notice.'[1]

In both respects, answering the call again to civil and political duty and, this time at least, realising that the moment was indeed historic and thus worth recording in some detail, led to the pages that now follow.

First, though, a brief backstory, or several of them rolled into one ...

Woody Allen once noted: 'If most of success in life is showing up, the other ten per cent is what you're showing up for.' In the contemporary history of this country, both chance and choice allowed me to 'show up' at some hinge points in our national story. The first was in the 1990s when I was a thirtysomething backbench MP, and a new constitutional order was in the making at the jerry-built and misnamed World Trade Centre in Kempton Park, near Johannesburg's international airport. There, amid high drama in which I was a bit player, the titans of modern times, Nelson Mandela and FW de Klerk, clashed and finally compromised over four turbulent years and constructed the new order.

In the first Parliament of the new democracy, from 1994 onwards, I had a ringside seat. This was again the case in 2000 when, as party leader, I was instrumental in negotiating the merger of two bitterly divided parties (DP and NNP), which led to the formation of the DA, the largest opposition party in South African politics for the decades that followed.

In various books and articles, and in many lectures, I have recounted a lot of the detail and some of the background colour of those epic events. But, beyond some fragmentary notes and a half-kept diary, the subsequent write-ups and talks depended heavily on memory, press cuttings and various minutes and memoranda.

During all those encounters – from breakfasts with Nelson Mandela (one of which, in early 1997, had on the menu his tempting offer, ultimately declined, to join his cabinet) to the near immolation of the DA and many lesser dramas in between – I never thought of myself as 'living history'. Rather, it was a case of going to work, doing the job and just getting through the mire of brutal politics, or navigating murky waters in the hope of getting to shore or at least to a safe harbour.

From my later perch after departing frontline politics in 2009, I determined that should I be placed in the centre of a political drama again, I would keep a careful account of what happened and when it happened and reflect contemporaneously on the dramatis personae involved.

I did not expect that to happen. And then the phone rang...

29 May 2024: 'Judgment day'

On 29 May 2024, election day, an earthquake erupted under the body politic of South Africa. On the back of the lowest percentage poll (just over 58 per cent) ever recorded since the advent of full-blown democracy, the mighty ANC, which loftily viewed itself as 'the vanguard of the people', crashed down to earth with its worst result in 30 years, barely a 40 per cent share of the national vote. The party was 17 per cent down from its 2019 total, and even that was a precipitous fall from its all-time high of 69 per cent in 2004.

This dramatic shifting of the hitherto static political tectonic plates had several interlinked causes, each of seismic impact. The voting public had endured years of ever-increasing misery, from electricity blackouts to the highest unemployment rate in the world, to pluck just two items from the national menu of state decline. Corruption, now metastasised across practically the whole of government, was so closely and correctly identified by voters with the ruling ANC that the election became a sort of judgment day on the party's malperformance and utter inability to 'self-correct' – a pet phrase of the ruling elite, observed largely in the breach.

Zuma's revenge changes the game

But the biggest cause of the ANC's poll punishment, and of my unanticipated return to national politics for a few weeks, was tinged with bitter irony. And it owed little to an upsurge of support for the party which I first led, nor to the stout efforts of its current standard bearers, since the DA's 22 per cent vote share indicated a basic electoral standstill. Rather, the cause of this earth-shattering eruption was a person who by rights should have been consigned to isolation and ignominy, or indeed to a prison cell.

Jacob Zuma, whose nine-year presidency (2009–2018) ended in disgrace after he ransacked the state and its institutions, having been captured by the émigré Gupta family (currently fugitives from justice), was facing criminal trial on election day.

However, in December 2023, weeks before the election campaign commenced, he embarked on a revenge mission against his successor, President Cyril Ramaphosa. This was seeded by an implacable hatred of the latter and the firm support of many who, notionally at least, still claimed allegiance to the ANC.

Zuma's rackety Umkhonto we Sizwe Party (MKP, or just MK), running on a platform of atavistic populism, succeeded in spectacular fashion, not only by dividing the ANC vote, along with that of another ANC renegade, Julius Malema's Economic Freedom Fighters (EFF), but also by tapping into a deep well of both pride and resentment among Zulu traditionalists.

His lavish campaign, apparently funded by Russian money, was populated by a rogues' gallery of rum characters who had been front and centre, along with their patron, during the state-capture years, which had crashed the country, beggared its economy and emptied its treasury.

Zuma's 2.3 million voters were unburdened by any of these political sins, even though his prison sentence for lesser crimes than corruption – in this case for defying a court order – nullified his election to Parliament.

MK emerged with 14.66 per cent of the national vote, the third highest behind the ANC and DA. In my and his home province of KwaZulu-Natal, Zuma finished first, with 45 per cent of the vote. It was the best achievement ever by a startup political formation in South Africa, although in truth MK was a feudal, anti-constitutional version of the ANC, fronted by arguably the best-known and most infamous political figure in the country.

Ramaphosa tried, cack-handedly, a populist tribute act but never convinced in this role. For example, he signed into law the uncosted and potentially ruinous National Health Insurance Bill (which would have bankrupted the state and destroyed private healthcare) two weeks before election day. But this was the precise moment when support for the ANC plummeted in the opinion polls.

Final result and a 'first rough draft of history'

When the result of this mould-breaking poll was declared on Sunday 2 June by the Independent Electoral Commission (IEC), no party had obtained remotely close to the 50 per cent proportion of the votes that would allow a single party to elect a president two weeks hence (as prescribed by the Constitution).

Only an agreement between the ANC and DA, on the one hand, or the so-called doomsday alliance of the ANC and MK and perhaps the EFF (which lost support and registered 9.52 per cent of the vote), on the other, could secure the presidency and a cabinet for the next five years.

Another party of significance was the Inkatha Freedom Party (IFP), although it ran a curious election campaign that featured its recently deceased founding leader, Mangosuthu Buthelezi, on its posters (see Chapter 18). The IFP's very modest national vote share (3.38 per cent) was compensated by its haul in KwaZulu-Natal: there, its 16 per cent support would, as events proved, make it indispensable in forming the provincial government. It was also, theoretically at least, an electoral ally of the DA in the multiparty charter formed as an anti-ANC alliance before the election. However, the lure of power proved, for both parties, stronger than any binding commitment to this pact.

In the helter-skelter of the 30 days that followed the IEC announcement, and which immersed me again in the rough waters of South African politics, a new government would be fashioned. What follows here is an account of that process – the good, the bad and the often very ugly. While it was fascinating to be part of the process, this brief but intense plunge back into politics was also a sharp reminder of my original wisdom in departing from it in 2009.

My 'first rough draft of history' (with apologies to Philip Graham of *The Washington Post*, who popularised that definition of journalism) appears below. It is edited from a diary I wrote during the 30 days that swept away some settled views of the country and who would govern it.

Or whether in fact it was governable at all.

Day 1: Monday 3 June 2024

The team John has appointed to head the negotiations with the ANC reflects his choices and consists of me, my former strategist Ryan Coetzee – quite one of the smartest and most opinionated people I know but now based in Dubai – and Alan Winde, an old 'comrade' and freshly re-elected premier of the Western Cape. He is the only DA member with current governing experience. While Alan, Ryan and I go back decades, the fourth member of our quartet I know only slightly: Siviwe Gwarube, the parliamentary chief whip, a young rising star in the party firmament.

But John's choices do not meet with the approval of his suspicious federal executive (fedex). And I have barely begun packing for Johannesburg, where the talks with other parties will be centred, than we receive a WhatsApp group message from fedex chair Helen Zille. She advises that not only has the fedex inserted her and party chairman Ivan Meyer into the mix, but she will take charge of the group!

Further, the same fedex has 'instructed' us to pursue 'limited' terms of reference for the first stage of discussions. Absurdly, Ryan and I thought anyway that we would also have to receive a further mandate from them on a potential deal.

I mention to John that this fedex (a lot different from my time at the top) seem determined to control a process of which they were not part. Ryan is even blunter: 'Why don't these clever people there [tinged with deep sarcasm] do the negotiations themselves?'

As events move on, it is clear that Helen holds considerable sway over the fedex she chairs (and, amazingly enough, also simultaneously takes the minutes in shorthand and offers an interpretation of them), while John is less certain of all the members' loyalties or to whom they are owed.

It is interesting (in the Chinese sense) to be inspanned again with Helen. She replaced me as party leader in 2007 and – by her own account – had for some years before been plotting my exit, although I was intending to quit anyway without any push from her quarter.

There is much to admire in her outsize personality: some six years older than me, she has the undimmed energies of someone 20 years younger than her 72-year-old self. She has a piercing intelligence and considerable personal and political courage. And when not at daggers drawn, as we will sometimes be in the weeks ahead, we have a warm mutual understanding.

But, like the poet Wordsworth, she has 'the defects of her qualities' – an adamantine obstinacy, a zeal of righteous conviction and total belief in the potency of her own analysis. She adds a great deal of rigour to the party management, but I doubt the party brand is enhanced by her continued presence at the top of the organisation. Her relish for public confrontation often takes the shine and attention away from the leader, John.

But she is both former leader and current executive chair and I am simply the ex-leader, with the ear of the current leader. And, usefully in these new times, I had direct experience in the 1991–1996 constitutional arrangements that led to the first (and failed) government of national unity, and I am no innocent when it comes to the manoeuvrings of the ANC.

I think it says much about John's self confidence that he is happy to have two of his predecessors in the negotiations mix, but the fedex seems determined to control much of the process going forward. Ryan and I remind the team that when the DP negotiated with the NNP to form the DA, a different federal council and fedex gave a broad mandate and received the final offer at the end of the process to either accept or reject. Different times now, it appears.

In the meantime, we obtain the fedex's so-called bottom lines (most of which are contained in the final agreement), of which the key one is 'we will not go into any governing arrangement that includes the MK or EFF' (to which the body later included a no-go for Gayton McKenzie's Patriotic Alliance [PA], which in fact went into the GNU alongside the DA). Further, the 'instructions' note that 'we will not support a government headed either by [party chair Gwede] Mantashe or [deputy president] Paul Mashatile', the former an ideological dinosaur and the latter implicated in deeply questionable dealings. In other words, a Ramaphosa presidency is the price of admission for the DA.

I am a little surprised, but suppose it is a fast-moving situation, to discover that Helen and Siviwe (who are already in Johannesburg, while Alan, Ivan and I arrive only tomorrow and Ryan on Wednesday) have already held initial meetings with both the ANC and the IFP.

Helen advises that the meeting she and Siv held with the ANC was 'urgent', as their team – headed by Mantashe, secretary-general Fikile Mbalula and members of the national executive committee (NEC) including Parks Tau, Nkenke Kekana and Nomvula Mokonyane (implicated in corrupt activities by the Zondo Commission) – had to brief their party structures. Helen describes the meeting as 'comfortable and without animosity'. Bottom line is there is no bottom line at this stage: the ANC wants a broad-based GNU (no doubt to disguise the fact of a coalition government with the DA) and, unlike the DA at this stage, the participation of MK or EFF in government is 'not a red line for them'.

But the ANC – according to Helen – is very divided on precisely what shape the new government will take: a minority government of the ANC solo? A confidence and supply agreement with the DA, primarily, where the DA backs a Ramaphosa presidency ('confidence') and supports the budget ('supply') in exchange for some policy agreements and positions outside government, in Parliament and the like?

I regard 'confidence and supply' as very weak tea indeed, but the DA has yet to determine precisely what it wants and in which shape and form.

Helen notes that the ANC team looked at each other 'very carefully'.

Helen and Siviwe then met with the IFP, who regard KwaZulu-Natal as 'mission critical' particularly in securing – in a four-party arrangement (IFP, ANC, DA, NFP [National Freedom Party]) – the premiership for themselves.

The problem, which will mushroom over the next few days, is how little time there is for all these agreements, if there are any, to be inked.

The Constitution mandates that Parliament must meet 14 days after the election results are declared, which is now just 11 days away. By then we must decide whether, and on what terms, we are going to vote for Ramaphosa as president. In most other countries, negotiations on forming new governments of several parties take months. South Africa has but a few days. The proverbial clock ticks relentlessly down.

Day 2: Tuesday 4 June

I arrive in Johannesburg. It is bone-chillingly cold, with icy winds encasing the Highveld, and particularly the ramshackle Balalaika Hotel, in Sandton, where our team is housed. I remembered going there as a student for Friday-evening drinking sessions, but the years since have seen its rebranding, minus extensive refurbishment, as a bland Protea Hotel. The warm and efficient staff compensate for the freezing conditions in my room.

Before our first team get-together, I receive an outreach from an international banker, on a brief visit from his head office in London, who requests an urgent meeting.

This is the first of many such requests, which pour in from then on: some from people I hold in high regard, others from favour seekers, influence pedlars and special pleaders – sundry people, some I barely know but who seek to influence the unfolding process and its outcome. I am quite amazed at the urgent messages I am sent, often in detail and in this case from an eminence I have never met before.

My visitor, who meets me in the hotel lobby for a brief coffee, falls between several categories. His financial house has a huge interest, via its investments, in the shape and form of the new government. Yet his opening remarks are truly strange: 'Tony, I don't think there is much appetite in the ANC for doing a deal with you guys, indeed there appears to be much resistance.'

I parry: 'Well, why tell me that? I think you should address such reluctance to the ANC and not to us. We are perfectly open to a fair deal with them.'

He responds that, after our coffee klatsch, he is to meet ANC deputy president Paul Mashatile, presumably not to provide him with advice on ethical governance. I do ask him, though, to spell out to the ANC high command that the alternative to doing business with us is a tie-up with the EFF or MK. He demurs but does advise, 'If that happens, the response of the markets will be immediate and completely pulverising.'

I am confident, as I bid the banker goodbye, that he will be far more deferential to the ANC number-two man. I hasten to an upstairs meeting room for our negotiations group meeting.

If Lincoln's cabinet was 'a team of rivals', our group will, over the next few weeks, prove to be more a reminder of Churchill's wisdom that 'there is only one thing worse than fighting with allies, and that is fighting without them'.

Helen holds court in the York Room, leading Ryan, who is on Zoom from Dubai until he arrives tomorrow, to quip, 'The Grand Old Duke of York and all that – I wonder who and which party will be marching up or down this hill?'

The DA is internally divided on what it wants: confidence and supply or full-blown coalition.

'Confidence and supply', an impeccably Westminster term, now enters the local lexicon in possible assistance for the beleaguered 'national democratic revolution' of the ANC. It means simply that a minority government (such as the ANC, with its 40 per cent vote share) receives the support of another party (such as the 22 per cent DA) in votes of confidence and for the budget in Parliament, subject to an agreement that could include policy and some positions outside the cabinet.

Helen clearly at this stage strongly favours confidence and supply and angles the group in this direction, while John messages me that he is strongly minded towards a coalition. (Later that evening, when he arrives at our hotel, I go to his room, where he is accompanied by his close confidant Leon Schreiber, and forcefully suggest to him that this strategic ambiguity can't continue. If he wants to enter government at cabinet level, then he needs to get his fedex to support his view. In the subsequent fedex meeting, he prevails.)

I remind both our negotiations group earlier and John and Leon later of the lesson from history offered by the US response to the Yom Kippur War of 1973. President Richard Nixon had to decide what sort of arms airlift to send to Israel following the surprise attack by Egypt and Syria. There was serious disagreement among his cabinet members on how large or small the weapons supply should be. Nixon, according to his secretary of state, Henry Kissinger, settled the matter decisively: 'We are going to be blamed as much for three planes or for three hundred. Send anything that flies.'

The politics of half measures, like being half pregnant, is often an illusion. Voters will be perplexed that their party has lent its support to a government but has no effective way, or power, of influencing its outcomes. The DA has correctly settled on pursuing a full-blown coalition, with sharing of executive offices, as its preferred model for engagement.

Helen later messages the group to advise that the ANC – via its secretary-general, Fikile Mbalula – wants an informal 'talks about talks' meeting tomorrow but restricted to her and Siviwe. Ivan Meyer and I push back hard and advise her to tell the ANC that they can't choose our team for us, and since we are only six in total, it could hardly be an issue. Helen duly informs the ANC of this.

Helen says that the ANC is 'paranoid' about leaks at this stage – a crowning irony, since in the days ahead it won't require a Roto-Rooter to detect that most of the leaks are from their side! Their concern, apparently, is that their comrades will round on them if they pursue talks with us before a formal mandate to do so from their NEC, which meets in two days' time. Not fast decision-makers on the other side, apparently.

Or I think it could be a ruse and the ANC will keep things idling along for as long as possible. As I advise our group, this was their tactic at Codesa: rush an agreement at the last possible moment to exert maximum pressure and force concessions from your adversaries. Encrusted on that historic event is the 'nimbus of myth', but the basic reality there was that the incoming power (the ANC) out-negotiated all their adversaries. Will history repeat itself now?

Meanwhile, in the world beyond our hotel, there is a press and social media storm brewing, applying loads of pressure and much noise on the negotiators. Some are pushing hard for an all-in DA, IFP and ANC deal, while others, particularly the poison pens of Iqbal Survé's Independent Media (ferocious opponents of both Ramaphosa and the DA), push in the other direction. And, in fine South African fashion, it's all being racialised. 'Don't sell out the revolution to white racists,' et cetera, scream the RET (radical economic transformation) crowd.

I have since last week started conversations with two people whom I have known quite well over the decades: Roelf Meyer, who was the NP chief negotiator at Codesa with Cyril Ramaphosa, and Pravin Gordhan, a recently retired ANC minister. My old friend and occasional political sparring partner, former judge Dennis Davis, reconnected me to Pravin.

Both are adamant that the EFF or MK entry into government would be disastrous, and that the 'constitutionalists' need to keep that option far away. Pravin is keener on a loose DA-ANC tie-up, while Roelf favours a coalition of 'the centrists', as he puts it.

I have a very disturbed night's sleep, and not just due to the frozen conditions in my hotel room. I feel, maybe because I am now 20 years older since I was last involved in such high-level negotiations, more weighed down by the prospects of failure.

What if we can't strike a deal? What if our bottom lines send the

ANC scuttling off to the EFF, dooming the country to disaster? What if we do get a deal but its terms condemn the DA to a sort of political zombie status, peripherally part of government and condemned to future electoral oblivion? I kept remembering FW de Klerk's unhappy role in the previous GNU, which he later described as being on a 'political death row'.

And I keep reminding myself, to calm myself to sleep, that I am not in charge anymore. I can only offer my counsel, and I have the advantage of not being personally invested in the outcome, since I am not going to be a cabinet minister in a future arrangement – if there is one. But, as a citizen rather than a partisan, I deeply fear the prospects of kleptocratic constitutional vandals and Chávez-inspired economic looters entering the government.

Day 3: Wednesday 5 June

My late-night ruminations lead to an early rising. At least I clarify one pending matter: our scheduled midday informal meeting with the ANC has been bedevilled by the issue of finding a suitably discreet and neutral venue.

I call my close friend Sandra Botha, with whom I served (alongside her husband, Andries), in Parliament. Beyond the gift of their friendship, the Bothas also personified an oxymoron as Free State liberals.

Sandra's daughter Dominique, an accomplished writer and poet, is married to Adi Enthoven, who heads a billion-dollar enterprise invested in a clutch of businesses, from Nando's restaurants to Hollard Insurance and private equity. He is a key but uber-discreet business leader who has done much, below the radar, to improve private- and public-sector cooperation.

Adi and Dominique are highly intelligent but, mercifully, also irreverent. Their passionate commitment to the country and its well-being is an antidote to the caricature of business and the wealthy as rapacious extractors and exploiters. This impressive duo are 'do-gooders' – in the best sense of the term – with a sense of humour. In their informal but effective way, both will do much to advance the process in which we are immersed.

Sandra had often told me that the couple's Johannesburg residence in Westcliff was a haven of refined, well-secured and walled-off comfort. Phone calls to Adi and Dominique secure the venue for our meetings (and in fact for future bilateral meetings between the parties).

We will spend many hours and days in this suburban idyll, both with the ANC and waiting around for their – always delayed – team to arrive. Originally erected in 1902 as a stable house for the neighbouring Randlord mansion, the Herbert Baker-designed home offers a tasteful blend of antiquity and all mod cons. The sweeping views from its lush garden over the green canopy of northern Johannesburg offset the gritty business at hand.

One hour late, in the sun-baked conservatory overlooking these perfectly manicured lawns, I meet, for the first time, not the ANC as such but two of its significant emissaries.

Fikile Mbalula is someone I have not met before. In public, both as a minister and latterly as the front man (secretary-general) for his party, he is a cartoonish motormouth, peddling absurdities and conspiracy theories. He was described as 'the class clown' by the *Mail & Guardian* when he rushed off to Moscow, praising Vladimir Putin, two weeks after Russia's invasion of Ukraine in February 2022.[2]

Yet this afternoon he presents a far more nuanced and thoughtful persona. He tells us that the meeting is, mystifyingly, 'a whispering session'. His party has put all options and all other parties on the table and has not committed to any of them yet.

However, he commences his 'whispers' with an undeniable truth: 'The problem for us [the ANC and DA] is that we have spent the past 30 years demonising each other – and now we have only a few days to overcome this history.'

Mbalula is also quite reflective on the pounding his party took at the recent polls. He mentions that in KwaZulu-Natal, so many voters 'wore our T shirts, sang our songs and went into the polling stations and voted for Zuma'.

CREATION

We suggest to the ANC duo that we will draft a document, and send it to them soon, that will set out our view on cooperation and a possible framework for the next government. Mbalula seems very interested, although he advises that 'the ANC doesn't have a document. We do everything on a handshake.' Over the next few days, this and future documents will be a matter of the fiercest contestation.

I had, back in 1994, served in Parliament with the other ANC official who accompanies Mbalula to our get-together: Nkenke Kekana. He left Parliament in 2003 and obtained, via black economic empowerment (BEE) businesses, apparently significant riches. Kekana speaks far less than the voluble Mbalula, to whom he is apparently very close. And he has ties to Paul Mashatile.

Dominique, in the meantime, has arranged a lunch for us – appropriately, of Nando's chicken pieces, plus delicious French fries. As we tuck in to our food, Nkenke takes me aback when he says, 'Tony, I thought you were living in Israel these days.'

I was somewhat stung by this remark, since not only was it completely wrong but suggested, beyond reminding us of the ANC obsession with Palestine (which spectacularly backfired in the recent elections), that somehow I was not fully South African. I joke in response, 'Actually, Nkenke I have never lived there, but since I couldn't persuade any local to marry me, I had to import an Israeli bride.' A titter of laughter follows.

Afterwards, I tell Helen that I thought the remark was intended to offend. 'Nonsense,' she responds, 'you are being paranoid.' 'Ha,' I retort, 'and this from the queen of paranoia.' We have a good laugh as we head back to the hotel.

The most striking feature of this initial meeting, aside from the general amity and constructiveness of the discussion, is the relative intimacy displayed between Helen and the ANC honchos. She is often portrayed in the media as a caricature, a sort of Wicked Witch of the West, hellbent on preserving the barricades of racial privilege. Yet, as the meeting reveals, she and 'Nkenks', as she calls Kekana, go back to the days of the struggle when she assisted activists from the ANC. And she calls Mbalula, her opposite number on the ANC side, 'Fix'. Public and private personae at odds with each other, in this case at least.

We will meet the full ANC team, they advise, once their endless internal consultations conclude.

It is quite clear that, outside our get-together, there are a lot of 'noises off'. Geordin Hill-Lewis (Cape Town mayor), who has a close working relationship with (finance minister) Enoch Godongwana, is messaged by him that under no circumstances 'should the DA stop talking to the ANC', as the 'constitutionalists will win the day' inside his party at the current national working committee (NWC) meeting. But then that parody of a struggle queen, the dethroned Lindiwe Sisulu, vents that any deal with the DA would mean 'spitting on the graves of our ancestors'. Classy.

Here is another significant difference between this negotiation round and the 1990s constitutional talks. Back then, there was no social media and no 24/7 news cycle. Now, the background noise cranks up, via Twitter (X), and the weaponisation of clickbait comments and 'fake news' supplants serious journalism.

There is strong pushback inside the ANC on deal-making with the DA. We keep hearing how Mashatile and Mantashe are pushing for closer ties between the ANC and the EFF and MK. At least that is clarifying, and we decide to sit back a little and allow either that option to ripen, with all its consequences, or for the EFF (which has demanded the finance ministry for its number-two man, Floyd Shivambu) and MK (which has demanded Ramaphosa's head) to start excluding themselves.

I meet for a late-night drink at the hotel with Alan Winde, who also thinks the direction of political travel is journeying away from us towards an ANC-EFF tie-up. Ever one to fixate on the odds, I ask him the percentage chance of a DA-ANC deal. About 30 per cent, he reckons.

And the bond and currency markets start to tank as news seeps out from the NWC meeting that the ANC is seeking a broad government of all comers, including the EFF, rather than a narrower and more market-friendly option with the DA and IFP. We let the media know, off the books, that any inclusion of the 'red berets' (as the EFF are called) will automatically exclude us. A binary choice. In other words, Cyril, always conflict-averse, must decide.

As Ryan, who emerges as the strategic glue binding our group, puts it: 'It is the essential and legitimate choice for Ramaphosa and his party. Does he go with the modern social democrats or with the race nationalists?' How the ANC answers or ducks that question will be the business in the days ahead.

Day 4: Thursday 6 June

We finalise a document that Ryan has drafted to offset and reclaim the narrative, and to ground our approach to the ANC and the wider public in values and policy choices and not as a seat grab.

'A Framework for Multi-Party Government' will not win an award for sexy titling. But its sober and precise language is very clear: it commits the DA to a government that protects and promotes the Constitution and Bill of Rights *in their entirety* (including the property clause), the independence of the Reserve Bank, a corruption-free public service, a 'sustainable fiscal framework' (by targeting a budget deficit maximised at 3.5 per cent of GDP by 2027, for example) and the full implementation of Ramaphosa's reform menu housed in Operation Vulindlela.

There are a lot of advantages to this approach: it contains the overlap of both DA and ANC positions (theoretically at least in their case, though much ignored in practice). Key elements go against the positions of MK and the EFF, and it has the singular plus of shifting the conversation towards the DA, and on a more elevated plane than 'Who gets which job?' The media and business types to whom it is sent give it a big thumbs-up. We also send it to the ANC and will discuss it when we meet them tomorrow.

Roelf Meyer comes from Pretoria to the hotel for lunch with me, and I invite Ryan to join us. I am keen to get Meyer's insights, and he is also close to people close to Ramaphosa and might have some useful suggestions for advancing the process.

I haven't seen him in person for some years. Although he is now almost entirely bald, he defies the ravages of time (or his 76 years), perhaps explicably by his very modest menu choice of a bowl of soup. Ryan and I opt for heartier fare – 'comfort food' is in order here.

Speaking of his considerable experience of the past government of national unity, Roelf believes the essential for any future success will be a good and open relationship between Cyril and John. But, as he knows well from his own attempts to secure such a one-on-one meeting between them, Ramaphosa has ignored such requests. In fact, Alan Winde, who has Cyril's number on speed dial, was advised by Ramaphosa that such a meeting would be a good idea but was entirely non-committal on its happening. John, too, has messaged him, with zilch reply.

Is this a strategic game or is Ramaphosa not interested at all? (In fact, the first face-to-face meeting only happens one week later, on the eve of the crunch vote in Parliament on 14 June; see below.)

Much later that night, at around 10.30 pm, when most normal folk are safely asleep, and hours behind schedule, Ramaphosa finally appears on TV following his party's marathon NWC meeting, to announce how the divided circles inside his party will be squared.

But, as one analyst notes, in familiar fashion Ramaphosa kicks the can down the road. Yes, there will be an 'ANC-led' government of national unity, and he cites (unhappily, I think, since it didn't last long) the 1994 precedent. His party is in talks with 'all parties'. But what form and shape it will take is left unanswered.

The only sliver of hope from his word salad of general pieties is that Ramaphosa cautions that future partners in government must commit to 'respect for the Constitution and the rule of law'. Since both the EFF and MK stand quite outside such a commitment, this could lead to their exclusion. But if their thirst for power and plunder is strong, a mere signature on a document won't be too bothersome for non-believers.

CREATION

Day 5: Friday 7 June

The day of our first full-blown bilateral meeting with the ANC negotiating team. Except, in fact, it isn't: the ANC messages us that they are still busy with internal consultations with their NEC and outside allies and request a postponement until Saturday.

I take this small gap to rush to the airport to fly to Durban to honour a long-standing commitment I did not expect to meet this evening – the 50th (!) anniversary celebrations of my matric class at Kearsney College.

Arriving that night, with my oldest friend, Steve du Toit, for the founders' dinner held in a windswept marquee at the school in Botha's Hill, midway between Durban and Pietermaritzburg, is completely surreal.

Before recently being thrust back into political intrigues, I had contemplated this evening with anticipation – a reunion with friends from decades past, reminiscing about old times and some of the highlights and horrors of our spartan boarding-school years (see Chapter 20). It is also salutary to be informed by the event organiser that of approximately 85 boys from our 1974 class, 15 are dead – 'absent friends' is the euphemism used.

In fact, at the dinner I am distracted from the revelry of the well-lubricated evening and more focused on the looming and uncertain outcomes I left behind in Johannesburg. My distraction is compounded by the number of old boys who ask about progress in the negotiations. I maintain my *omerta*, but the evening is a useful vox populi of upper-middle-class, racially diverse South Africa (a good taxonomy of the school alumni present). Most who entreat me are freaked out at the prospects of an ANC-MK-EFF government. 'You must stop this from happening, Tony,' one flush-faced inebriate implores me. As if it is in my gift!

Day 6: Saturday 8 June

Back on the Highveld after the overnight dash to Durban, I join our team in the hotel to strategise on our approach to the imminent meeting with the ANC.

A point in our favour to introduce into the discussion is that in the two provinces where there is no overall control (Gauteng and KwaZulu-Natal), the DA has a 'kingmaker' role, in which our votes will determine who is elected premier. We will not sever the national arrangements from the provincial ones, and vice versa. (This is the theory anyway: subsequent events prove the wisdom of boxing champ Mike Tyson, who said, 'Everyone has a plan until they get punched in the face.')

We arrive before schedule in the early afternoon chez Enthoven for the meeting. This time, our larger meeting is held in a modernistic guest house, below the main house, whose conference table easily seats our delegations.

The large ANC delegation arrives punctually, minus their chairman, Gwede Mantashe, who bursts in some 45 minutes late profusely apologising. He was taken to the nearby Westcliff Hotel in error. It makes one think of how many more important matters of state might also be subject to such a haphazard misstep. But this is not a time to cavil and carp.

The ANC team is essentially its top leadership minus Ramaphosa and Mashatile, plus some additionals who will, over the next few days, form their negotiating core: Fébé Potgieter, articulate and bright; Ronald Lamola, outgoing minister of justice; Enoch Godongwana; Andries Nel, with whom I served in Parliament and who has carried water for his team for decades now; former Johannesburg mayor Parks Tau; and Nkenke Kekana. Missing from the line-up, due to illness, is David Makhura, who heads the party's governance unit. (In future meetings he will prove indispensable as the rational voice who gets the deal done.)

It is striking, to me anyway, given the splendid lack of deference and hierarchy on the DA side of the table, quite how all members on team ANC defer to 'comrade chair' Mantashe. Even the normally voluble Mbalula is relatively muted in his presence.

CREATION

Mantashe rumbles in a low baritone with introductory comments. Little of it is remarkable or alarming – generalities such as 'we must act with speed to advance goals for a progressive agenda' and the country's needs. Beyond forming a new government, he advises us that his NEC is punting a 'national dialogue' with the whole of society, whatever this might mean? Is it a smokescreen for undermining the multiparty government? Who knows?

He does, though, compliment the DA for its 'interest in taking matters forward' with the ANC, which he advises is in a race against time to form a new government and, unlike some 'other parties' (unnamed by him), has not 'rejected the idea of a GNU'. But, he says, 'we [the ANC] are open-minded but it is not an open-ended process.'

Mantashe, who is chairing the proceedings, attempts to swat away the youngest (by far) member of our team, Siviwe Gwarube, when she interjects to offer a thought. 'No,' says the status-minded old trade unionist, 'You can only speak after your chairperson' (a reference to another of our team, Ivan Meyer). Siv, undeterred, ignores him and proceeds.

Helen, who is simultaneously transcribing proceedings on her laptop and disconcertingly also leading the discussion from our side, turns to the DA framework document as the basis for cooperation. Others offer comments, of which the more interesting are those of ANC treasurer Gwen Ramokgopa, dressed in an impressive and no doubt expensive grey ensemble, that 'redress must be at the core of the new government'. Better than looting the state at least, I think to myself. Next to her sits Nomvula Mokonyane, finely robed as well. She is a member of the top ANC leadership whom the Zondo Commission referred for investigation and prosecution for corruption. More than two years on, the lethargic National Prosecuting Authority has yet to act.

On sartorial matters, in an inversion of popular caricature, the ANC side of the table is clothed in ultra-expensive designer garb and coiffed to match. Mantashe, though, does not do fashion. Our side, far from the rich capitalist class representatives we are alleged to be, is decidedly more downmarket: Cape Union Mart and Uniqlo puffer jackets for us.

Lamola punts the confidence and supply model as the most likely outcome, while Parks Tau finds some agreement with the DA document on matters economic (which is no surprise, since many of these points were copied from National Treasury policy).

Fébé Potgieter gets into the weeds on some important issues – 'the devil' of it. How will minority vetoes in cabinet work? This, she advises, 'could be a problem'. She also flags the difference between the DA-favoured devolution-of-power approach and the ANC model of 'cooperative governance'. She warns that in looking at these details we need to remember that 'we have not exactly been *ad idem* with each other these past 30 years but have voted against each other far more than we have ever agreed on things'. This is another reminder that we must cross boundaries and collapse historic divisions in a few days. I jot down the words 'Mission Impossible?'

I decide to play the Codesa card and remind the meeting – via 'comrade chair', as I dub Mantashe – of Joe Slovo's appeal back then for the gathering to 'lift ourselves above ourselves' to reach common ground. It is clanging cliché but I think its provenance might appeal to the comrades. I also remind the meeting, no doubt unnecessarily, of the basic parliamentary arithmetic that 40% +22% (our respective seat haul) = stability.

The back and forth has lasted no more than an hour when Mantashe announces their departure to keep a commitment to meet with the red berets. We learn later this evening that these talks have gone very badly and – per one ANC insider – 'the EFF walked away'. This suits us – to be the last party of size standing at the end of the process.

Today's meeting reminds me of the adage about administering chicken soup to a sick child: 'Might not help but can do no harm.'

Our next meetings (right through to the end of the process) will be between the ANC core group ('the technical team') and ourselves. And, in the final settlement, between Ramaphosa and Steenhuisen.

CREATION

Day 7: Sunday 9 June

The Sunday papers are filled with detail, rumour and gossip on the talks. In the past few days, I have found myself in the unusual position of declining most media enquiries and ducking interview requests.

Not that this prevents my mug, along with those of the other team members, being paraded in print. One of the few interviews I give is a brief Q&A to an intrepid reporter from *Rapport*, the Afrikaans broadsheet.

Marizanne Kok managed to convince me, after I told her flat out I would offer no word on current matters, by asking me to reflect only on the 1990s constitutional negotiations and on the Argentinian experience of governmental disasters. I am somewhat amazed that my unremarkable utterances on both topics merit a big colour splash inside the paper today under the headline 'Dís die nagmerrie wat SA nie wil hê nie' (This is the nightmare that SA doesn't need). (Through populist misgovernance, Argentina holds the world record for sovereign debt defaults, to which I was an eyewitness during my ambassadorship there in 2009–2012 [see Chapter 19].) The EFF economic proposals would plunge South Africa off the same fiscal cliff.

The *Sunday Times* accurately headlines its article on the negotiating teams with the reminder that the people involved 'have a heavy responsibility – and not much time'. No pressure, then.

More instructive is the tabloid *Sunday World*, heavily briefed, it seems, by the ANC's rejectionist faction. The front page screams boldly: 'Cyril faces revolt over DA pact' (not that there is one, actually). It quotes two inside sources who advise that 'Prospect of an ANC-DA coalition divides NEC as majority aligned with Mantashe is said to be against deal "selling out black people".'

Yet, with just five days to go to D-Day (14 June), we have barely got into groove on likely arrangements. Meantime, from Durban, Dean Macpherson – the party provincial chairman and a good friend – calls to say that he has lined up both the IFP and ANC on a provincial power-sharing deal contingent on a national arrangement being in place.

I am impressed by his political deftness and surprised, by contrast, at the relative muteness of our Gauteng leadership. On the other hand, the Gauteng ANC is headed by an unpopular populist, Panyaza Lesufi, who crashed his party to a record low vote share (just 34 per cent) but behaves as though he is King of Gauteng, with a divine right to rule and no need to engage with the runner-up (the DA, with an unimpressive but determinative 27 per cent of the vote and seats in the provincial legislature).

I head back home to Cape Town to sort out my real life, some domestic and business matters, until we meet again with the ANC on Tuesday.

We also get some intel (who knows whether real or not) that the ANC is looking at an alternative line-up to secure a parliamentary majority by bypassing the DA and EFF and MK entirely. Our smart staff whizz Johann Coetzee quickly, via WhatsApp, crunches the numbers: ANC (159) + IFP (21) + Gayton McKenzie's PA (9) + Freedom Front Plus (6) added to nine other 'rats and mice' single-digit entities gets them to 204 votes – four more than needed to elect the president. Interesting option but of course highly unstable too.

Day 8: Monday 10 June

Once again, the ANC messages to request a meeting between us and their 'technical team' before the next bilateral round. Helen and Ryan in Johannesburg meet the ANC trio (Fébé Potgieter, Parks Tau and David Makhura).

Afterwards, our group receives a report-back from Ryan, who advises that the political aspect of the discussion yielded at least some insights for both sides. On our side, we said, whatever the technical modalities might be, the DA could not enter any arrangement which did not give the party 'some actual power' and in fact, with a multiparty arrangement, the balance of power.

The ANC anxiety appears to focus on KwaZulu-Natal and a real fear there of a conflagration and people dying. For the ANC, the GNU construction that they are punting is designed to prevent MK from going down the pathway of insurrection. It also provides a fig leaf (our interpretation) to cover the fact that such a government of national unity will in effect be an ANC-DA-IFP grand coalition.

Helen and Ryan underline to the ANC that we cannot vote for Cyril as president on Friday without an ironclad agreement beforehand that protects our interests. Let's see how all this pans out over the next few days ...

I fly back to Johannesburg to rejoin our negotiators.

Day 9: Tuesday 11 June

Our lawyers draft a 'framework agreement' to present at our noon meeting with the ANC team. In essence it repeats the previous spiel on non-negotiable principles and policies we outlined in Ryan's earlier framework document. This time, though, we get down to brass tacks on the quids for the quos of electing Ramaphosa president in three days' time.

It leaves blank the names and parties to be elected for the other positions of speaker, deputy speaker, etc. But it details that the ministers and deputies and their provincial equivalents will be determined by each party to the agreement (ANC, DA and IFP).

It specifies that such positions 'shall be divided broadly according to the proportion of each participating party's support within the GNU'. In other words, the DA proportion is calculated by dividing its number of seats in the National Assembly by the total number of seats of all GNU parties (ANC, DA and IFP) in the National Assembly.

We helpfully but pointedly insert these percentages for national government positions in the document: ANC 60 per cent; DA 33 per cent; IFP 7 per cent. (Subsequent arm wrestling over this clause nearly capsizes the GNU before it is even launched, and events will extravagantly prove how the DA plan gets the full Mike Tyson 'punch in the face' treatment.)

The other crunch issue detailed in the draft is the resolution of disputes in the multiparty cabinet. This is based on 'general consensus'. In the event of this happy state being unobtainable, however, then 'sufficient consensus' is deemed to be reached when 'parties in the GNU representing 60 per cent in the National Assembly' agree.

We deliberately borrow the term 'sufficient consensus' from the lore of Codesa. There Ramaphosa, the ANC chief negotiator, defined it with some brutality and crudity as 'sufficient consensus exists when the ANC and NP agree on something, then everyone else can get stuffed'. This time we codify it, more elegantly, to mean the same thing, except the DA now stands in for the vanquished NP. (This crucial clause survives unscathed in the final agreement.)

Among ourselves, we agree that there will be no provincial agreements absent a national deal with the ANC. Also, beyond the detail in our draft, we reckon that the urgency of the Friday deadline means that the issue of cabinet appointments will have to be rolled over beyond Friday for the next phase of the negotiations. And then, at some indeterminate future point, come decisions on government policy. Once again, all this is theoretical; we still have no agreement, even in outline, with the ANC.

We head off to the Enthovens' to see whether the minds will meet or how far apart we really are.

I realise in this meeting with the ANC core group (Enoch Godongwana, Fébé Potgieter, Parks Tau and David Makhura) that we are dealing with the visible tip of a much larger iceberg. It might not be easy, but we can certainly do business with this quartet. Unknown to us, except via leaks and rumours, is the much larger submerged body – whom we never sight. They are the fractious and often snarling majority who constitute the party's NEC. And they, ultimately, will have to approve any deal.

David Makhura advises that Godongwana is present to represent 'the markets' – and not without concern, given their gyrations as the investment community uncertainly awaits the outcome of the talks.

But there is a moment of light relief. Someone, known to both sides, has floated a kite for his own preferment and advised the media that the DA has proposed that Ramaphosa 'appoint a finance minister who is not in the ANC but recruited from respected financial institutions'. We assure Godongwana, whom we hold in high regard, that this is an invention. There seems to be a lot of special pleading and mythmaking in the media right now.

Helen repeats that the DA is in 'good faith' in these talks, but we need specific 'modalities' in seeking a genuine coalition that will not be a repeat of the 1994 version of the GNU.

As she says this, I remember an instructive conversation I had in 1997 when Nelson Mandela offered me a place in his cabinet. I was warned by one of FW de Klerk's former ministers (Dr Rina Venter) that the failure of that GNU was because 'De Klerk failed to pin down Mandela as to precise ground rules for minority parties in the coalition government'. Helen avers, correctly, that this minority party in 2024 is not intending to repeat the mistakes – and omissions – of 1994. 'History does not repeat, but it does instruct,' as American historian Timothy Snyder wrote.[3]

Helen is expert at riding her hobby-horses; the current favourite is the Basic Education Laws Amendment Bill, or BELA, which she quickly introduces into the conversation. Fair enough, Afrikaans groups think it the death knell for mother-tongue education. I rather think the economic trajectory we are on is more vital, but I keep my counsel.

We then get into some of the nitty-gritty. For example, we agree that there will be no 'sealed mandates' (meaning simply ministers in specific portfolios conducting affairs entirely independently of the rest of government). And there is some discussion of our document, which raises some concern on the ANC side of the table, especially on the issue of percentages for breaking deadlocks.

I chime in that the detail is one thing, but the governing reality is another: 'We accept that the DA is a 22 per cent party, but equally the ANC today is a 40 per cent party, not the 62 per cent you were in 1994.' I offer this in muted and decidedly non-aggressive tones, simply to underscore reality.

Fébé responds, 'We accept that we are a 40 per cent party.' (This acknowledgement will be undercut soon enough when the ANC behaves like a 70 per cent party not needing to share power with others, but this lies in the future.)

Much talk again from the ANC about the importance of the 'national dialogue', which is intended to be an outreach to 'the 22 million South Africans who have opted out of voting or registering', as Fébé explains it. I, of course, think this is a diversion from the task at hand, especially when David Makhura reminds the meeting that 'we don't have much time, and if we take too long to reach agreement, violence could erupt in KZN and spread elsewhere'.

He is the epitome of calm rationality, though, and tells us that while the county today suffers from many serious ailments, 'we also cannot be held to ransom by people who want to storm the Bastille.'

Given that the ANC sees itself as a revolutionary movement, I draw comfort that one of its key figures aligns against the local insurrectionists – an unstated but clear reference to MK and the EFF.

There is some concern from the ANC that our draft agreement effectively provides the DA with a veto over the ANC. 'This will spook people,' Parks Tau advises and questions whether aspects of our proposal will 'neuter the president and his prerogative powers'. We indicate in response that our proposal recognises the ANC majority relative to other parties, but 'sharing power must mean that we have some of it'.

Anyway, the biggest takeaway from today is that the ANC has removed the option it first preferred – a confidence and supply agreement to prop up a minority government. It has shifted onto our preferred terrain of a coalition government, although in ANC-speak this arrangement 'dare not speak its name', hence the acronym GNU.

There is some further discussion, and we end the meeting on a positive note. The ANC tells us it now 'understands where the DA stands'. They will go back to their national committee and report on our talks, and we agree to meet again tomorrow to take matters forward.

CREATION

Day 10: Wednesday 12 June

We awake this morning to alarming messages from our leadership in KwaZulu-Natal. The rumour mill there, in this most combustible of regions, is in overdrive. With the election of the provincial premier scheduled in two days, a political party is apparently offering bribes of more than R5 million per provincial legislator for ANC members to defect during the secret ballot to elect the top man.

We head off to a conference room at the hotel for an urgent Zoom session with the IFP and DA provincial honchos. Francois Rodgers, the DA leader in KwaZulu-Natal, says that not even certain DA legislators might be immune from the cash (perhaps of Russian provenance?) being spread about by a political party he names, but the IFP is firmly on board for an all-in deal with us, the ANC and themselves, plus the crucial swing vote of the single NFP member. This combination will get us just over the line to form a majority and block the MK-EFF alternative.

The IFP leadership assures us that their commitment to working with the DA both provincially and nationally is ironclad and there will be strict proportionality in allocating the new provincial executive (cabinet): IFP 4, ANC 3, DA 2 and NFP 1. And Thulasizwe Buthelezi, an IFP leader, promises 'full information sharing' on all approaches his party receives from the ANC. (In the event, two days hence, and absent any of the predicted drama, the IFP premier is elected, and the provincial cabinet allocation is exactly as predicted.)

Amity and light with the IFP, then. We now head back to Westcliff for our scheduled next round with the ANC at 11 am. Outlook more clouded there.

Dominique Botha greets us in the splendid winter sunshine, which bathes the stone house in dazzling light. She tells us that to move things in the right direction, she has arranged a splendid lunch for our delegations. 'Not Nando's this time!' she promises.

'Hurry up and wait' is the order of today, though. We sit around and wait and wait for the non-arriving ANC group. Helen receives a message from them advising that they 'are stuck in meetings'.

In anticipation of a long and conclusive meeting, we are all booked on the last flight out of Johannesburg tonight. From tomorrow, the drama moves to Cape Town, where Parliament is to meet on Friday.

I walk across to the edge of the lawn and take in the sweeping view of the treetop-level beauty of Johannesburg, where I have spent most of my life and where I launched my political career back in 1986 as a Johannesburg city councillor. From the elevation of Westcliff ridge, there is no sign of the decay and dysfunction into which the current municipal leadership (or, more precisely, the lack of it) has plunged the City of Gold.

Dominique did not exaggerate: the buffet lunch is an epicurean feast, and we much enjoy the fine foods, which Helen thoughtfully films and sends to Fébé Potgieter 'stuck in meetings', with the message 'See what you are missing!' But I can't help thinking that not only is the ANC rude in not showing up, but clearly there must be problems inside the comrades' camp over their proposed tie-up with the DA.

The always informed News24 journalists message me and the other DA negotiators requesting confirmation that the 'ANC has stood you up' for today's meeting. I decide to ignore this, although Helen confirms their no-show. The ANC never actually advises that our meeting is off, so we hang about.

Despite the delights of the sumptuous hospitality, lots of laughs with Adi and Dominique and a fascinating tour of their library (where first editions of the now sadly obscure South African author Sarah Gertrude Millin, who once lived in this house, are prominently displayed), today is essentially a complete waste of time. And time is the one essential there is very little of as the clock ticks down to Friday.

Later this evening, after arriving back in Cape Town, Helen relays a message from the ANC negotiators: 'They profoundly apologise for not pitching to our meeting today but their meetings with their tripartite partners [trade union federation Cosatu and the SACP] ran on to 1800. They are very edgy about the news that their talks with us never happened, as this is moving the markets.' They request a meeting with us tomorrow morning in Cape Town. Meanwhile,

Cyril finally messages John to request a meeting with him tomorrow afternoon.

Our concern is that the ANC is using all these postponements to rush us into a deal ahead of Friday's vote for president without essential details in place to govern the coalition. Helen sends Nkenke Kekana a message: 'Let me be blunt (as I tend to be). We cannot vote on Friday for President Ramaphosa unless we have a signed and sealed agreement that includes the clauses we put into that [framework] document.'

She is 100 per cent correct. Let's see what we can sign and seal tomorrow.

Day 11: Thursday 13 June

D-Day minus one for South Africa (although the actual D-Day, 6 June 1944, was commemorated exactly one week ago). And, as we will tonight burn the midnight oil, spilling into the next morning, this too will be 'the longest day'.

If the Enthovens' Johannesburg home is steeped in history and elegance, our venue today in Cape Town – the SunSquare Hotel in the City Bowl – is a monument to corporate blandness. We repair downstairs to a basement conference room to await the ANC. Miraculously, this time they are only 28 minutes late for our scheduled noon start.

Profuse apologies from them for yesterday's no-show, and David Makhura explains, 'We don't want you to get the impression that that meeting wasn't important to us. It is, but we had so many internal meetings to conclude.' Fair enough, as is his next statement: 'South Africa is on edge about what could happen tomorrow.' Too true, as reflected in the blizzard of messages on this topic that light up my phone.

Our meeting today, the longest with the ANC so far, stretches on for more than three hours.

The ANC regards our draft document as 'too legalistic' (not surprising, since it was drafted by lawyers) and too elaborate. Certain clauses of it, in their view, undermine both the Constitution and government practice. They also disdain the formula we offer of a three-party agreement (ANC, DA and IFP) as a 'grand coalition' or an 'elite pact', which for them is 'political suicide'. Their demand is for a broad-based 'government of national unity'. This, they advise, will offset their refusal to do an ANC-EFF-MK deal, which is now off the table.

For us, on the basis of 'a rose by any other name', form and title are far less important than substance, and we drill down into our essential non-negotiables. We have no mandate to speak for the IFP, we advise, but our bottom lines are the requirements of proportionality in cabinet composition, the precise definition of 'sufficient consensus' to break deadlocks, and real power-sharing where it matters, such as input and influence on the budget. We also need sight of which other parties the ANC intends to bring into these arrangements. We advise then that whichever other parties join this government jamboree, we 'don't want our power in it to be diluted' by minnow parties with minimal support from the electorate.

We agree that we will draft a new, pared-down 'statement of intent' that will, in the first instance, be signed by the ANC and the DA and later by other participating parties. It will (per David Makhura) 'not be too legalistic'. We agree tonight to exchange drafts and, hopefully, reach agreement – before Parliament votes on the election of the president tomorrow at around 10 am. Makhura advises that the 'President's word is his bond, agreements he reaches with [Steenhuisen] will be honoured.'

Before we leave, Helen tells the meeting that whatever statement we agree to must be signed by both parties to formalise the deal. I pipe up, as the self-described 'detribalised lawyer' in the room, that this is not crucial: in law, only agreements on the sale of land need a signature; for most others, the basic law of contract suffices (offer and acceptance equals agreement).

As Helen and I walk out of the hotel to the nearby DA offices, we have a blazing row. She feels I undermined her in the meeting. I vehemently object, with some choice expletives, to her dismissive waving of her hand in my face. Childish indeed, and I am later chastened both by my rudeness and by Siviwe's rueful remark: 'You and Helen behave like an old married couple, always arguing!' Indeed. We soon enough patch up our quarrel. In truth, my bad behaviour is the result of relentless pressure placing all our team under strain. Little do we know then that it is soon going to get a lot worse …

We now meet John in the DA offices for his report on his first meeting with Ramaphosa since the 29 May election.

He says that their coffee date went well enough. He confirms that Cyril, whom he describes as extremely relaxed and convivial, will make him, after his election as president tomorrow, 'a serious and substantive offer' for the DA to join the government. John advises that he cheekily told His Excellency not to suggest the DA takes up 'the ministry of women and children'. Cyril also tells John which parties he intends to invite into the cabinet. (On this matter, at least, Ramaphosa's commitment is honoured when the final cabinet is announced ten days later.)

All that is now needed, John cheerily informs us, is a solid agreement with the ANC to conclude this phase. Easier said than achieved, as the next 20 hours prove.

It is now midnight, and I am at home, nursing a stiff Scotch and checking my phone. Earlier this evening, sequestered in the hotel basement, we had another series of back-to-back meetings, first with the ANC (on Zoom), then with the IFP in person, and with later feedback to the DA federal executive. Our lawyers (Elzanne Jonker and Michael Bishop) are also in the mix and rapidly convert tentative agreements reached on this statement of intent into (we hope) bulletproof language.

Day 12: Friday 14 June

At 1.48 am we have now draft 10 (!) of the statement of intent, which the parties need to conclude and sign before 10 this morning. There is a lot of haggling between our side and the ANC on the wording of three specific clauses relating to the proportionality requirement for cabinet appointments (reflecting the seats of each party in Parliament); the dear old definition of 'sufficient consensus' to break deadlocks on disputes in the executive; and, finally, who has the veto, and how it is exercised, on adding new parties to the GNU beyond the ANC, DA and IFP.

These three clauses, and changing versions of them, fly back and forth through cyberspace into the wee hours. (I finally go to sleep around 2 am and pick up the thread at 6.30.)

We agree to some changes without conceding our bottom lines on these clauses; John, at 5.44 am, messages the president with our proposals and advises him that he can discuss these with Ramaphosa 'at any time' but that we need to agree these to get 'over the line' before Parliament sits this morning. He ends his message with the hope that 'this is a historic moment for our country'.

At 7.58 am the Presidency send back their changes, which are epic and threaten to derail the entire deal. Ramaphosa proposes to junk the words 'broadly proportional' to seats won in the National Assembly in forming the cabinet and replace them with the nebulous statement that the GNU shall reflect 'genuine inclusiveness'. He also strikes out the requirement that parties (ANC and DA effectively) representing 60 per cent of the National Assembly have the final say in determining 'sufficient consensus' and removes the veto right of signatory parties to new admissions to the GNU.

At 7.30 am I rush from home to the Westin Hotel, opposite the Cape Town International Convention Centre, where Parliament is about to meet. What is it about basement conference rooms? This one is where the DA parliamentary caucus is assembling, and I huddle with John and Leon Schreiber as we weigh the meaning of Cyril's last-minute radical changes.

In my view, this rewriting by Cyril (or his team) is an act of bad faith, completely at variance with what his negotiators concluded with us a few hours before. It is a deal breaker. Helen, on the phone and now en route to the hotel, is even more vehement. John and Leon are deeply anxious as the deal starts to unravel. Though I do manage to inject some humour into the gathering gloom by offering the thought,

'What would the DA do without its Leons?' Nervous laughter from John and (the other) Leon.

Helen messages Fébé Potgieter that the 'president's version has changed the definition of two clauses that are cardinal to us and this we cannot accept'. John follows up with a message to Ramaphosa saying that the clauses he changed regarding proportionality and the 60 per cent requirement for sufficient consensus ('to prevent the ganging up of small parties against the two largest parties to the agreement') are not only compromises on our part from our starting point but their retention is 'fundamental to our participation'. Helen goes outside and tells the media pack that 'there will be no deal until the DA is satisfied with the clauses on proportional representation and sufficient consensus'. Amen to that. We have basically yielded the issue of other parties entering the GNU, with John accepting Cyril's word on who will be sitting around the cabinet table.

Yet the clock ticks ever down and we appear no closer on the two clauses outstanding, although at this stage Andries Nel takes over as the anchor from the ANC side. There is little movement on the substance.

The DA MPs troop across the road to the convention centre to be sworn into office, although they have yet to be instructed on whom to vote for as speaker and then president. Helen, Ivan Meyer and I take our seats behind the cordon of the makeshift venue, and I have not a jot of regret for being, this time, an observer and not a member of the new Parliament. But I have some anxiety on how the rest of the morning will unfold and whether, for the first time ever, my party will enter national power. Or remain, as before, on the opposition benches.

At 11.21,[4] John, from his seat inside, confirms that there is no deal without resolution on these clauses and we inform Andries Nel. A few minutes later, he sends a refreshed version headed 'Final Final Final'. But is it, in fact? Anyway, given Helen's insistence on a signed contract, there is no time both to check the new wording and to get the signatures from both sides.

The 'final version' also appends the party designations for the three posts up for imminent election by the just-constituted Parliament: president (ANC), speaker (ANC) and deputy speaker (DA).

Providence, in the improbable form of the EFF's Floyd Shivambu, then lends a hand: for some inexplicable reason, he calls for a half-hour 'caucus break', which the presiding officer, Chief Justice Zondo, grants. Whew.

We now check the changes: the 60 per cent requirement (meaning the ANC and DA have final say on disputes) is reinserted as per our original draft. The other contested clause – number 16 – appears more as a word salad, with bits and pieces from both sides tossed into the document. It constitutes the government of national unity on the basis of 'genuine inclusiveness' of the contracting parties, 'broadly taking into account the number of seats parties have in the National Assembly and the need to advance the national interest. The President shall in constituting the executive take into account the electoral outcomes.'

We think this meets our essentials, if barely (a battle royal on its meaning lies ahead), and sign the document.

The Rubicon was a small stream separating Cisalpine Gaul from Rome. When Julius Caesar crossed it in 49 BC, with fatal consequences, he muttered, 'The die is cast.' Some 1 975 years on, we cross our own great divide. We throw in our lot with the ANC, and the DA votes in the ANC's Thoko Didiza as speaker, Annelie Lotriet (DA) as deputy speaker and, finally, Cyril Ramaphosa as president.

John addresses a packed press conference on this historic moment, while Geordin Hill-Lewis hosts a lunch for a few of us in his private dining room (a nice perk of being mayor and joint landlord of the convention centre). We reminisce on all the battles past, won and often lost, that have brought us to this point.

Later that evening, after dear Michal treats us to a splendid dinner *à deux* at a local fine-dining place, I return home, very tired but quite unexpectedly moved by the enormity of this day.

I write with some feeling to John, whom I first met in 1996 as a young campaign activist in Durban: 'John, I felt a deep sense of pride today ... you are the very first of us to enter the portal of power and on far better terms than those offered to me by Mandela in 1997. Strength for this journey.'

He replies immediately and with excessive generosity: 'Thanks AJ. None of this would have been possible without the foundation that you, Douglas [Gibson], James [Selfe], Dene [Smuts] and many others laid for us to be where we are today.'

In thanking me for the work done on getting this over the line, neither he nor I know that the worst, most dangerous part of the journey lies just ahead.

Day 13: Saturday 15 June

Finally, quiet time at home after the tumult of recent days. My phone rings. It is Michael Katz on the line. Michael still heads the huge law firm ENS in Johannesburg. He was my first boss when I served articles of clerkship as an attorney at Edward Nathan & Friedland (as ENS was then called) way back in 1983. We have a warm chat, and he marvels at the achievement of yesterday and the worst-case outcome avoided with the agreement embodied in the statement of intent.

And then he, arguably the ablest commercial lawyer in the country, adds: 'Of course, Tony, this document is not enforceable in law. You can't go to court if there is a dispute on its terms. It is a political statement, and it rests on the politicians to make it work.' Those words will prove very instructive in the days ahead.

9
Endgame

Day 15: Monday 17 June

Shepherds? Guide dogs? Minders? What, I ask myself, is the role of us negotiators as we face the grittier task of finalising the party's participation in the new and yet unformed government of national unity. I settle on the image of the sherpa who helps the mountaineer reach the summit, hopefully intact.

Friday's vote in Parliament for Ramaphosa's re-election as president (like the provincial votes for the ANC's Panyaza Lesufi as premier of Gauteng and the IFP's Thami Ntuli as premier of KwaZulu-Natal) was based on an agreement. Yet its last-minute provisions will allow much scope for manoeuvring in terms of seats (both in number and influence) at a cabinet table still being designed. The days ahead will see endless name-calling and back-and-forth bids and counterbids, while the pinnacle will be ever more obscure.

Captain Hindsight soon suggests that we should have got something more ironclad, yet objectively time didn't allow for that. On the other hand, I now think part of the explanation for why the ANC kept delaying and cancelling meetings was to pressure last-minute changes in the document, then get our votes for Ramaphosa and later reinterpret key clauses to our disadvantage. Let's see how this all pans out ...

The DA sherpas meet in late afternoon with John and the other Leon (Schreiber) at the DA head office in Gardens, Cape Town, to navigate the way ahead. The ANC has announced that other parties are joining the GNU with no reference to us, despite understanding that we should first have been consulted. Helen sends off a note of protest on this to Mbalula. (They later spar on TV.) Then we consider the quantum and sorts of cabinet posts we should seek. 'We don't have a deal, just a piece of paper,' one of our number gloomily concludes. Eerie silence from the ANC on further engagement with us to sort all this out. Clearly, John needs a follow-up meeting with Ramaphosa to clear things up.

Meanwhile, the JSE, on the back of Friday's agreement, hits an all-time high, with stocks surging like the song 'Kumbaya', unaware of discordant notes soon to sound.

Joshua Dickinson, a DA staff member, works out that in a 30-seat cabinet, the DA proportional share (after proportionally diluting to allow smaller parties to enter) would be nine ministers, and the ANC's 17. We also compile a wish list of posts, including deputy president or minister in the Presidency, plus energy, justice, public service, trade, industry and competition, transport, public works and infrastructure, and home affairs, and deputy minister of finance. (In the end, only three of those are obtained, with one-third fewer ministries than our entitlement.) How to achieve any of this is the business of the next few days.

Day 16: Tuesday 18 June

Silence from the ANC side. John and the other MPs decamp to Pretoria for Ramaphosa's inauguration the next day.

Off for supper to our friends Doug and Sue Band. I find it almost surreal, but comforting in another sense, to know that people have lives outside the carapace in which I have been encased these past weeks. I let off some steam on the frustration of the past days and dimmed expectations for the week ahead. We have lots of laughs about the absurdities of politics and some politicians, although I remind myself that for much of my life, I was a member of this peculiar tribe.

Day 17: Wednesday 19 June

Cyril is inaugurated with the usual pomp and gives an unusually inclusive and conciliatory speech, more about the country and far less about the ANC.

John sends him a message of congratulations and tells him, 'It is imperative that you and I meet to discuss the DA component in the executive. I am concerned that our respective parties are speaking past each other, including in public ... I am available to meet at your earliest convenience as I do not believe that allowing a vacuum to take shape will be conducive to getting the GNU off to a good start.' In response, Ramaphosa suggests a get-together on Friday morning at his official residence, Mahlamba Ndlopfu, in Pretoria.

Day 18: Thursday 20 June

This morning, the always informed Pieter du Toit, deputy editor of News24, has a trenchant opinion article on the portal, South Africa's best-read news site, for which I am a weekly columnist (on leave owing to my current involvement). He writes, '[T]he ANC's decision-making process is laborious, messy, often contradictory, exceedingly chaotic and always noisy ...

'In the week preceding Ramaphosa's announcement of the NEC's decision to support the idea of a government of national unity, the loudest voices were those antagonistic towards the idea ... But as the moment that the ANC will have to hand some executive power to the DA is approaching, dissenting and angry voices and groups [fully ventilated on Twitter by the SACP and Cosatu, among others] are again becoming louder.'

He concludes: 'Ramaphosa has very little choice. His party have agreed to a model [encapsulated in the statement of intent], and they need the DA to ensure stability ... The next few days will be crucial.'

We will now see how strong that 'need' is.[1]

At the ANC's request, we meet on Zoom with their core group at noon. By far the tensest meeting to date. The ANC are very upset at 'how some are communicating', this being a reference to Helen's TV interview on the meaning of the statement of intent and her interpretation of it, and her claim that the ANC secretary-general (Mbalula) had clearly not read the document he signed.

David Makhura avers that detractors of the pact 'say it won't last a day'. And he reminds the meeting, 'We have a duty to find each other.'

Ryan messages our group that he can play either the bad cop or Mother Teresa – 'I have a range.' He then reads out to the meeting a rather triumphalist tweet from Fikile Mbalula: 'It's essential to dispel any misconceptions regarding any party's ability to outmanoeuvre the ANC's vision ... The GNU, an ANC-led initiative, ensures than no single party, whether DA, IFP or others, can hold our national agenda hostage.'

Public spats are a two-way street.

We move to a lesson in constitutional civics, à la ANC. Ronald Lamola reminds the meeting that the ANC is 'a party of constitutionalists', which is good to know even if the same constitutionalists were on holiday during the nine years of Zuma. Anyway, we are informed that the president's prerogative powers can't be trumped by our agreement. At one level this is a truism, but at another it is completely misleading, since the statement of intent references both these powers and the limitations the agreement places on them. (Lamola's line soon enough enters the public domain, via the president's spokesman, Vincent Magwenya.)

Before the argument proceeds further, I excuse myself from the meeting. The family of James Selfe has requested that I speak at his memorial service this afternoon. He died a few weeks ago. He had endured years of struggle with the debilitating multiple system atrophy disease, which imprisoned him in a failing body while his steely mind remained sharp to the very end.

'Jimmy,' as I always called him, served the party – under five leaders – for more than 40 years. He chaired the federal executive for 20 of them, his ego never outshining the leader, whatever he thought of the different incumbents. He was a true servant-leader – with a wry sense of humour to boot. During recent days, Alan (Winde), Ryan and I have lamented his absence from the current negotiations round.

In my eulogy to the packed auditorium at Kirstenbosch Botanical Garden, populated with many figures from the party hierarchy past and present, I offer his legacy from past times for the new realities facing both country and party.

'Whatever the future holds in the brave and uncertain new world of coalition South Africa and the breaking of the ANC's hegemony, James's life and example will accompany the DA leadership forward like a stable and constant shadow.'

I choke up at the end of my tribute to our gallant, now-departed friend, a true soldier for democracy.

Day 19: Friday 21 June

I have a useful chat with Bobby Godsell, in the 1980s the interlocutor for mining giant Anglo American and Cyril Ramaphosa, who then headed the National Union of Mineworkers. More directly for me, Bobby was the leader of the Young Progressives in Durban when I joined the movement way back in 1970, the first step in a long political journey. Bobby, as ever, is a fount of encouragement and pithy advice on the current saga, and offers general encouragement and some specific views on how to get this thing over the line.

John reports back on his just-concluded discussion with Ramaphosa. Bottom line: Cyril intends to appoint a multiparty government of around eight parties in cabinet but to reward the DA with just three ministerial posts, and he would like our reaction to this. John says that he gave the president a 'tentative no' to his offer. I frankly don't understand his tentativeness; I would have thrown it back at him. Ramaphosa asks him to respond after party consultations. He wants to announce the cabinet two days hence, on Sunday. (This happens a week later, on 29 June.)

Reaction in our group call is fast and furious: 'He is lowballing us,' is the polite, though objective, response from Siwiwe. Ryan says, 'It is a game of chicken and let's see where this ends.'

We agree to draft a comprehensive written response to Ramaphosa. We don't want to be suborned and we have the balance of power. But we know we 'gave away' our maximum leverage on Friday (when we voted to re-elect Ramaphosa). On the other hand, we will be blamed by all and sundry, not least by business, if this deal collapses, although the markets are closed until Monday. And a lot of instant polling shows strong support among the DA voter base for participating in the GNU. A dilemma.

Day 20: Saturday 22 June

Yesterday we sent our response to Ramaphosa under John's signature. After observing the usual courtesies, it advised the president of our interpretation of the phrases 'respecting the will of the people through the election result' (a much-repeated ANC trope) and 'the need for inclusivity'.

Our letter offers our proportionate dilution of some of our cabinet entitlement to accommodate the five smaller parties (outside of ANC, DA and IFP) Ramaphosa wishes to bring in. Then we compute our entitlement (as a percentage share of parties participating in the cabinet) to mean nine posts for the DA and 15 for the ANC, based on fact that the ANC has 56 per cent of the seats of parties participating in the new government and we have 30 per cent.

John then drops his original demand (made at the Friday meeting with Ramaphosa) for the deputy presidency, noting, 'This is despite this position traditionally going to the second-largest party' in a coalition. He forcefully dismisses the derisory offer of three seats for us, and states, 'It is essential for the party to be represented across the five clusters of government.'

That triptych of ideal politics is about to be severely tested today and over the next week. Pushback comes informally when a trusted business intermediary advises, on impeccable authority, that the ANC is prepared to offer us seven cabinet posts plus the crucial deputy ministry of finance (though cancelled out to an extent by the idea that the ANC will generously allocate itself an additional deputy ministry of finance too).

Our group notes how the ANC is trying to diminish our 22 per cent of the total National Assembly seats (30 per cent among participating GNU parties) and how to counter this.

Sure enough, in late afternoon, we receive a formal response from the ANC secretary-general precisely along these lines. Mbalula claims, per his letter, that he is mandated by Ramaphosa to respond, since the negotiations are between two parties (ANC and DA) and both sides are 'deadlocked' on the meaning of clause 16 in the agreement on the meaning of 'proportionality' in composing the cabinet. This 'difference of understanding', as he delicately describes it, boils down to whether seats in the new government (or executive) are assigned as a percentage of the total number of seats in cabinet (DA proposal) or as a reflection of the number of seats in the National Assembly (ANC proposal). Hitherto, we were unaware of such a difference of opinion resulting in a 'deadlock'; clearly, the ANC is laying the ground for its new approach.

However, he makes nonsense of his own argument when he inserts a table in the letter that blanks out all other participating parties in the GNU, including the ANC, and assigns six cabinet (and seven deputy) ministers to the DA. How is this computed? He offers only this non sequitur: 'We believe [it] to be a fair and reasonable manner of determining the number of positions in the cabinet.'

He ends his note advising, 'The nation awaits the conclusion of these discussions.' And wait it will until we figure out a response to this. First, we decide, informally, to break our silence and start some selective briefings of our own to key media (the ANC has been doing this all week), and second, tomorrow, to send a robust response to Mbalula.

Ryan thinks the ANC doesn't really want to share power: 'CR [Ramaphosa] wants the DA in cabinet but to be neutered and disempowered – but with fringe benefits.' John, on the other hand, believes the party will suffer deeply if it is seen to walk away from even a sub-par power-sharing deal.

An immersion into normalcy: Michal and I go for dinner to our dear friend the indomitable Audrey Hamilton Russell (who is also the cousin of Sandra Botha and Dominique Botha). At 87 years of age, Audrey has the zest and enthusiasm of someone in her forties. She has prepared a wonderful feast (or my idea of one: roast lamb and crisp potatoes). She is, as ever, warmly supportive and encouraging. I remind her how we first bonded more than 20 years ago: an admired political colleague of that time had just published a thuddingly dull memoir. Audrey, who reads voraciously on all topics, naturally had read it. At the time, I asked her opinion of it. 'After page 20, I lost the will to live,' was her verdict. Typical!

Day 21: Sunday 23 June

President Harry Truman once said, 'If you want a friend in Washington, get a dog.' Throughout my political career, and long before, I was surrounded by hounds. We are now on our third set of dachshunds in 24 years. Jack and Lyla, the current duo, are typical of the breed: loving, demanding and endlessly greedy. But their morning expectation – signalled by a barked demand or whine – is a brisk walk. Never mind lesser matters such as the fate of the nation: their needs are to be answered. So I head out with them into the warm, wintry morning of our Constantia neighbourhood.

On my return, I read the Sunday papers, which contain plenty of off-the-books briefings from both sides. However, we are not responsible for the screaming headline in the tabloid *Sunday World*, 'Government of National Unity faces collapse'. (They usually are impeccably briefed by the anti-Ramaphosa-ites in the NEC.) Survé's poison pens at Independent Media have a confected story advising that there is a

5 pm deadline today for the DA to accept the cabinet proposals or be excluded. Entirely fake news, as the ANC messages us to confirm.

Ryan, when our group meets, thinks the DA at this moment has 'massive leverage', since we are the difference between a stable government and a minority coalition. And he sets out to draft our response to Mbalula. (In the event, ironically, since Helen, as fedex chair, signs off on the letter it is she, not Ryan, who will bear the brunt of public anger after it is published. Not that Helen minds publicity – *au contraire*!)

We all chip in with amendments. Broadly, I remind my fellow negotiators that the essence of a negotiation is to be prepared to walk away from it. Anyway, Ryan borrows from Lenin's playbook: 'Probe with bayonets: if you encounter mush, you proceed; if you meet steel, you withdraw.' That is the idea anyway.

Our 'bayonets' letter is premised on rejecting the ANC view that cabinet numbers can be distributed among all parties in the whole of Parliament, since this would include all parties, including those in opposition to the GNU.

'It is obvious that the distribution of positions in cabinet can only start with a consideration of the relative size of the parties participating in government. Governments, by definition, are made up of parties participating in government. They are not made up of parties in opposition – that is what Parliament is for.'

We reiterate our demand for a fair shake, as quantified before, and for cabinet representation across all the clusters (economic sectors, social protection, governance, justice and crime prevention, and international cooperation), with a list of preferred ministries under each heading.

However, the final 'demand' in our response will soon be weaponised by both the ANC and several civil society and media pearl-clutchers to suggest that the DA is intent on setting up a parallel state based on an illegal foundation. We push the envelope here stating that any directors general in departments headed by DA ministers should be 'reconsidered in light of our concern that incumbents may not be amenable to direction from DA ministers, especially given the ANC's cadre deployment strategy'.

In retrospect, this paragraph was clumsy in its construction, because it allowed the normal circle of critics, and a few new ones, to paint the party as unconstitutional. In fact, the plain evidence of the ANC stuffing the upper reaches of the state administration with party loyalists was a demonstrable fact, not the imaginings of the politically paranoid.

We also call for any tenders awarded by such departments, since election day, to be subject to review. Here we have in mind the possibility of last-minute departmental manoeuvring to handcuff DA ministers before they enter government.

We also remind the ANC that our participation in governments in Gauteng and KwaZulu-Natal depends 'on our participation in government at national level'.

Barely has the letter landed (via email) than we receive furious blowback. Mbalula is incandescent and tells Helen that the missive is 'a deal breaker'. And then Ramaphosa messages John to meet him tomorrow in Johannesburg 'to resolve issues'.

Day 22: Monday 24 June

Every Monday morning the firm I chair, Resolve Communications, has its weekly staff meeting. I edge my way slowly through the grinding traffic (there is no option given its density) to our offices in Gardens, Cape Town. En route I listen to a lot of chatter and comment on the CapeTalk radio call-in show on the negotiations. 'Why can't they finish this thing?' asks one irate caller. Another suggests the 'DA is being arrogant' (a favoured depiction of the party by its opponents), and many sound off on the horrors of the EFF entering the government. Lots of vox populi on-point.

John flies out from Cape Town early this morning for his midday meeting with Ramaphosa at the president's private residence in Hyde Park, Johannesburg.

Before this meeting, a business friend with access to key ANC members advises that 'the DA is demanding too much and the most posts the DA would get is six, and if there is no agreement today, they [the ANC] will go without the DA.' Is it a feint to pile the pressure on or is it their bottom line?

While waiting on our chat group for John's report-back from his meeting, I message him, with a nod to papal elections, and ask if the outcome is 'white smoke, black smoke, no smoke'? He replies, 'grey smoke'. He soon gives us the lowdown: 'Cyril told me he was very upset with our letter – "It didn't just put a cat on the table, it was a leopard." He also rejected our assertions on directors general as being legally problematic.'

However, after this prelude, the president then offered six cabinet posts for the DA in a seven-party government (ANC, DA, IFP, Freedom Front Plus, Patriotic Alliance, Good and Pan Africanist Congress). Two small parties (United Democratic Movement and Al Jama-ah) are represented at sub-cabinet level, with a deputy ministry each. And while the quantum is modest, to put matters at their mildest, the qualitative offer impresses.

The DA is offered the ministries of trade, industry and competition, home affairs, public works and infrastructure, communications, basic education and forestry, fisheries and environment. Four deputy ministries are also thrown in.

Our collective dismay at the total is offset by the real opportunity offered by these key posts to both exercise meaningful power and offer change to the lives of millions of people.

Of the half-dozen ministries, by far the most significant is the Department of Trade, Industry and Competition (DTIC). This ministry sits at the heart of the economy. Under outgoing minister Ebrahim Patel, a micromanaging ideologue, it was ground zero for statism, protectionism and deindustrialisation. The mind boggles at the liberating effect a business-friendly, growth-oriented DA person could bring to this office.

How to respond? The president requests John to do so as soon as possible since he wants to finalise the cabinet.

While we settle on a response, the public space is filled by the leaking of our original letter to the ANC on Sunday. A media house confirms it was sent to them by 'ANC sources'. As Helen puts it, 'The amount of hate mail that has been generated against us this past 24 hours since Fikile [Mbalula] released the letter has led to an [explosion] on social media and my own inbox is brimming.' Clearly, the narrative being set by ANC and their media supporters is to cast the DA as the villain of the piece. (It will soon get a whole lot worse.)

We send back to Ramaphosa a letter under Steenhuisen's signature. We agree that we should accept the six ministries offered and explain why an additional two will seal the deal for us.

John's letter thanks Ramaphosa for 'the constructive meeting' and for the cabinet proposals, which he accepts and regards as 'a serious offer'. Then he adds this caveat: 'It is going to be extremely difficult for me to get my party to accept one-third (ie six posts) of the ANC's allocation when we won more than half the number of votes of the ANC.' He advises Ramaphosa that his original offer does not give expression to clause 16, on proportionality, in the statement of intent.

To 'clear the final hurdle' he proposes a compromise – a climb-down from the nine we believe to be our entitlement but an improvement on Cyril's modest offer. Rather, he suggests that, in addition to the six positions, 'another two' be allocated to the DA, chosen from any of sports, arts and culture, rural development and land reform, agriculture and public service and administration. He also indicates there should be an equivalent number of deputy ministers since 'there is no rationale for reducing the number to only four'.

He asks for the president's 'considered feedback ... to get us over the line'.

This time, it is not long in coming (it lands next afternoon; see below), although history will not likely judge it to be 'considered'. Rather, Ramaphosa's response is dripping in barely contained (feigned?) fury, righteous indignation and false assertions, and is histrionic, even bullying in tone.

One of my oldest friends from Johannesburg, Cliff Garrun, comes round for dinner with his daughter Kim. I find it hard to concentrate on social matters, with all the background negotiations drama playing in my head. But Cliff – whom I recruited into both student and municipal politics (what are friends for?) – is ever-patient and understanding. We have been in many rodeos together over 40 years, but I am not as hopeful as Kim is (youthful idealism?) that there will be a good outcome on this one.

Later, I go to sleep not expecting a positive response from the Presidency and wonder whether the past three weeks have been an exercise in utter futility.

Day 23: Tuesday 25 June

The alarm wakes me at the absurdly early time of 4.30 am. I am due to fly at first light to Johannesburg for a business meeting. On rising, I receive a message that it is now postponed. This allows me, over coffee, to look at the pile of messages and media reports that crowd my inbox. None of it makes for pleasant reading.

Yesterday, the normally even-handed Fébé Potgieter – one of the ANC's core negotiators – took to social media to denounce John's and Helen's letters as 'outlandish and ridiculous'. And she is allegedly part of the reasonable faction of that fractured organisation!

Helen, whose usual high energy has succumbed overnight to illness, sends a sobering message (at 2.36 am!) to our group: 'We cannot walk away. The DA will be blamed 100 per cent. The country will go into a deep and collective depression over a very long period and blame it all on us. We have taken the country with us to this point. We will lose them just as quickly. Whatever we say, Cyril will come across as having made us a reasonable offer that we rejected ...'

Later this morning, she elaborates that it will be 'extremely difficult to get the media and the public to understand that WE are being short-changed here. Most probably they think Cyril is being generous ... There will be an enormous cost to walking away. Greater than we can imagine.'

I am deeply taken by her view. Helen commenced this process as a coalition hawk who didn't want to touch the corrupt ANC with the proverbial bargepole nor have the DA contaminated by the ANC's sins of misgovernance. Her comment here shows her adaptive side and reading, in my view accurately, of the current – and likely future – political weather.

At 8 am, we have a group call. John reports back on a late-night phone chat he had with Ramaphosa, who advised him he can't go beyond the six posts offered, as 'he has got a lot of internal problems due to the "DA letter of demand".' (This no doubt explains the tone of his letter to John, soon to arrive.) John's view is that we must call it: 'We will remain in opposition.'

Ryan takes the contra view to Helen: 'It is not about whether it is six or eight seats. It is all about the ANC seeking to neutralise and undermine the agreement and the DA with it. We are going to land up in a burning house and we won't be able to get out of it. We should be prepared to walk away, and those people who don't like us will blame us anyway.'

Even the usually emollient Alan Winde is downbeat. He suggests that 'six seats for us out of 30 is just unacceptable. The ANC wants the DA to save the ANC so it can keep governing in the usual way it has always done without changing.'

I am deeply ambivalent on it all, except to offer the rather unhelpful view that 'better no deal than a bad one'. A very fatigued Siwiwe seems the keenest of our group to keep the conversation going with the ANC.

We do agree, though, that a further discussion between John and Cyril might be worth it. Leon Schreiber injects some humour into it all by asking whether it is 'Hiroshima (all blown up) or Stalingrad (surrounded and captured) for us?' Having read several books on Operation Barbarossa (the German invasion of the Soviet Union), I interject: 'The danger is that the DA will go in and become the modern equivalent of Field Marshal Paulus!' (He infamously led the German Sixth Army to surrender at Stalingrad in 1943 and then spent nine years in a Soviet prison camp.) Alan Winde, at least, is amused by my gallows humour.

The press is even gloomier than our conversation, as are the declining markets. 'Tensions rise in the GNU as DA states demands' is the front-page headline in *Business Day*. Ramaphosa is quoted [from his weekly newsletter] as advising, 'The GNU cannot be preoccupied with jockeying for positions, tussles over appointments or squabbles within and between parties.'[2] Sophistry of a high order from the presidential pen.

Our group adjourns and reaches out individually to various opinion formers, influencers and ANC whisperers to see if we can nudge matters in a more positive direction.

Mid-afternoon, Cyril's reply to John arrives. Gone is the avuncular charm of earlier meetings. This is a blistering, full-frontal attack.

He commences by lamenting that 'the habit of negotiating through correspondence, as adopted by the DA, can be problematic'. I suppose a paper trail is inconvenient for him.

But the real kicker is his spurious suggestion that this 'can make parties play to the public gallery of public opinion through media leakages'. Were it not for more serious charges to follow in short order in his letter, this would be truly hilarious: we know as fact that it is the ANC which has done the leaking, which allows its president to now ride his high horse of indignation!

Then he goes on to advise that our proposals 'jeopardised the foundation of the GNU'. He states that the request for the two additional cabinet seats amounts to 'moving the goalposts'. Quite how our polite response to his modest offer of six positions, way below the proportionality demarcated by the statement of intent, is 'undermining' is not explained. And didn't he ask us to respond to his offer just one day ago?

What he does elucidate at some length is his understanding of the same agreement, far removed from our own. In his view, the wording of the now infamous clause [16], which he emphasises in bold, 'broadly taking into account' electoral outcomes in composing the government, is entirely subservient, in his opinion, to 'the full appreciation of the President retaining discretion to constitute the Cabinet'.

His view of things seems to involve having his cake (the presidential power to select the cabinet) and eating it (the undertaking in the statement of intent to respect proportionality). He accordingly advises on his prerogative powers to appoint ministers: 'I have duly and sufficiently tempered them to fulfil the commitment of the statement of intent.'

The question left begging in his missive is staggering: Ramaphosa alone, it seems, will deem what the rules of the agreement are, and he will red-card players who, in his view, violate the rules. Further, he will be judge and jury on what and who aligns with the statement of intent. This, in his view, has been sabotaged by us: 'The latest proposals by the DA ... undermines the process. We are unable to accede to the latest proposals, nor its continuously changing of the meaning of the statement of intent and moving of the goalposts.'

It is quite clear that the statement of intent, particularly the vexed clause 16, with all its imprecisions and ambiguities, is now being used by one of the signatories (the ANC) as a weapon of attack against the other signatory, namely the DA.

My first impression on reading his aggressive jeremiad is to throw it in the bin; my second is to ask whether we are in fact in a proper, or any, negotiation at all. Or are we simply to scoop up any crumbs that are scattered from President Cyril's table?

My sour response is aggravated by other, less important morsels that his letter contains. He accuses the DA, for example our proposal for reviewing director general appointments (see above), of being 'legally incompetent ... and misguided' He also claims that other suggestions made early in the negotiations but never advanced (such as sealed mandates) amount to the party 'wanting to set up a parallel government that would operate outside the framework of and parameters of the constitution-based method and protocols of running the government of the Republic of South Africa'.

This pompous put-down – aimed at Helen's letter of 22 June – is pure confection. It is also hypocrisy on stilts. Ramaphosa himself served in a rogue government headed by Jacob Zuma that the Zondo Commission found to be both constitutionally delinquent and protocol-busting.

The only opening for further engagement comes right at the end of his diatribe: 'I intend to conclude all negotiations and consultations this week. Until then I remain open to having further discussions with you.'

John thinks the letter is 'sabre-rattling'. We all agree that his letter is designed to be leaked by the ANC – par for this very rocky and endless course. Ryan reminds us that a top journalist told him that 'Cyril is very thin-skinned', which might explain his tone. Inelegantly, I scribble in the margin of the letter, this is 'a fat FO from CR'.

Helen moans that 'from experience, I am the scapegoat for everything. Lightning rod.'

Later this afternoon, John takes the small gap offered in the letter to engage Cyril on its contents. The president advises John that our letters have created 'much rancour' for the comrades, that his (Ramaphosa's) offer is now 'under review' and he will do his best to 'reverse the damage done within the ANC and in the public by our letters'. This is almost comic: his side does the leaking and he, an old mining unionist, could hardly have expected us to accept gratefully any opening offer he made without countering it.

John, though, uses his time with Ramaphosa to ask the essential question: 'Do you want us to be in government with you or not?' John advises that the response was 'Yes, we need the DA in government for stability', and dealing with the EFF and MK is a no-go. 'Too ghastly to contemplate' is John's interpretation of this.

Ramaphosa promises to revert tomorrow with an outcome.

Day 24: Wednesday 26 June

In the lull waiting for some presidential response, I answer my unattended messages and emails. The inbox overflows with mostly beseeching requests to do a deal – on any terms. There is also a clutch – ranging from good friends in business and banking to casual once-off cocktail-party types who mine gossip and monetise it – ferreting out information on progress, or its lack. I offer little in response to most.

None of my correspondents, though, is as unintentionally amusing as the note which Geordin (Hill-Lewis) sends about an investor call he took this morning. 'Someone who earns money as an "analyst" asked me: "The DA argument on proportionality makes complete sense. But don't you think the ANC needs a transition period (!!!) in which they get used to what it means to share power. Perhaps you need to give them the mental space to do so."'

We also receive leaks from the ANC meetings that Ramaphosa is facing pushback against dealing with the DA, and some party leaders are seeking a rapprochement with Zuma and MK. Whether this is genuine or designed to soften us up is hard to gauge.

At 7 pm, Ramaphosa messages John to advise that he has just finished all his (party) meetings and asks John to await a call from him in '30 to 45 minutes'. At the height of 'Ramaphoria', which gripped the country when he replaced the disgraced Zuma in 2018, there was a photo of Ramaphosa pointing to his wristwatch and demanding on-time meetings. Presidential punctuality has, alas, slipped since then. John only hears from Cyril at 9 pm.

He advises John that there is 'good and bad news'. The 'good' part of it, in the president's view, is that he can finally offer the DA six cabinet and six deputy posts. The 'bad' part is that he needs to withdraw the offer of the DTIC ministry and replace it with tourism!

I am flabbergasted. Tourism as an economic sector is significant. But as a political post it is the equivalent of Siberia – the place you send the unimportant figures who need to be fobbed off with ministerial perks. I think here of party-hopping, one-seat wonder Patricia de Lille – the outgoing minister. Or, further back, when the first English speaker was appointed to the NP cabinet: tourism was where Frank Waring was dumped – a ministry of utmost unimportance.

(We later learn that Mashatile and Mantashe forced Ramaphosa to withdraw the DTIC offer: all the BEE regulations, the eye-watering tenders, the entirety of government interventions in the economy are housed in the ministry. Handing it to the ideologically opposite, goody two-shoes DA was a big no for them. Cyril folded.)

Ramaphosa asks John to consider the new offer and revert to him the next day.

I message John and the group: 'My pre-bed and very depressing view of things is that in truth there is no good option here. Either we take a deal with the ANC (even if we finally get a better ministry than tourism) and land up for five years with people we don't trust and who go back on their word, etc. Or we walk away and surrender the country to the tender mercies of an ANC-MK-EFF government and take the blame for it.'

We agree to meet tomorrow and concur that unless there is, as a minimum, an improvement on the tourism ministry, we will walk. Regardless of consequence.

Day 25: Thursday 27 June

Our group ends up meeting three times today as our position hardens – no deal with the ANC unless it substitutes the tourism ministry for something 'more meaningful' (transport plus Transnet is our preference). Or increases our cabinet allotment. Preferably both.

Various big-business potentates (after pressuring us enough these past days) message Cyril directly (or via third parties). One message reads, in part: 'I see the country looking for a real partnership in your new government and the reaction of the rand and economic sentiment makes it clear that the expectation is for the DA to end up with a ministry of real economic substance.'

I take a call from another billionaire, a social acquaintance, who offers much earthier advice: 'Tony,' he purrs down the line, 'I am here to offer the coward's counsel – DA should go into GNU even on unsatisfactory terms. Just get a foot in the door – it will do wonders for investment here. And I am not sure we have any economic future at all if the EFF gets in.' He promises to call Ramaphosa with the same message.

The press today – after the DA took a drubbing earlier in the week – turns more in our favour.

Veteran and influential commentator Peter Bruce writes in

Business Day. Noting the 'media hysteria and wild misreporting' of the Zille letter, he turns his columnist guns on the ANC and fires off an apt fusillade: 'The ANC will absolutely hate the thought of having to go into government with the DA, however many new DA ministers may eventually be involved. It simply doesn't want to do it. Its denial is so bad that the party leadership has almost lost its ability to read for meaning [this referring to Ramaphosa's intemperate letter to Steenhuisen].

'It is not as if the ANC has much say in the matter. It would be the largest party in the GNU but it could survive only with the support of the others, perhaps especially the DA. It simply has to choose, and by late Wednesday you could almost hear the silent screams of denial.'[3]

We decide not to give a direct response, yet, to Ramaphosa but to suggest another meeting. Let's see how the pressure builds overnight.

Just before 6 pm, John messages the president (after consulting us and his federal executive) to advise, 'There is acceptance of the ministers and deputy ministerial positions except for Tourism. I will be able to travel to Pretoria tomorrow to take the discussion further and to seek potential alternatives, if you are amenable to such a meeting.' They will meet in person tomorrow at 2.30 pm.

John, whose wife Terry and daughter Olivia (my goddaughter) are away on a coastal break, arrives at our home for a kitchen supper with us. Given the weight of events, he is surprisingly relaxed, even chipper.

Over Michal's excellent lamb shanks – which he and I savour – she asks in her forthright way: 'John, do you really want this to happen?' 'Yes, I do,' he replies.

After dinner, I manage to devour an entire slab of chocolate and blame my indiscipline on anxiety.

Day 26: Friday 28 June

At the behest of News24, I write a column this morning on current events. I tread carefully not to disclose any inside information on which I sit. So, I couch the situation, writing 'as one of many midwives involved in this messy process', in more general terms and remind the ANC that it faces a choice: 'Does it want a stable inclusive government which commands a decent majority in Parliament and where parties are committed to ... the foundational principles ... embedded in the statement of intent?

'There are two other alternatives open to the ANC: on the one hand it can strike a deal with the EFF and MK ... This will give the government a sort of security in numbers, though looking at the local government accords [where local coalitions with the EFF were collapsing] not too much of it. But it certainly won't achieve most of the principles and programmes outlined in the agreement the ANC signed two weeks back. In fact, it will be a violation of them.'

The final alternative, I write, would be to 'limp along as a minority government, hostage vote-by-parliamentary-vote to the vagaries of uncertain outcomes'.

I conclude, 'None of these choices are either perfect or even very good for any of the parties. But choosing the worst outcome is the surest recipe for future country failure.'[4]

An inventive sub-editor headlined the article 'The ANC faces its own "Sophie's Choice"', this being a reference to an excruciating decision faced by the title character in William Styron's novel (made into a movie starring Meryl Streep). I have begun to think, though, that, for the DA at least, it is Hobson's choice. It doesn't really have any option but to hold its nose and go into government.

Late afternoon, John arranges a group call with the sherpas to report back on his meeting with Ramaphosa. The president offers the DA the ministry of agriculture in lieu of tourism. He says that transport needs to be close to the Presidency and he needs a top ANC person there who can ring the changes (Barbara Creecy).

There is a collective silence from the normally chatty group as we absorb the latest final offer. I am nonplussed at this pedestrian proposal, better than tourism but not by much, though Ivan Meyer and Alan Winde are more optimistic. They point out that agriculture is hugely important to a big slice of our voters and the ministry sits in the important economic cluster of cabinet.

John asks us all to sleep on it and to convene again early tomorrow.

ENDGAME

Day 27: Saturday 29 June

Overnight we are ensconced at a magnificent Hermanus beachside place that Michal has booked us for the weekend.

I awake to a view of the cliff path, the glistening waters of Walker Bay enveloped in the early-morning winter sunshine. Perfecto. However, on the business to hand there is a message from John: 'What does your gut feel on this proposal, AJ, your really basic feel on it?'

I respond: 'It is 50-50: It is a mediocre deal but not taking it will be worse. But you need to take real fighters into government with you, not wokeists or time servers who will fall in love with their new surroundings.' He agrees.

Our Zoom meeting happens at 9 am: There is now no dissent – an acceptance all round that we are going in and will have to make the best of it.

On the upside, the portfolios are quite serious ones and offer the chance for the party to make a meaningful difference in the lives of millions of people. They will also provide a unique opportunity for the party to shake off the spurious but weighty image of an organisation promoting white privilege and inimical to black advancement.

John motivates going into government by reprising a conversation we had before the 29 May election. I told him then that the DA in its current form was, if not at the end of the road, then at least (as the election results proved) at a significant fork in it. And, to sustain the metaphor, the party would, on its current voter base, soon run out of road. It needed a reformation, though how and with whom was unclear.

Entering the government, alongside a declining but still large ANC, could conceivably lead in future to an amalgamation of the centrists and constitutionalists. This could be a chance both to build a new movement and to provide a shield against the predatory, deeply divisive political vandals massing outside the citadels of power, determined to storm in at some future time.

John also tells the meeting that his discussions yesterday were the 'warmest and frankest' he has ever held with Ramaphosa. The president is, at least on his telling, not in denial on the significance of the ANC's power loss on 29 May.

Ryan, who was the most sceptical about the unfolding deal during the week, now, correctly, suggests we craft communications stressing the upside of it and the far worse alternative waiting in the wings.

That alternative, the EFF, now makes a clumsy, last-minute foray to grasp at a bit of power. Having early in the process overbid its weak hand and left the table of negotiations, it wants to return.

The Inanda Club in Johannesburg's northern suburbs was, in its heyday, a WASP enclave replete with polo ponies and players on its fields, G&Ts on the terrace and Rolls-Royces for the Randlords in the car park. Far more recently, the ANC has used the same club as a venue for meetings, suggesting that while the ruling class has changed hands, some old haunts remain intact.

Yesterday at Inanda, the ANC and EFF had a last-gasp meeting where the red berets put in their pitch to enter the GNU as an improbable partner.

This afternoon, a letter from EFF secretary-general Marshall Dlamini, addressed to Mbalula, on the contents of the meeting was released to the public. Gone was the previous EFF bluster that the ANC was a sellout, irredeemably corrupt organisation deserving electoral extinction, etc. The letter upgraded the ANC to the legions of the righteous: 'The EFF acknowledges the ANC as a progressive movement that has played a gallant role in the advancement of the liberation of the oppressed,' Dlamini gushed.

Next, the EFF did an abrupt turn on its revolutionary agenda. Now its conversion was to 'the rule of law, supremacy of the constitution, anti-corruption [sic] and transparency' – a direct crib from the statement of intent, however awkward.

The reason for this cringing kowtowing to the ANC, despite voting against Ramaphosa's election as president just two weeks ago? It wants to feed at the GNU trough. It advised the ANC that it was 'willing to participate in an ANC-led government with other parties, with the exception of the Democratic Alliance and the Freedom Front

Plus [a right-wing white party, soon to enter the GNU]'. The DA and Freedom Front Plus are, in the considered view of the EFF, guilty of advancing an agenda that is 'imperialist, counter-revolutionary, white supremacist'.

As a spectacular U-turn, this missive stands in a league of its own, and its beseeching, desperate tone towards the end of the note is unintentionally hilarious: 'We would like to state that we are not on a mission to pursue cabinet positions for careerist purposes.' God forbid.

Rather, the selfless purpose of the EFF proposal is to stop 'the counter-revolutionary imperialist and domestic forces [who] are closing in on the ANC to institute a soft coup and undo the historic gains of the oppressed.'

The pseudo-revolutionary claptrap in the letter cannot hide the whiff of desperation from the ever-changing EFF. Their strategic incompetence and tactical ineptitude have left it stranded, along with a poor election result, ever further from power.

No one in our battalion of the 'counter-revolutionary imperialist forces' thinks the EFF initiative will succeed in derailing the coming GNU train steaming ahead (nor did it).

John, who gets plenty of barbs for his lack of post-school qualifications, is in fact extremely well-read. This he evinces when, in the late afternoon, he sends me his choices for DA cabinet members (to be announced by Ramaphosa tomorrow evening). The message ends with a quotation from Shakespeare's *Macbeth* on the call and the cost of ambition: 'I go, and it is done; the bell invites me. / Hear it not, Duncan, for it is a knell / That summons thee to heaven or to hell.'

Day 28: Sunday 30 June

Only the sound of seagulls outside our beach house in Hermanus disturbs the quiet this morning. For the first time in three weeks or more, there are no Zoom meetings, no urgent texts or frantic calls.

The *Sunday Times* leads with 'It's A Done Deal', but its final contours and contents will only be announced tonight on TV by Ramaphosa. In his column inside the paper, Peter Bruce, well fed with morsels from both sides, distils the essence of the ANC-DA deal: 'In all, the DA rewards have been muted ... Once in the cabinet the DA will be in office, but will its people be in power? It promises political stability to Ramaphosa but can't protect him from his own party.'

He underlines, though, why Steenhuisen had to take the deal on the table on Friday: 'rather than risk of being blamed for the insecurity that would result from pulling out altogether, he had no option [but to take it]'.[5]

Dean Macpherson calls in the afternoon, delighted that he is to be appointed, meritoriously, as minister of public works and infrastructure. He thanks me for the role I played and promises to deliver a bottle of Dom Pérignon champagne. (He makes good on this later.)

The ever-unpunctual Ramaphosa finally, 47 minutes after the scheduled 9 pm broadcast time, announces the new cabinet in his televised address. Very late and very large could be the takeaway on the super-sized cabinet he unveils: 32 ministers (two more than before) and 43 deputies.

The DA was never consulted (nor, to be fair, did we enquire) on the final size of the cabinet and discovers its expected modest slice of executive power even more diminished, to around 18 per cent of the total.

It is interesting, though, as Ramaphosa reads out the list, to see how the fortunes of the core negotiators have risen: Siviwe gets the basic education ministry, a vast and hugely important job, though in some ways the proverbial 'hospital pass', with its failing standards and hostile trade unions to confront or conciliate. Leon Schreiber gets home affairs, another site of current dysfunction but potential opportunity, and John (who got to assign which DA members went in, and in what posts) takes agriculture for himself. 'Farmer Jones' I dub him – after the proprietor in *Animal Farm*.

The remaining trio of DA ministers, Dion George (forestry, fisheries and the environment), Dean Macpherson (public works and infrastructure) and Solly Malatsi (communications and digital technologies), will have their work cut out.

On the ANC side, two of their key negotiators get significant promotion: Ronald Lamola is appointed minister of international relations (and can only be an improvement on his predecessor, that Israel-bashing, Hamas-conciliating diplomat, Naledi Pandor). The contested DTIC is awarded to Parks Tau, who is less of an ideological zealot than the previous incumbent at least. (Future events will prove this assumption entirely incorrect; see next chapter.) The third ANC minister we closely interacted with these past weeks, Enoch Godongwana, retains as expected the key finance ministry.

What is striking about the 'kortbroek [short pants] ministers', as the legion of deputy ministers were once dubbed, is how, apparently to checkmate the DA here, Ramaphosa has appointed an ANC deputy to mark each of the six DA deputies he appointed.

Day 29: Monday 1 July

My national service is now wrapping up.

Today, though, the once-vaunted ace in our pack, the balance of power in Gauteng province, disappears. There, ANC premier Lesufi declines to allot the DA even remotely a fair proportion of cabinet posts. Worse, during his hostile negotiations with us, he refuses to indicate which portfolios are on offer and which other parties are participating in his government. He intends his 'offer' to be rejected, and so it is. Lesufi, one of the worst and most scandal-plagued ANC premiers (it is an overcrowded field) is both a vote loser (the ANC vote fell by 15.43 per cent compared to 2019) and an implacable foe of our party. He also helms the anti-Ramaphosa faction inside his own party. He will head a minority government: good luck to him.

Sir Mick Davis is a London-based friend and former South African businessman and liberal philanthropist. He is a thoughtful and engaged observer of global and local politics. Over the past weeks, he has offered very helpful suggestions during the negotiations process.

Today he messages me with an elegant and accurate summary of the state of play:

'In the game of chicken, you must be able to live with the outcome if the other side does not turn away. An outcome of the ANC and EFF et al in government would have been catastrophic and therefore the DA was always playing one trump short. At least they have negative control going forward – they must use it judiciously.'

Day 31: Wednesday 3 July

Yet another hotel basement, for the final scene in this lengthy drama. However, the swish Red Room Asian restaurant, at the stately Mount Nelson Hotel, is an upgrade from the previous venues.

It is a celebratory dinner for both the DA negotiations team and the crop of newly appointed ministers and deputy ministers from the party, sworn into office earlier today.

The convivial evening – augmented by fine food and excellent wines – is a very happy, even light-hearted affair, where we swap our war stories and reprise recent events and peer a little into the very uncertain future.

I meet, for the first time, some of the new DA deputy ministers. One of them, a young man from Potchefstroom, Sello Seitlholo (deputy minister of water and sanitation), tells me he was born in September 1989, the exact month and year when I was first elected, aged 32, to Parliament.

As I think back to all the plateaus and plummets of recent days, I realise in this peak moment that a new generation, appropriately, will shape the future.

10
Aftermath

'Imperfect information, too little time'

In 2007, I was awarded a Fall fellowship at Harvard University's impressive and immersive Institute of Politics, at the John F Kennedy School of Government. One of the other fellows, Dr Meghan O'Sullivan, provided a pithy summary of the pressures of making consequential decisions against a pressing deadline.

Meghan joined our fellowship directly from the administration of President George W Bush, having served as Special Assistant to the President on Afghanistan and Iraq. She described her job as 'making big decisions with real consequences with imperfect information and with too little time'.

The preceding chapters suggest that this definition applies, in spades, to the helter-skelter negotiations that led to the founding of the current GNU in South Africa.

Could the DA have struck a better deal? Who bluffed whom in the fraught and concertinaed process from which South Africa emerged in the second half of 2024? These questions lingered as the country emerged into a new political world: the ANC shorn of its majority, the DA in the cabinet and the markets cheering. For example, at the end of August 2024, the once-falling rand hit a 13-month high, 'riding a wave of optimism' according to analysts, who cited 'investors looking more favourably at South African assets' following the formation of the ANC-DA coalition.[1] Most citizens were relieved that while the battered, almost bankrupt (state debt topped R5 trillion in 2024) country still was on the cliff edge, at least it hadn't plunged off.

The mood music certainly improved post the GNU formation, primarily by shutting out the discordant populist tunes sung in the MK/EFF chorus, although, as referenced below, that danger still lurked. Simply the large improvement in the national psyche, and renewed investor interest from abroad, meant that a stock exchange surge – after years of flat-lining – and a strengthened currency and falling bond rates made the enormous national debt more sustainable to finance.

In mid-December 2024, I attended the annual lunch hosted by Investec (a high-end South African and UK bank) at their gleaming new Cape Town headquarters in the ever-expanding V&A Waterfront. What was striking, beyond the reminder of the serious wealth of the country assembled there, was the great appreciation expressed for the existence of the GNU. It mattered little, based on some casual conversations over lunch, the intricacies or compromises in the new government, or even the achievements (or lack of them) in the six months of its existence. What really counted for these folk, an accurate barometer of general business sentiment, was that it was the DA that was in the new arrangement, not the EFF and MK – the far worse alternative for them and the economy.

This glimpse into the soul of the economic weather-makers suggested an impressive vindication of the DA decision to throw in its lot with the ANC. But, as the first major bust-up in the new government would painfully indicate, it also revealed just how difficult it would be for the DA to exit the government. The party's business backers would be appalled if the DA departure meant the entry into office of those determined to blow up the economy and reduce to smithereens the accumulated wealth gathered around the lunch tables, and elsewhere across the country. (See below.)

AFTERMATH

An intimation of discomfort

Meanwhile, in late August 2024, a few weeks after the GNU was formed, a local television channel, eNCA, flighted a documentary on the negotiations that had preceded it, entitled '29 Days in June'. Both Helen Zille and I were interviewed and gave full voice to our version of recent history.

However, one crucial insight gave me pause in my own take on events. This was provided by our interlocuter from the ANC, the estimably smart Fébé Potgieter. When pressed by journalist Annika Larsen on the 'unfair' or at least meagre share of cabinet posts given to the DA in the arrangement, Potgieter offered that the negotiations were a give-and-take affair. True enough.

She then said that the DA had succeeded in its demand for 'sufficient consensus' on cabinet decision-making (clause 19), effectively requiring the agreement of both the ANC and the DA, that is, parties to the GNU representing 60 per cent of the seats in the National Assembly. Also true.

She then set out to justify the over-reward of the ANC in cabinet seats relative to its proportion of the vote, and the under-representation of the DA in government. In her view, and doubtless her party's, the DA failed to obtain its original demand that parties should, in the main, be allocated cabinet posts proportionate to their size.

Indeed, as described in the previous chapter, the six executive positions which the DA obtained were at least one-third short of its proportional entitlement, while the ANC generously over-rewarded itself in the allocation.

Watching this interview allowed me to recall how, during the negotiations process, the ANC, from the president down, kept insisting that 'presidential prerogatives' needed to be respected and preserved when it came to selecting his cabinet. This, at one level, was constitutionally correct. Yet, the ANC – lacking a majority – had also signed a statement of intent with the DA that tempered this prerogative and qualified it in terms 'broadly proportional' to the participating parties' strength. But the clause in the agreement that governed this question also contained such nebulous phrases as 'taking into account the national interest' when it came to composing the new government.

The ambiguities in the agreement allowed Ramaphosa to drive a coach and horses through our quest for the DA to obtain representation in cabinet, which quantitively and qualitatively would reflect the votes we brought into the new government.

The word salad in the agreement barely met our demand for proper representation but did not totally undermine it either. And the limits of both time and overwhelming public and market pressures nixed our walking away for want of a perfect formulation. But both the pressures and the wiliness of Ramaphosa allowed him to construct a cabinet table fashioned very much, though not entirely, to his party's specifications.

Watching the interview with Fébé Potgieter reminded me of a vague discomfort I had experienced, but not articulated, when the agreement between the parties was being finalised. I had wondered why the president and his party had yielded to our demand that disagreements in cabinet be settled by 'sufficient consensus'. The clause in question precisely defined the obtaining of such consensus as meaning that 'sufficient consensus exists when parties to the GNU representing 60 per cent of seats in the National Assembly agree'. In simple terms, this meant that it was obtained when both the ANC (40 per cent) and DA (22 per cent) agreed, allowing each party a veto right in the event of a dispute.

It dawned on me afterwards that perhaps the ANC had thrown this in as a sop, since the cabinet would not itself be deciding much of real consequence.

It is one, and an important, thing to have your hand on the brake, but that can only be consequential if the vehicle itself is in motion.

Limits on the veto

There were some intimations early in the life of the sapling GNU that the mechanism on which the DA had spent considerable negotiating capital – an effective veto right on decisions – might be hard to operate.

Thus, in the first two months of the new government's life, the cabinet had only two formal meetings, and the leader of the second-largest party (Steenhuisen of the DA) did not have a single sit-down alone with the president. If, per Roelf Meyer's advice, the glue holding the fabric together was the personal chemistry between Ramaphosa and Steenhuisen, theirs was very much a slow-burn relationship. In early 2025, for example, the duo sat down to lunch in an attempt to thrash out issues of contention (see below), but this, extraordinarily, was only the second or third such meeting *à deux* since the government had been founded.

I couldn't help but contrast this position, where the DA now had real power, since its votes in Parliament were necessary for the government to continue and its budgets to be approved, with the first days of full democracy on these shores in 1994.

Back then, when I headed a small seven-seat party, Nelson Mandela made conspicuous efforts to meet with me, have telephone chats and confer presidential time on a party that had no power to affect his government's hold on office (see Chapter 16). I also was not shy to approach the president on matters of concern when I felt Mandela could assist in resolving an issue. Steenhuisen, by contrast, often seemed reluctant to press, initially at least, the far more objective power he held to pursue his and the party's agenda. Perhaps, though, it was Ramaphosa who was parsimonious in offering time to his coalition partner to sort matters.

Steenhuisen also got off to a rocky start with his decision to appoint alt-right shock jock Roman Cabanac as his chief of staff. I offered him the unsolicited advice that this appointment, whatever merits Cabanac had, would at best be an enormous distraction from his multiple tasks: getting to grips with his portfolio, running the party and leading his DA cabinet in the difficult and new terrain they now held. He persisted with it for a few weeks, until he attempted (difficult in view of the strenuously pro-employee labour laws) to dismiss Cabanac, who refused to quit.

The concentration of power

Far more than personalities, though, there is the issue of where power resides. Commentators such as former Deputy Chief Justice Dikgang Moseneke have observed that the South African Constitution places enormous, barely unfettered, powers in the office and person of the president. In 2014, at the height of Jacob Zuma's corrosive destruction of the state and its institutions, Moseneke noted: '[A] careful examination of the powers of the national executive chapter in the constitution displays a remarkable concentration of the president's powers of appointment.'

These appointments range from the deputy president, chief justice and all judges to the auditor-general and the heads of the National Prosecuting Authority, police, military, reserve bank and revenue service. While there are some limits and checks on this appointing authority, many are slight or illusory.

Moseneke concluded his survey and remarks with an ominous warning: 'This uncanny concentration of power is a matter which going forward we may ignore, but only at our peril.'[2]

And perilous this proved under the rapacious hand of Zuma.

Ramaphosa was far more benign and less corrosive to the constitutional project than Zuma, although he inflated the size and reach of the Presidency to a far greater degree. Also, the 'remarkable concentration of the president's powers' would prove very handy after May 2024, when he was forced to bring other parties into his government but still held the trump card of his powers of appointment.

His hand was also vastly increased, and that of parties such as the DA diminished, not just by the president's power to select the key mandarins of state authority but also by the location of the true centre of power itself. And it clearly wasn't in the oversized cabinet.

Rather, it was inside the Presidency itself that the engine of government was fuelled, and the vehicle of state sent in a direction of travel largely directed from the president's office. To be perfectly fair, though, thanks to the disabled condition of the state, the car often did not arrive at all or ran out of fuel on the journey.

Under Ramaphosa, the Presidency consisted of no fewer than four ministers reporting directly to him and housed in his expansive, super-sized office. The key lieutenant directing the flow of government business was Maropene Ramokgopa, the minister of planning, monitoring and evaluation.

Of even more significance was the motivation I advanced, early in the negotiations process, to press for full-blown participation in government and the cabinet rather than the weak brew of so-called confidence and supply. The latter would have given the party enhanced oversight and power in Parliament and no say at executive level. My preference was based, in large measure, on the vast discretionary powers that more and more legislative instruments placed in the hands of ministers whose power to rule by regulation, often outside any effective parliamentary scrutiny, was an increasing feature of lawmaking in South Africa.

For example, in January 2025, without any buy-in (and over the objections of the DA deputy minister Andrew Whitfield), the DTIC published draconian, investment-crushing regulations. One set, arguably illegal and unconstitutional since it was regulated sans a general revenue bill, imposed a three per cent after-profit tax on all companies to fund a proposed R100 billion money pot for Black industrialists. Another set mandated steep percentages for law firms in respect of Black management and ownership. The voices of both the DA and the affected industries and sectors were either ignored or bypassed.

Crumbs, concessions and clusters

And, while having a seat at the table of power was better than being outside the door, if the sextet of DA ministers were marooned in their individual fiefs of power but excluded from direct involvement in or influence over most government departments, then this power could be ephemeral. This danger exercised the minds of the DA government cohort, especially after Ryan Coetzee, who had anchored the negotiations process for the party, was drafted in to strategise their role in cabinet.

It is also true today that, in countries with explicitly parliamentary systems, power is becoming concentrated in the executive arm. A prime example is Britain, where power has increasingly seeped from both cabinet and Parliament to the prime minister's office in Downing Street. After the inconclusive general election of May 2010, Prime Minister David Cameron formed a coalition with the Liberal Democrats, with proper levers and formalised mechanisms for the junior partner (Lib Dems) to have real buy-in on policy and processes.

This was not the case with South Africa's GNU, headed by an all-powerful Presidency. For example, the scrapping of the standalone ministry of public enterprises saw hundreds of state-owned companies coming under the control of another presidential minder who was slated to head a state holding company where these mostly flailing enterprises were to be housed. And so power flowed upwards, if not noticeably increasing efficiency and good governance, then markedly removing more and more control from cabinet committees and the body itself to the Presidency.

As for the cabinet clusters, where a lot of government work is done and directed between the largely formal meetings of the body itself, here too the electorally diminished ANC retained dominance. The seven government clusters, created to 'foster an integrated approach to government', cover the table of ministries, from economics to justice. But the ANC very generously allocated precisely one co-chairpersonship to the DA: Dion George, minister of forestry, fisheries and environment, was appointed, alongside the ANC's Ronald Lamola, to head the international cooperation, trade and security cluster. The IFP also received one co-chairmanship. The ANC obtained five. The DA's early insistence on a leadership role in the key economics sector cluster was either never advanced or quietly forgotten. For a party with only 40 per cent of the seats in Parliament, the president had allocated the ANC 70 per cent of the cabinet cluster chairs.

There was a deep irony in the angry fusillade Ramaphosa fired at the DA in the early stage of our negotiations, when he accused the party of 'attempting to set up a parallel government' (see previous chapter).

Governance expert Professor William Gumede, of Wits University, pointed out that this was precisely what Ramaphosa himself had done: 'Ministers in the presidency are unheard of in other countries. It causes more duplication and chaos because you have ministers and then ministers in the presidency ... [Ramaphosa] is creating a parallel cabinet inside the Presidency, which will cause more inefficiencies and duplication.'[3]

In their second meeting before the formation of the GNU, Ramaphosa directly advised Steenhuisen that the Presidency and its ministries were off limits to DA entrants. It was not difficult, after the formation of the cabinet, to conclude that 'the inefficiencies and duplications' were a small downpayment for Ramaphosa for the far larger prize of retaining most of the power and all the control beyond the reach of any non-ANC member of the new executive.

There is wisdom in the Washington, DC, truism that 'personnel are policy'. Who is deployed where in government tells us quite a bit about the design of the state and its likely outcomes. But what of policy itself? Would there be a step change in direction and approach by the new multiparty government? Or would it be largely the same old failed ANC policies slightly dressed up and more efficiently and incorruptibly implemented by one-time staunch opponents of the ruling party and its orthodoxy?

Too early to tell: 2025 isn't 1994

By early 2025, it was too early in the life of the GNU to forecast with any certainty how matters would evolve and whether in fact, and over time, the DA (and the smaller coalition parties) would be able to effect real, or any, change and alter the thrust of policies and practices at variance with their interests and beliefs. Or whether these parties had been 'played', their support used to prop up Ramaphosa and the ANC. From the opposition perspective, some of the detail narrated above suggested little change in government policy. The 'national democratic revolution', whose policy prescripts had tanked the economy and employment prospects, seemed unaffected by the changing of the government guard. The new entrants from outside the ANC now inside the government received a few concessionary crumbs from the table of ANC power – the generous privileges of cabinet perquisites. A classic case of 'being in office but not in power'.

On the other hand, the first requirement of a politician is arithmetical – the ability to count. And the DA, with just 22 per cent of the vote, could not with its percentage alter the entire national political trajectory. It could only choose key battles, and even then – as this account suggests – its victories would be both few and uncertain. This did not constrain the ranks of the party's critics who harrumphed frequently that the party had been, for example, 'outfoxed or outboxed' – actually, the electorate had largely determined this.

The GNU's short-lived predecessor, the 1994 model, offers no helpful precedent. It lasted just two years, and its formation was a consequence of the interim constitution, not an inconclusive election result. Back then, the ANC held 62 per cent of the seats in the National Assembly, and the arrival or – in the case of the NNP's exit in 1996 – departure of parties from the government did not affect the ANC's hold on power.

By contrast, post-2024 South Africa is in a brave and uncertain new political world. If, for example, the DA went nuclear and pulled the trigger on its participation, the current government would, at a stroke, lose its parliamentary majority.

But that decision, an extremity, can only be made once. It carries an echo of the Cold War concept of 'mutually assured destruction', according to which the superpowers possessed sufficient thermonuclear missiles in their respective arsenals to blow up their opponents, indeed most of the world, but in so doing would trigger the destruction of their own countries. Less dramatically, the partners in the GNU could detonate the government, but at the likely cost of burning themselves in the process.

Further, while the 1994 experience indeed differs in fundamental respects from the GNU of 2024, not every warning from that era should be ignored. In June 1996, FW de Klerk left the first GNU, in which his party, like the DA today, had six cabinet seats, but he had the consolation of being a deputy president. Afterwards, he told Parliament: 'Continued participation [in the GNU] would be equivalent to detention on a kind of political death row. The survival of multiparty democracy, which depends on the existence of a strong and credible opposition, was being threatened by our continued participation in the GNU.'[4]

Budget blues

Hopefully, history will not repeat itself three decades on. A party such as the DA will need to assert itself, tactfully at first and then forcefully, if indicated, without collapsing the enterprise itself. This attribute the DA, finally, demonstrated in mid-February 2025, when it refused to support the tax-hiking budget of the minister of finance. This forced a humbled ANC to postpone the budget speech, a parliamentary first, and go back to the drawing board, spooking the markets and forcing a government rethink.

A hastily redrafted budget was tabled by the minister of finance on 12 March. It retained a (smaller) VAT increase and few spending cuts. The DA opposed this as well. Now both the budget and the future of the GNU itself were at risk and both faced unknown outcomes, pending the final vote in Parliament, at the time of this writing.

Red lights, amber warnings

Shortly after the formation of the GNU, I spoke to some of the new DA ministers. They were still finding their feet under their new desks. They also experienced quotidian trivial examples of being leaked against by hostile colleagues or excluded from events (such as the president's *imbizo*s, lavish public talking shops where the head of state interacts with citizens). On enquiry, a DA minister was informed, 'Oh, so sorry you didn't get notice of it.' Of course, given the inefficiencies of the state from top to bottom, cock-up was as probable an explanation as a grand conspiracy to exclude. Of more significance were issues of policy and personnel. If not red-light stops for the DA, these issues suggested an amber warning flash or two.

This triviality paled when, in mid-December 2024, the government, absent any consultation with coalition colleagues, unilaterally announced that a 'national dialogue' would be convened. The ANC had always referenced this idea during the GNU negotiations, perhaps, benignly, to reclaim public trust or, ominously, to impose new policies on the cabinet via the back door. Who knew? Certainly not the party's 'partners' in government. However, once again the chronic disorganisation at the heart of government rescued the situation from becoming another chokepoint in the coalition. The 'national dialogue' much spoken of was, like many other grand projects conjured up by the ANC, postponed to an indeterminate future date owing to the lack of both planning and project management for the event.

Despite having been in government for more than three decades, the ANC had obviously, in matters grand and small, never read the memo from Thomas Edison that 'vision without execution is hallucination'. Indeed, it might be said that the comrades in the movement were high on their own rhetoric, not so much on doing the hard yards that determine the fate and future of nations.

A ministerial misadventure and the DA pushback

Enter, from stage left, health minister Aaron Motsoaledi, one of the most arrogant, implacably ideological and least efficient ministers – he left behind a huge mess in his last post, at home affairs – and an avowed foe of the DA in the cabinet.

After the formation of the GNU, Motsoaledi announced – despite strenuous opposition from many parties, including partners in the coalition, and also the most representative bodies of both business and the medical community and health funders – that he was pressing ahead with the National Health Insurance Act, the legislative vehicle for the proposed National Health Insurance (NHI) scheme.

Before the election, Ramaphosa had signed the legislation authorising the creation of a state fund and scheme for universal healthcare access for all. It is a laudable idea but certainly unaffordable, unconstitutional and untested.

AFTERMATH

At the signing ceremony in May 2024, just weeks before polling day, Ramaphosa – once heralded as political heir to the reconciliatory Mandela – railed against 'the well to do, the rich' and whites in general for 'opposing universal healthcare'. Condemned by many for overemphasising consensus-seeking at the expense of decisive action, on this occasion he warned, 'NHI is coming whether you like it or not.'

It is beyond the compass of this account to detail the disaster-in-the-making that is this presidential and ministerial misadventure, but some headline observations are useful.

Politically, the National Health Insurance Act was dead on arrival, since the ANC's precipitous plunge in the opinion polls on the eve of the election directly followed the signing ceremony. Opposition to the legislation, contra Ramaphosa and Motsoaledi, united both the middle class and many working-class members, of all races, who contribute to private medical aid schemes.

Under the legislation, all medical aid funds and most providers would be nationalised, and the provision of any health service offered by the state (however badly or theoretically) would preclude the private medical aids from covering the costs for the same service. Instead, a national health fund would be set up, to be financed by mandatory contributions from taxpayers. Not a word or thought was offered on how the estimated R200 billion funding required for NHI would be achieved. However, Business Unity South Africa estimated it would require, as a minimum, a 31 per cent hike in personal taxes and a rise in VAT from 15 to 21.5 per cent.[5]

The track record of wholesale looting by officials and politicians of so many state-owned companies and, pertinently, of the procurement budgets of provincial hospitals did not inspire confidence that a gargantuan health fund of this magnitude would somehow escape the grasp of rapacious and predatory cadres.

South Africa's extremely narrow tax base (for all government receipts bar VAT) was revealed in an alarming set of statistics published early in 2024: there are only seven million personal taxpayers in the country, of whom just 1.4 per cent pay a whopping 59 per cent of all personal taxes. Just 770 companies contribute 60 per cent of all corporate taxes to the fiscus. Ranged against this are some 28 million citizens who receive one or another state social grant.[6] The system is currently unsustainable and will become unsupportable if the swingeing tax increases for NHI are levied. In the event, most of the 1.4 per cent who pay the lion's share of the taxes, the most skilled and the most mobile people and corporates in the net, will leave the country.

Whether there would be enough competent doctors to provide the service – if ever implemented – was laid bare in a survey: it revealed that 38 per cent of the 17 000 members of the South African Medical Association planned to emigrate due to NHI's arrival.[7]

The NHI scheme was also contra the DA's (and most of business's) value set. It offended against the constitutional principles of freedom of choice and devolution of power (since health is primarily a provincial, not a national, competence).

In Parliament, and via one of many legal challenges to this legislative monstrosity, NHI was opposed strenuously by the DA. At cabinet level, Steenhuisen took a more emollient approach, advising an interviewer, 'We are going to try to find each other [the DA and ANC], at the end of the day we want the same thing ... universal access to basic healthcare for all.'

But the radically different means of its achievement, on current reading, suggests a fundamental irreconcilability. Not a single DA voter, nor many beyond the party's constituency, will acquiesce in the destruction of the private health sector and the ban on its use or the scrapping of private medical aids.

Some DA insiders waved away these concerns, dismissing health minister Motsoaledi as an incompetent blowhard who did not have the ear of the president or many ministerial colleagues either. But then why, I wondered, had Ramaphosa spent so much political capital on the enactment of NHI? I was, in any event, far less sanguine than some in the party. Even if Motsoaledi was as described, his key officials were bright, efficient and deeply zealous.

The veto that the DA exercised on this became necessary when the party refused Motsoaledi's demand for the mini-budget tabled in October to provide for the effective elimination of private medical aid schemes within five years. In classic Ramaphosa style, this was sent off for 'further negotiation' – a filibuster at least, if not a final victory over dogmatic madness. However, the minister possesses a vast regulatory arsenal to introduce aspects of control over the private healthcare sector and medical aids which will not, at first blush, be in the purview of his cabinet colleagues.

In October 2024, the mini-budget was tabled, shorn of the ideological obsessions of the ANC (NHI and a new and costly push for the localisation of industries). This signalled a DA pushback and a readiness for more visible public scraps with the ANC.

The NHI saga continued unresolved into the new year. The DA declared a dispute on the most combustible aspects of this elephantine overhaul of the health sector, based on its total opposition (along with organised business) to the NHI's stated intent of forcing private patients into the NHI system and limiting the rights of citizens to purchase private health insurance. Some sort of resolution on this was apparently achieved between the parties – as ever, the devil would be in the future detail. A crisis if not averted was, in the best local tradition, postponed to an indeterminate date.

BELA blows up

The future of NHI is, at the time of writing, unresolved. But before its resolution was in sight, a more immediate chokepoint threatened the GNU. This came in the form of the Basic Education Laws Amendment Act, known by the acronym BELA.

There was not much beauty in it, though, for either the DA or its Afrikaans-speaking supporters – a pillar of the party's electoral base. Around 90 per cent of Afrikaans South Africans voted for the party in 2024.

The big difference here was that while the health ministry was headed by the ANC's Motsoaledi, the notional authority for BELA was the basic education minister, the DA's Siviwe Gwarube. She opposed the Bill being signed into law by Ramaphosa. He ignored her, so she boycotted the signing ceremony in mid-September 2024.

I recorded earlier how, in our GNU negotiations, Helen Zille had advised our counterparty that the legislation (then awaiting the presidential imprimatur) was a 'red line' for the DA.

The opposition to the new law, amplified on the highly effective and voluble platforms of two leading Afrikaans civil society groups – AfriForum and the Solidarity trade union – related to two controversial, indeed combustible, clauses. One would allow the provincial head of education, not the school governing body, to override a school's language policy; another would remove the power of controlling admissions to schools from the governing body to the provincial administration.

For many, especially in Afrikaans communities, this was the death knell for mother-tongue education, and in their view the demise of Afrikaans. It was a deeply felt emotional issue for a minority that saw its fundamental rights being overridden.

However, in addition to mounting a court challenge against the legislation, Steenhuisen, by dint of his access to Ramaphosa, persuaded the president to discuss the concerns directly with the Afrikaans groups. This he did, and the result was a fudge, or at least more breathing space. Ramaphosa announced at the signing ceremony that he would pause operationalising the two key clauses for three months, to 'give parties time to deliberate ... and make proposals on how the different views may be accommodated'.

This apparent velvet glove concealed an iron fist: he simultaneously said that should no agreement be reached, 'we will proceed with a full implementation of all the parts of the Bill'.[8]

Before this happened, Steenhuisen joined a mass march, organised by the two Afrikaans civic organisations, in Pretoria to publicise opposition to the legislation. He proclaimed to an appreciative audience that the BELA Act – or its contentious clauses – 'give the state too much control over who gets an education at any particular school, and in what language ... we cannot allow authority for [school decisions] to be handed over to an official in a provincial office, far removed from the needs and wants of community members.' This is precisely what the contested sections (4 and 5) did.

These stirring public words were strikingly at odds with what was happening in the background. BELA became, for the circling internal opponents of Ramaphosa, led by the egregious populist premier of Gauteng, Panyaza Lesufi, a battering ram to beat down the fragile walls of the GNU. He and his allies demanded the full implementation, voetstoots, of the BELA Act without amendment. Little concerned with the well-being of pupils, in my opinion their essential purpose was to pressure Ramaphosa to do their bidding or face a potential motion of recall and the entry of the MK and EFF (closely allied to Lesufi and the anti-Ramaphosa faction) into government.

The DA – the party that had drawn the 'red line' on the BELA Act – now faced its own reckoning. It was boxed in by its Afrikaans allies in Solidarity and AfriForum, who were unfussy in threatening the party that if any final settlement of this issue did not meet their requirements, then there would be hell to pay (worded more elegantly, but that was the essential drift).

Meanwhile, the cabinet had established a 'clearing house' where contentious disagreements between parties in the coalition were sent for processing and resolution. This is where BELA ended up, after a detour to statutory body Nedlac, where state, business and labour thrashed out issues of contention.

What was striking in all this manoeuvring was, as foretold earlier in this account, the complete absence of the 'sufficient consensus' mechanism detailed in the statement of intent signed by all parties participating in the GNU. It had, on this and all previous disputes, never been operationalised or even triggered. Just to remind readers: clause 19 of the statement of intent mandates that in the event of a disagreement between parties in the government, an agreement reached by parties representing 60 per cent of the seats in the National Assembly (ANC and DA) would determine the matter.

No one, at least on the DA side, could properly explain why, on this core and disputatious issue of mother-tongue education, there had been no recourse to the mandated dispute-resolution process where the DA held the power of veto. (Finally, in January 2025, the DA triggered this clause in respect of other contentious legislation, NHI and the Expropriation Act [see below], but whether this would move the dial at all remained questionable.)

And so, on 20 December 2024, Ramaphosa announced that, in agreement with all the parties, including the DA, BELA would be enacted in full 'immediately', shorn of any amendments.

'We were royally fucked' was the response of one DA insider when I enquired about the mysterious disappearance of the party's 'red line' – now apparently written in invisible ink.

I did subsequently join a discussion with the key DA personalities enjoined on the issue, and the terms of the 'settlement' became both clear and somewhat dispiriting. On the upside, the party, via its minister for basic education, Siviwe Gwarube, would be responsible for drawing up the 'regulations, norms and standards' underpinning the legislation. This gave some comfort to AfriForum and Solidarity, although soon enough both bodies commenced court proceedings to stop it. No doubt a battle royal will emerge when these norms and standards are published in final form. The crisis had not been resolved but, in the best local tradition, kicked down the road.

Of course, in instrumental terms, there was another option open to the DA. The operationalisation of any legislation, such as the BELA Act, requires the signature of both the president and the relevant minister, in this case Gwarube. One suggestion made within the DA was for Gwarube to refuse to countersign the legislation until after the new regulations had been published. This in turn – as the Presidency made clear – would constitute ministerial insubordination, leading Ramaphosa to fire her, which in turn would cause the DA to leave the government.

As one key advisor to the party spelt it out: 'In simple terms, this means BELA will be the hill on which the party dies.' Not a single person inside the conclave thought many of the party's voters, not least its business supporters, would understand such a dramatic and drastic step.

So the party stayed its hand. At one level, it was a comprehensive win for the radicals in the ANC and the ever-malleable Ramaphosa. However, there is much wisdom in Jean-Paul Sartre's remark that 'if a victory is told in detail, one can no longer distinguish it from a defeat'.

This applies to the future, no less, of the GNU itself. While the DA was 'outboxed or outfoxed' on this matter, it will not, if it is to sustain credibility and self-respect, allow itself to be the willing agent of other ANC policies, such as NHI. For the DA, this is the hill on which the GNU could collapse if the legislation is pushed ahead.

But the 'defeat in victory' label adheres most closely to Ramaphosa himself. He has, in some essential matters, far more in common with the DA than he does with Lesufi and the populist faction of his own party. He handed them a win with the outcome of BELA so far (unadorned with the regulations to come). But he might well have handed them a sword as well; emboldened by this victory, they could in time sever his head.

The ANC elective conference in 2027, when Ramaphosa's successor as party president will be elected, will likely render Ramaphosa the lamest of hobbled ducks for the remainder of his presidency of the republic. But since the manoeuvrings until then will be fought with intensity, even a recall motion for the president is not off the table. It is salutary to recall that neither of his predecessors, Mbeki and Zuma, completed their second terms in office. Mandela wisely elected to serve a single term.

Expropriating good faith

A New Year surprise awaited the minister of public works and infrastructure, Dean Macpherson, when Ramaphosa signed into law the contentious Expropriation Bill, which had lain on his desk for some ten months since its enactment by Parliament in March 2024.

The Bill divided experts on its reach and meaning. Opponents of it (which at the time included the DA then in opposition) stated that it threatened land ownership security, while some experts stated that the legislation simply aligned the concept of expropriation with the prescripts of the Constitution and its property clause (section 25).[9]

While the merits and demerits of the legislation remained contested, what was incontestable was the process, or lack of one, that resulted in the presidential pen signing the legislation into operation: some months before the signing ceremony, Macpherson had sent Ramaphosa a detailed legal opinion on the internal contradictions in the Bill, which in senior counsel's view rendered it unconstitutional. Ramaphosa simply never responded to his own minister's view and, further, gave him no advance notice of his intention to sign the legislation into law. Added to the bad-faith aspect that encased this grubby saga was the fact that Macpherson's deputy in the ministry, the ANC's Sihle Zikalala, was clearly briefed by the Presidency in advance of the signing. He issued a statement of support at the very time his minister was only finding out about the event.

The Expropriation Act also attracted notorious attention from no less a figure than newly inaugurated US President Donald Trump. On 7 February 2025, he fired off an executive order 'addressing egregious actions of the Republic of South Africa'. Among its bill of indictments was this legislation, which the president claimed '[enabled] the government of South Africa to seize ethnic minority Afrikaners' agricultural property without compensation'. This was a very strained, arguably incorrect, reading of the legislation, but it proved that local acts had global consequences. The same order halted all US aid and assistance to the country, and offered to 'promote resettlement of Afrikaner refugees' fleeing South Africa for the US.[10]

Ramaphosa's (mis)handling of the Expropriation Act recalled the schoolboy play of 'silly buggers'. It is, though, no way to run an adult government, least of all one requiring a serious approach to the cascade of problems flooding the country.

11
Fractures and Finesses

The problem of personnel

The adage 'politics makes strange bedfellows' applied with interest to the people the DA was now in bed with, in a marriage based on political necessity, not personal amity.

The DA had spent three decades in opposition exposing the twin evils of corruption and the deployment of underperforming and compromised cadres in government. In the courts it had unleashed its effective 'lawfare' against the most egregious of these. Yet, suddenly, it was in government alongside some of these shifty elements. All ANC cabinet ministers, for example, are drawn from the ranks of the party's NEC.

In January 2025, Adriaan Basson, editor-in-chief of News24, revealed that no fewer than four of the DA's cabinet colleagues from the ANC were in the crosshairs of various criminal probes by state law enforcement agencies.[1]

Deputy President Paul Mashatile was under investigation for undue benefits, relating to luxury housing he enjoys, sourced from dubious figures and family members who were enriched with tenders while he was a Gauteng provincial minister.

Gwede Mantashe, ANC chairman and minister of minerals, had been fingered by the Zondo Commission for unjustified enrichment from tender-milking entity Bosasa. (He was challenging the findings in court.)

Minister in the Presidency Khumbudzo Ntshavheni was in the frame following a much earlier court judgment (now the subject of potentially imminent prosecution) relating to her alleged misconduct as a municipal manager; the court found the award of a contract by her was 'repugnant and devastating'.[2]

The final member of this rogues' gallery was human settlements minister Thembi Simelane. Ramaphosa had half-heartedly acted against her when her previous post as justice minister became unsustainable after revelations proved conclusively that she had benefited from monies received from a third-party middleman criminally accused in the looting – from widows and orphans, literally – of VBS Bank, a finance house into which, as a municipal mayor, her council had made illegal deposits. In Simelane's case, typically, Ramaphosa could not wield the axe. He simply shuffled her off to a lesser portfolio.

A report by the Centre for Risk Analysis, published after the formation of the GNU, made uncomfortable reading for new parties, especially the exponents of clean governance, in the arrangement: 25 of the 87 members of the ANC NEC were 'linked to serious corruption' (either detailed in the Zondo report or under investigation by the Special Investigating Unit). A further 26 members had been identified by the media (often after scrupulous deep-dive investigations) as implicated in corruption, while ten of their colleagues were only 'weakly implicated' in wrongdoing. Extraordinarily, or not, given its reputation, just 26 members, a minority, of this august body 'have zero known links to allegations of corruption'. In analysing this report, journalist Natasha Marrian pointed to the absurdity that the same NEC is 'tasked with reforming and renewing the ANC'.[3]

The DA was not joined with the ANC on its Sisyphean quest for party reform and renewal. But there is the danger of collateral association and the difficulty of marrying respect for cabinet collegiality with the presence of some very dubious figures, on the one hand, and with keeping corruption at bay in Parliament and calling it to account, on the other. Needle-threading of such a high order needs a deft hand.

Marching to Pretoria

One of the more impressive new DA leaders is Cilliers Brink. I met him when he was still a schoolboy some 20 years ago and was struck by both his political precocity and his easy charm and impeccable manners. After he qualified as a lawyer, his ascent through the party ranks was impressively and appropriately swift. After serving in Parliament for four years, in March 2023 he was elected mayor of Tshwane, the municipality centred on Pretoria, the capital city of the country.

His tenure was troubled, though not because of any lack of competence or courage. He inherited a deeply dysfunctional, bankrupt and corrupt municipal administration, populated by rafts of hostile ANC deployees. He also headed a fractious multiparty governing coalition.

Brink's attempts to right the listing ship were thwarted by many forces. Beyond the usual suspects on the opposition benches, headed by the ANC and EFF, Brink was finally felled from within. This happened when his coalition partner, the mercurial and strategically inept ActionSA, decided to go back on the promise of its leader, Herman Mashaba, never to cooperate with 'the criminal ANC'. Mashaba did precisely that when ActionSA, smarting from its paltry national election debut (a measly 1.2 per cent), decided to exact revenge on the DA. This was exacerbated by the fact that most ActionSA representatives were defectors from the DA. A combination of ANC, EFF and ActionSA votes saw Brink removed from his post in late September 2024.

The return of the ANC and lesser parties to power in Pretoria was bad news for the city's residents, given the path to perdition the parties piloted when last in office. However, since the drive to remove Brink and the DA from power was driven essentially by the ANC's Gauteng provincial leadership, headed by Panyaza Lesufi, this led to a lot of unanswered questions – not least for Brink's party.

The DA had lent its parliamentary votes to elect Ramaphosa as president in June. But here we were, just three months later, and the ANC returned the favour by ousting a DA mayor in Tshwane.

Theoretically at least, the answer to this was structural: the national agreement between the ANC and DA did not extend vertically to embrace power-sharing at the provincial and municipal levels.

But in the realpolitik of the matter, some in the DA began to ask why their leader had not strenuously arm-twisted Ramaphosa to prevent this. Or perhaps he had, but Ramaphosa was unwilling or unable to intervene. It was no secret that the ANC in Gauteng was an outpost of resistance to dealing with the DA and far preferred a comradely coalition with the EFF, with ActionSA performing the classic function of useful idiots to enable it.

Lesufi was said to fancy himself as Ramaphosa's successor, his failures as provincial premier, in a scandal-ridden, vote-shedding administration, proving – in his estimation at least – no bar to falling upward.

A fine balance

All the DA ministers I spoke to said broadly the same thing: 'Tony, we are not afraid to walk if need be.' One of them, on moving into his new ministerial home in the leafiest of Cape Town's suburbs, said, 'Mentally, I am keeping my suitcase packed in the event of an early exit.'

That initial approach changed after a few months in office. Instead of DA ministers preparing for the exit door, if necessary, the strategy changed and hardened. This was expressed to me by an insider, a keen sports follower, in the cabinet grouping in October 2024: 'Strategically, there is now a shift. The question mustn't be: will the DA walk away? The question must be: will CR [Ramaphosa] remove the DA? Because he can't. Just as we can't easily leave, he can't easily fire us. Put the ball in his court. Play the game in his half.'

The strategy soon enough informed the party's tactics. Assertively and, in my opinion, correctly, the DA dissented on the president's unilateralism in foreign policy, such as his dark proclamation of pitiless Russian dictator Vladimir Putin as a 'valued friend and ally'. Not that such noting and protesting of foreign relationships made much difference to policy and practice. The ANC apparently regards international relations as its own 'sealed mandate', walled off from other inputs. Doubtless the return to office of Donald Trump as US president, determined to write his own rules of international engagement, will be far more effective in causing South Africa to pause its embrace of American enemies, from Iran and Hamas to China, than any local pressures.

Then, since the ANC was oft to forget that it had lost its majority in Parliament, the DA made necessary common cause with its ideological foes there (MK and EFF) to create, amid strenuous and futile ANC opposition, an oversight mechanism to hold the president and his department accountable to the National Assembly. Ramaphosa fumed at this idea of Parliament doing, 30 years late, its core function: holding the Presidency and executive to account. (Hitherto, the Presidency, alone of all government departments, had had no portfolio committee in Parliament to report to.)

On the other hand, there was also a heightened degree of responsibility on the DA side, and doubtless among their more serious-minded ANC counterparts. The most futile exercise in a life in politics, and in the world beyond it, is to prepare for every contingency but success. Having thrown in their lot with the new GNU, an early departure by the DA might not only burn down the ANC's house but could also be, as noted above, self-immolating.

And some early wins were recorded by new DA ministers making the political weather, with reforms and resets and exposing sloth and malfeasance in departments such as home affairs and public works and infrastructure. Here, Leon Schreiber and Dean Macpherson were both fleet-footed in trumpeting achievements and not afraid of a good scrap to promote their agendas. Behind the scenes, in the National Treasury, deputy finance minister Ashor Sarupen proved very effective.

My late colleague Colin Eglin was a veteran party leader of yesteryear. He was immersed in the constitutional negotiations between 1991 and 1996 that led to South Africa's new order. He said, after the finalisation of the Constitution, 'If we were stupid enough to do this, we certainly should be stupid enough to make it work.' Useful advice for working alongside previous political opponents for the benefit of the public weal.

But not at all costs. There is a very fine balance, and great wisdom is needed to strike it. An eyes-wide-open optimism – despite the early challenges – is the best approach.

Totalitarian temptation

The glue holding the sometimes fractious, certainly fragile GNU in place was the totalitarian temptation lurking just outside the gates of government. The alternative, an ANC-MK-EFF coalition, had been stopped, for the time being at least, by the entrance of the DA into governing arrangements with the ruling party. But it had hardly disappeared.

The diminished SACP barely had a constituency to speak of and its ideology was as rusty as its unrefreshed leadership. Its national chair, Blade Nzimande, was 66 years old. He had presided over multiple departmental failures and scandals but remained in the cabinet. And the SACP remained part of the tripartite alliance, along with the ANC and trade union federation Cosatu.

In an impressive exercise in political schizophrenia, the presence of several SACP members in the GNU, including Nzimande, Gwede Mantashe and key deputy finance minister David Masondo, did not deter the SACP from criticising the composition of the GNU itself.

Within weeks of the formation of the new government, SACP general secretary Solly Mapaila vented his disapproval. In September 2024, he told an interviewer that the presence of the DA in government was 'a betrayal ... the political choice the ANC made, it's a gross error ... because there were other possibilities for the ANC not to collaborate with the DA'. He dismissed the ANC's coalition partner as a 'party of white interest, of the white minority, the imperial regime's interest, the apartheid regime's interest'.[4]

While even Karl Marx might have blushed at this crude referencing of race consciousness absent of any class interest, the general secretary was explicit in who the best partners were. He suggested that the 'betrayal and sell out' of Black interests could be remedied by an alignment with the MK and EFF.

One of the consequences of the DA's arrival in government was that it ceded its decades-long tenure as official opposition in Parliament to Zuma's MK Party, headed there by the disgraced and impeached judge John Hlophe. Hlophe was the first jurist in the recorded history of South Africa (since Union in 1910) to be impeached by the same Parliament in which he now served. In his maiden address to the assembly, he gave full vent to his (and presumably Zuma's) world view. He advised Parliament that 'transformative change ... across South Africa' could only be achieved by replacing Roman-Dutch law (which he had administered for two decades from the bench), which, he added, 'was imported into this country through the genocidal force and forced down our throats'.[5]

'African law' rather than the current Constitution was, in his view, the foundation stone for a transformed republic, without the impediment of any protection for individual or property rights, and with supremacy for traditional leadership. This was MK's ticket to the future. His party also favoured junking the Constitution in its entirety and restoring the apartheid-era arrangement of the supremacy of Parliament, meaning there would be no checks and balances on majoritarianism.

New home for state looters

Hlophe's MK Party ranks in Parliament would soon enough be augmented by some impressive looters of state coffers who had enjoyed pre-eminence and immunity during Zuma's presidency. They were the key architects of 'state capture' identified by the Zondo Commission who had plundered billions – from Transnet to Eskom and the Passenger Rail Agency of South Africa (Prasa) – and destroyed the national infrastructure. Now they were being sworn in as MK MPs. A veritable rogues' gallery was now the official opposition in Parliament.[6]

MK might be a cult party, with a gaseous, even poisonous, race-populist rhetoric and a ramshackle platform centred around Zuma, but it held sway with nearly half the voters in KwaZulu-Natal and registered just under 15 per cent in its national electoral debut, the best result ever recorded by a fledgling party.

It was capable of both cannibalising ANC votes and eroding the support base of the EFF, the previous *enfant terrible* of race nationalism in the country. Not only did the arrival of MK reduce the EFF to under ten per cent in the May election, but the red berets also bled some leading members – such as Malema's number two, Floyd Shivambu, and former national chair Dali Mpofu – to Zuma's outfit. The unity of the so-called progressive caucus could not survive the poaching by MK of EFF people, and it soon unravelled.

The numbers did not lie: between them, MK and the EFF enjoyed the support of 25 per cent of South African voters. It is difficult to locate the big-tent ANC on the ideological spectrum with any precision: its policy positions are many and often flatly contradict one another. However, it is fair to estimate that at least one-quarter of current ANC voters (and likely around that percentage of members of the ANC national executive) are attracted by policies that would junk any fiscal sustainability, destroy independent institutions such as the South African Reserve Bank, crater economic growth, purge foreign investment, accelerate the flight of the country's skilled population and crush the private sector.

A road to national ruin and a recent warning

It is hardly surprising, for example, that the political idol of Julius Malema is the late dictator of Venezuela, Hugo Chávez. Over more than a decade of misrule and democratic vandalism, Chávez converted what was once South America's most robust democracy and admired economy into a pitiless authoritarian sham and a state of beggary (despite having the world's greatest recorded oil deposits).

The arrival of either the EFF or MK, or both, into a reconfigured GNU, which many leading lights in the ANC, though not Ramaphosa, would support, would not only make the example of Venezuela, or perhaps Zimbabwe, the country's likely trajectory; it would also kill off both Ramaphosa's leadership and any prospect of national reform and renewal.

Just days after the current GNU was formed, a new report revealed that unemployment in South Africa had hit a record high of 8.38 million people in search of work who could not find any job. Of a labour force of 25 million people, more than 33.5 per cent were unemployed; on the expanded definition (including those who have given up the attempt to find work), the figure rose to 42.6 per cent (or around 12 million people).[7]

Curiously, this drew barely any response from the government, least of all from the ministry charged with employment. The DA justified its participation in the GNU on achieving an improvement in two interrelated metrics: driving up the economic growth rate and reducing the unemployment figures. It has set its own measurement for success or failure.

But this is hardly confined to the DA scoreboard. Reversing or denting significantly the 'worst unemployment crisis in the world', as analyst Ann Bernstein has termed it, is a national imperative. Continuing on the current failed path that has led to this catastrophe can only embolden – perhaps finally empower – the radical populists keen to take the reins of power themselves.

It is, of course, now settled knowledge that rapid economic growth is the only sustainable route out of the death spiral of South Africa's triple lock of inequality, unemployment and poverty.

In 2008, the conclusions of the Commission on Growth and Development, chaired by Nobel Prize-winning economist Michael Spence – and on which former ANC finance minister Trevor Manuel served – confirmed that there is no substitute for economic growth. The report approvingly quoted this assertion: 'Economic growth is not a mysterious force that strikes unpredictably or whose absence is inexplicable. On the contrary, growth is the fruit of two forces: the ability of people to recognize opportunities on the one hand, and the creation by government of a legal, fiscal, and regulatory framework in which it is worthwhile for people to exploit those opportunities.' Its other obvious remark is worth repeating: '[The] key is simply to put sensible policies in place, and then let the intelligence, industriousness, and ingenuity of the people do the rest'.[8.]

Extortionate shakedowns on businesses to fund racial transformation, and the demand that all law firms, regardless of areas of specialisation or expertise, must achieve a mandatory 30–50 per cent Black ownership and management of legal practices, as cited above, do not amount to 'sensible policies'.

Calls for economic reforms are made with regularity. But left unsaid by many business leaders who whisper in government's ear are some necessary home truths. These include that there is no short cut to avoid hard choices, and that you cannot be both pro-growth and simultaneously anti-business – the precise place where the ANC and its DTIC has placed the country.

Curiously, notwithstanding so much evidence to the contrary, Ramaphosa is still seen by some as pro-business and a change agent, although sightings of him in either role are vanishingly few. He too is a signed-up member of the 'growth club' and monotonously repeats calls for economic reform and investment. Yet he also wants to retain the 'national democratic revolution', racial percentages, job-crushing labour laws, the whole shebang.

Paul Romer, former chief economist of the World Bank and a Nobel laureate, reminds us of the gap between government rhetoric and real life: 'Everybody's in favour of growth, but nobody wants change.'[9]

V
THE EXPERIMENT

'People's opinions are mainly designed to make them feel comfortable. Truth, for most people, is a secondary consideration.'

– Bertrand Russell, philosopher

12
A Quiet Death, A Loud Aftermath

My father, Ray, led a distinguished and ethical life and was privileged to have a peaceful death. He was born in 1925, when King George V ruled a vast empire, and never switched on a computer or even a cellphone. I once suggested that he become au fait with the brave new world of technology and advised him that being computer illiterate in the 21st century was somewhat like being functionally illiterate in the 20th. With typical sang-froid, he replied, 'So be it.'

He thought Twitter was for the birds too. He had no concept of what an 'influencer' was, but he certainly influenced much of my life for the better and backed me up in the choices I made.

On 15 April 2018, he had reached the impressive age of 93 two weeks before. He arrived at this milestone absent some of the health horrors afflicting many nonagenarians, apart from some mild symptoms of senile dementia; for example, when I visited him, he would ask me three times in as many minutes where we were going for lunch!

That Sunday morning, after taking a shower, he told his carer, at the Durban retirement complex where he contentedly spent his last years, that he was feeling tired. As she recounted it, she asked him if he would like to lie down for a while. He readily agreed and closed his eyes for the final time. His quiet end, though, had a cacophonous aftermath.

BEING THERE

I was in London when Michal phoned with the sad but inevitable news of his passing, and I was pleased that, just a few weeks earlier, I had been with him on his birthday. I hastened home that evening to begin the rest of life's journey without his large, though recently fading, presence in it.

My mother died some 16 years before him. And so now it was a strange, sombre feeling, even at the age of 61, to be finally a full adult, which happens (I think) when the last barrier between your childhood and your own final demise is lifted.

I had barely arrived home, immersed both in mourning and in the distracting detail of planning his last send-off, when both print and social media went into overdrive on the news of Dad's death. The normal South African festival of hypocrisy, of brushing over inconvenient facts of life to mourn a notable passing, was absent in his case. Even though, in my father's case, the 'facts' were wrong. Not just false but entirely invented.

My father was a well-regarded Supreme Court judge in Natal from 1967 to 1987, at the height of the dark era of apartheid. He delivered many pioneering judgments – lifting censorship, removing restrictions on employment and using legal creativity to free detained persons. They were hallmarks of his liberal disposition and distaste for the authoritarian state. In his later ceremonial role, from 1983 to 1993, as chancellor of his alma mater, the University of Natal, he robustly championed academic freedom and free and dissenting speech during a challenging decade when both were under assault.

But he was also a stickler for the rules (as I often painfully learnt during wayward times of yore) and for the oath of his office. Although he expansively utilised judicial office to promote freedom and liberty, he also felt obliged to adhere to its strictures. When he was on the bench, the death sentence was mandatory in cases of murder without extenuation. He imposed it extremely rarely and always, as he recounted, with deep anguish. (On retirement, and freed from the constraints of office, he became a leading abolitionist.)

However, one case or appeal he never tried or adjudicated in any respect was that of Solomon Mahlangu, an ANC guerrilla who was sentenced to death as an accessory to murder, after a shootout in Johannesburg, by Judge CDJ Theron in the Rand Supreme Court in 1978.

Shortly after my father's death, all the Independent Media titles, the *Mail & Guardian* and the bots and bottom-feeders on Twitter (led largely by ANC and EFF supporters) published a montage featuring my father, the gallows, Solomon Mahlangu and me. The headlines were, in variations of exclamation and excitation, along the lines of 'Tony Leon's apartheid judge father who hanged Solomon Mahlangu dies' and 'Good riddance'. More economically, a simple 'good' often followed in the comments section.

The *Mail & Guardian* at least retracted and apologised. Twitter and the Iqbal Survé newspapers (Independent Media) did not. Nor were they bothered with accuracy, and the feat of placing my late father in a court in which he never sat, delivering a judgment he never gave to an accused person he never tried, went uncorrected. (Indeed, the same montage sometimes reappears on X, as Twitter is now called, when some anonymous keyboard warrior seeks to engage in thoughtful and meaningful debate with something I have written.)

The ANC guerrilla my father had in fact sentenced to death, in 1986, was Andrew Zondo, who killed five civilians and injured 40 others when, with premeditation and sans remorse, he placed a bomb in a shopping centre in Amanzimtoti, on the Natal South Coast, two days before Christmas 1985. This case, courtesy of the ANC, had been rehashed for at least 20 years before my father's death. However, the big differences between those cases meant smearing my father's name (and attempting to have a go at his son) with fake facts. They also simply de-individuated – essentially dehumanised – the people involved, Mahlangu and Zondo and their motives and victims, treating them as interchangeable instruments of posthumous propaganda. More likely, the Twitterati and so-called journalists were utterly unconcerned, completely ignorant of even the facts of each case.

Weighed in the balance against my father's much-loved presence, his good life and peaceful passing, it seems trite to concentrate on the fetid stew of social media concoctions and how it affected one family in grief. And battering the truth with 'alternative facts' has become the new (ab)normal. But my first-hand experience of this was hardly unique or localised.

The symphonies of hate on a lot of social media have had far more baleful effects on wider political events – from Brexit to Donald Trump to the demonisation of anti-corruption fighters in South Africa – as the merchants of loathing, disinformation and fake news have proven across the world. 'Things don't need to be true in order to be believed' was coined in a different age, but its currency was hot and reminted in the new digital age. And, three years after my dad's death, I would discover this anew with intense ferocity.

13

The Interview

After publishing a book, authors typically embark on a round of media interviews to promote interest and sales.

When my book *Future Tense: Reflections on My Troubled Land* was published in April 2021, I was doing the media sessions and launches in Johannesburg. An interview was arranged with a young journalist from News24, James de Villiers. (Ironically, the same journalist would in 2024 fall upwards and emerge as spokesman for my friend Dean Macpherson, the new minister of public works and infrastructure in the GNU.)

De Villiers, who at first blush came across as thoughtful and sincere, arrived at my brother Peter's home in Parkwood to interrogate me on the book and its contents. The article he subsequently wrote proved anew that first impressions are sometimes wrong.

When the interview was published a few days later, it contained scant reference to the book – not much beyond mentioning the title, and little about its contents. Certainly, its literary merits or demerits went unmentioned in the article.[1]

Rather, the interviewer spent inordinate space discussing the handsome furnishings, artworks and even the cats in my brother's home. Did I mention the interview was meant to be about the book and its author, not the interior decor of his older brother? In any event, the reason for the detailed descriptions of 'a satin white couch', 'the sizeable lounge' and even my 'silver watch' was evident from the headline slapped across the piece: 'Former DA leader Tony Leon: Checking your privilege is absolute garbage.'

'Gotcha' was one of the clear takeaways from this *engagé* reporter. The implication of the article was this: look at how well and finely he lives, and then he spouts about the absurd notion of white privilege. Even if, for this purpose, it was not my home that provided the background for the hit job.

None of the reporter's talent for describing home furnishings triggered much attention. Yet one line in the interview, naturally shorn of much context, lit the fire of the internet shortly after publication. It would blaze for at least two weeks afterwards, and its embers are still fanned on occasion today.

The offending paragraph read: 'Resting his right hand on his leg, Leon says [Mmusi] Maimane's election as DA leader "was an experiment that went wrong", as Maimane had never committed to the party's ideals before joining it.' Indeed, Mmusi Maimane on his own account had been an ANC voter until 2007, and his political hero was Thabo Mbeki, certainly not the leader of the opposition at that time (me). He only joined the DA in 2010.

Actually, in addition to the leader's lack of roots in the DA, as I advised the reporter, and as the book made clear in far more detail, the big risk, subsequently proven by events, in selecting Maimane as leader was simply this: '[In 2014] he entered Parliament for the first time and was promptly installed as parliamentary leader without a day's experience in the legislature.'[2]

One of the reasons why the 'experiment' quotation received such an outsize response was that even the threadbare context offered by the journalist was stripped out of the link that News24 used to promote the article. It simply read, 'Former DA leader Tony Leon speaks to News24 about his new book ... why Mmusi Maimane was "an experiment gone wrong"'. As clickbait, this was just the ticket for instant outrage, unless

THE INTERVIEW

the casual reader forked out the R75 required to read the full article behind the paywall. The one-liner suggested I was gratuitously and crudely insulting his person.

The book interrogated in some detail the question first asked by Ernest Hemingway in 'The Snows of Kilimanjaro': How did the leopard climb so high?

Maimane's swift ascent to the top was an attempt by his party to have a Black leader, and the book highlighted some of his gifts as he drifted upwards on a sea of hope and hype. But it also probed at some length how the party's loss of 400 000 votes in the 2019 election, when Maimane led it, was related to, indeed caused by, a battle for the soul of the party. On his watch, finding a coherent direction of political travel for his party resembled a modern version of trench warfare in World War I: a long fight over very barren terrain.

As I recounted, 'On the even more vexed issue of policy confusion and values and party ideology, one of the key outsiders we interviewed – a black intellectual – summed it up: "The DA has been captivated by the racial and nationalist narrative of the ANC."'

That interview on the DA's ANC-lite approach happened after Maimane appointed me (with strategist Ryan Coetzee and banker Michiel le Roux) to a panel to conduct a postmortem on the failed campaign and questions of leadership.

Maimane did not like the outcome of the report he had personally commissioned, which recommended that he and the top leadership resign. But, shortly afterwards, he quit the party and started on a new political journey. He founded his own outfit, Build One South Africa, or BOSA (the name filched from an old DA slogan), which in the 2024 election won just two seats with 0.41 per cent of the national vote, finishing in 14th place out of the 20 parties that obtained parliamentary representation. His election promise, 'A job in every home,' proved true for just two families – his own and the other MP elected to Parliament on the BOSA ticket.

No doubt, when the News24 article appeared, Maimane seized the moment to extract some revenge for the report he had commissioned and whose closely reasoned conclusions he resented. So, on publication of the 'book review' interview, he took to Twitter with all the injured innocence of a hapless victim to offer this thought: 'Hey, ore experiment ke mang? [Who is your experiment?] ... I am a human being. Not your science study.'

Maimane's humanity was not the object of the comment at all. As I read his response, though, I couldn't but reflect that what added to his sense of perceived or confected injury was another incontestable truth, which the 'offending' article did in fact contain and which led directly back to the aftermath of my father's death a few years before.

In the interview, I referenced the deep hypocrisy of Maimane at that time. After my father died, Maimane was one of the very first people to message me condolences and followed up by sending a large bouquet of flowers to our home with a message of sympathy. Yet, in the public space, he and the party said nothing (despite my dad being a founder of the Progressive Party in Durban and generous donor to the DA). Winnie Mandela, who died at the same time as my father, received from Maimane's DA a handsome public eulogy, without a single reservation on her public life and moral conduct, even though she detested the party and all it stood for.

Helen Zille wrote to me of the DA's public silence: 'We used to stand by the principle, and deal with the consequences. Now we predict the consequences (among people who would never vote for us anyway) and then ditch the principle. It is really infuriating and must have compounded your grief manyfold.'

14
Two Weeks Hate

I claim some credit, during my tenure as a party leader, for being a reasonable talent spotter. One mega-talent who served as my researcher was the very able James Myburgh, who went on to become the founder and editor of the essential website and news service Politicsweb. In 2021, he did a deep dive into the Maimane response and the furies it unleashed in the online echo chamber – the sewer of spite and insult that passed for commentary on Twitter and other social media platforms.[1]

Myburgh described the saga as 'the latest outpouring of national rage over nothing'. He called it *Two Weeks Hate* and suggested, citing many precedents, how a general pattern could be detected, of which my case was the most recent: 'The *Two Weeks Hate* commonly begins with a somewhat white-looking person ... or institution ... doing or saying something that could be perceived as discriminatory or insulting to someone from the racial majority. A consensus then coheres on social media, and the visage of this person becomes, for a period, the object of intense popular hatred.' But, as he noted, and as I experienced, 'the frenzy cannot sustain itself for too long however and usually, after about two weeks, it passes'.

That fortnight, give or take, seemed much longer. While no boy scout in such matters, I still felt a lot like a hare watching a hissing cobra: I could not take my eyes away from my phone as I viewed the bilious comments piling up, alternately shrugging them off or feeling silent outrage (except to family and close friends) at the responses, some crude, all ad hominem and mostly vicious.

Maimane had crashed his party and then fled the scene of the accident he had caused. He was now bathed in the aura of victimhood, often from people who had rubbished his leadership until recently. And it provided him with endless publicity, at the time when the oxygen of public attention for him and his new cause was in short supply.

However, one thing I decided to do, long before the storm passed, was not to apologise, since there was, on even the semblance of an objective view, nothing to apologise for.

Myburgh's typically forensic and unsparing analysis revealed that some of the very mouthpieces who piled on against me were themselves guilty of using precisely the same characterisation of Maimane, which in my hands they now branded as offensive, racist and even hateful.

I know that many people have the memory of a goldfish, but surely this does not apply to a major newspaper? Here, Myburgh provided a spectacular instance of the two sets of books kept by some of the nation's moral mouthpieces. Here is one example:

> The *Sowetan* [a national newspaper, though in steep decline] published an editorial criticising Leon's use of the phrase 'an experiment gone wrong', as it sought to 'reduce Maimane's leadership and agency to a mere exploratory effort by the party ... One of the traits of racism is precisely that – the use of power by white people to erase the significance of black people in the spaces they occupy.'

To this high-minded outrage, Myburgh excavated an inconvenient reminder: 'This is the same newspaper that commented on the occasion of Maimane's resignation as leader of the DA that he had been elected ... "on a ticket that he will transform the historically white party into a non-racial entity ... But the events of the last few days ... suggest that *the Maimane experiment* has now collapsed [my emphasis]."'

He also unearthed the fact that Maimane, at an election rally in 2019, during the very election in which he had achieved such prodigious vote-shedding, had branded the ANC 'as a party of government [as] a failed experiment'.

Encrustations of fact in place of myth held little appeal or didn't count for much when the narrative or trope pushed was 'white man attacks black man in dehumanising terms' (even if the offending term had been used before by the 'victim' himself). I recalled, and not for the first time either, the brilliant line from the 1962 movie *The Man Who Shot Liberty Valance*: 'When the legend becomes fact, print the legend.'

'The experiment' incident was also a jolting reminder that truth has a hard swim in the mephitic waters of cyberspace and in some of the parochial sections of the print media.

The wider world

My *Two Weeks Hate* was a reminder of two things I had experienced when on the political frontlines: first, you simply must, however much it sticks in the craw, suck up the criticism in the public domain. Enoch Powell, the British parliamentarian, once said: 'For a politician to complain about the press is like a ship's captain complaining about the sea.' Until writing this, I have adhered to this injunction.

Second, it was a further intimation of why I was pleased that I didn't have to deal with the media on a daily basis, unlike when I was party leader. I was also blessed – and a real gift it proved, with hindsight – that when I was at the helm of my party there was no Twitter, and Facebook arrived in the year I stood down as leader of the opposition in Parliament.

In politics, on both the thirst for publicity and the steep price paid, Matthew Parris, a great newspaper columnist and a former Tory parliamentarian, was on to something when he wrote, 'Being an MP feeds your vanity but starves your self-respect.' That applies to past, present and doubtless future parliamentarians.

However, hypocrisy, falsehood and self-esteem anxiety, coupled with feigned victimhood, are hardly confined to the local polity. Mark

Mazower, a British historian based at Columbia University, wrote in 2018 that the usual binary distinction between the durability and health of long-established democracies and the failures and lapses in polities with far shallower roots no longer applied – especially now in an age of internet furies driving the new recession in democracies.

The backstory was well described: '[T]he collapse of the Soviet Union seemed to leave democracy as the only game in town. By the beginning of this century, most political scientists ... had come to believe that liberal democracy was the new normal, something to which the entire world should aspire.'[2] Like many political predictions, Mazower observed, this one did not age well.

He noted that, in the decades since then, we have witnessed the Arab Spring crushed, the rise of Recep Tayyip Erdoğan in Türkiye and Viktor Orbán in Hungary (true believers in 'illiberal democracy'), the election of Donald Trump in the US in 2016 (and again in 2024) and the rise of populist (and worse) parties – and governments – in some of the most established democracies in Europe and in Asia.

In Israel, the Netanyahu government's assault on the judiciary is an example of the challenge to liberal democracy. In 2024, the rise of the far-right Alternative für Deutschland (AfD) party in Germany, with its echoes of a Nazi past, was another portent of popular disaffection with the liberal order in even apparently the most stable and moderate of modern democracies.

Democratic 'backsliding' of this range and variation, however, is not caused by conspiracy theories cooked up by internet Machiavellis (although it is certainly aggravated by them). These online echo chambers, though, close off contrary voices and reject information or news that does not align with a specific world view. Social media, which has now balkanised the flow of information, simply allows the reader or viewer to mentally omit any contrary evidence, however compelling. As a mental filter for the new age, social media is ideal for confirming bias and prejudice – and for strong opinions based on weak foundations. It is a reminder of the truth of Iris Murdoch's comment, 'We seem to know a great deal on the basis of very little.'

VI
THE REAPPRAISAL

*'History is lived forwards but it is written in retrospect.
We know the end before we consider the beginning
and we can never wholly recapture what it was
to know the beginning only.'*

– CV Wedgwood, *William the Silent*

15
What If?

In 1840, Thomas Carlyle suggested that 'Universal history ... is at bottom the History of the Great Men who have worked here ... the soul of the whole world's history, it may be considered justly, were the history of these.'[1]

In centuries since then, there has been a lot of pushback against this 'great man of history' thesis. For example, Marxists believe history is driven by class interests, 'motive forces' in the jargon, and Tolstoy wrote that leaders were merely 'history's slaves'. Of course, both threads play a role: the individual leaders who drive events and the 'structural zeitgeist' where huge events, the very arc of history, its forces and furies, trump the power of personality.

For South Africans, there is a rich cottage industry based on posing a series of contingencies, or 'what-if' scenarios on the dramatic and fraught transition from apartheid to democracy. What if, for example, nature had not intervened in 1989 and felled hard-line securocrat PW Botha, owing to a ruptured blood vessel in his brain, paving the way for the election of FW de Klerk as leader of the NP and state president? Or what if, instead of his triumphant release from 27 years in prison in February 1990, Nelson Mandela had died incarcerated?

Only a brave, or foolish, prognosticator could confidently suggest that either of these two contingencies (and some others) would not have altered the course of the country, likely in the wrong direction too.

I have written several books and many articles, and delivered a lot of lectures, on the sweep of events, in which I was fortunate to be a close participant, that culminated in South Africa's radical course correction and overturning of three centuries of more or less settled history in less than a decade. The last white general election (1989) and the enactment of the new constitutional order (1996) bookended a tumultuous chapter in the national story. And, of more personal salience, this period marked my first eight years as an MP.

While there were many actors in this national drama (or melodrama, it sometimes seemed), three leaders held the ring in determining the outcome of those tumultuous times. FW de Klerk, Nelson Mandela and Mangosuthu Buthelezi were the leading dramatis personae. Many writers and observers have attempted to explain their characters, their collaborations and their enmities. Their traversing of some peaks and precipices, at various times, has been well chronicled with degrees of accuracy, exaggeration and even full-blown revisionism, depending on the purpose and prejudice of the scribe.

In 2014, I wrote an entire book on Mandela,[2] and in a later work I probed the conversion – or apostasy – of De Klerk from conservative nationalist to progenitor of democracy.[3] Buthelezi, literally and figuratively the third man in this leadership trio, has also featured as the historical and political figure who imposed his outsize personality, needs and agenda on the other two, objectively more powerful and important figures.

Both past and present would have been considerably different in the absence of any or all of these three. It can be confidently asserted, too, that South Africa's avoidance of a full-blown racial civil war and/or descent into an authoritarian dystopia was never inevitable. In the words of a historian reflecting on Germany's descent from Weimar democracy to a Nazi dictatorship in the 1930s, it did not unravel inexorably. Rather, it was preceded by 'a series of ups and downs and a succession of unforeseeable contingencies, none of which seem to have

WHAT IF?

been inevitable.[4] In far less dramatic and dark circumstances, this is a good fit for South Africa's passage from past to present.

Aspects of the leadership and personalities of De Klerk, Mandela and Buthelezi should, in my view, be reappraised. Notably, they have all died since my last reflections (Mandela in 2013, De Klerk in 2021 and Buthelezi in 2023). Some new evidence and more distance from both the personalities and the events in each case enable a more considered and nuanced view of role and motivation.

Sophocles suggested, 'One must wait until the evening to see how splendid the day has been.' Ancient wisdom for these and immediate past times too. Certainly, when weighed on the scales of history, Mandela and De Klerk (Buthelezi less so) incontestably guided the country to the safe harbour of democracy, often navigating the most unforgiving seas. And they correctly deserve high praise for so doing, reflected in the award to Mandela and De Klerk of the Nobel Peace Prize in 1993.

Beyond hagiography, though, it is worth briefly pinpointing – in each case – the mythology that now encrusts these leaders and their times and concisely revisiting and revising some key traits central to each to provide a more realistic portrait.

16
FW de Klerk's Needle-threading

My late colleague Colin Eglin was a person of both high intelligence and gruff disposition. Observing FW de Klerk (state president 1989–1994, and deputy president 1994–1996), he offered the grudging view that 'He might not be a great man, but he certainly did a great thing.'

This equivocal remark about his one-time opponent relates to De Klerk's iconoclastic speech in Parliament on Friday 2 February 1990. And its meaning.

In perhaps the most shape-shifting address ever delivered in a Parliament that stood until then as a bulwark against majority representation and full democracy, De Klerk that day signalled the end of white minority rule. He might not have intended the full consequences of the political bombshell he detonated that morning, and a lot of evidence suggest he didn't, but he placed the country on an irreversible path. Within just four years it would see him, by his own hand, removed as the last white president of the country. There were many other forces at play, both internal and external, that hastened this reality, but the formal power at that moment rested with the state president. And, for perhaps the first time in the history of the republic, the incumbent head of state decided to get ahead of events rather than remain imprisoned by them.

FW DE KLERK'S NEEDLE-THREADING

At around 1 pm that day, just after De Klerk's extraordinary act of political heresy, the then co-leader of the DP, Wynand Malan, hosted a lunch for some newly arrived parliamentarians from his caucus, including me.

Sea Point's La Perla restaurant still stands today, defying both the ages and changing culinary attitudes (although its prices have skyrocketed). But every personality around the lunch table that day has long since left active politics.

Malan, who briefly served in the DP troika leadership, represented an enlightened strand of Afrikaner nationalist politics. Two years before the La Perla get-together, he had quit his lifetime allegiance to the National Party and won a seat in Parliament in 1987 on the platform that the timorous reforms of PW Botha, interspersed with lashings of state-sanctioned repression, provided no real answers for a country at war with itself and the wider world.

All the lunch guests mulled, in a state of surprise and disbelief, the meaning of De Klerk's address, just three hours before our meal, which famously upended 350 years of history.

De Klerk's speech caught everyone on the hop – the exiled ANC leadership in Lusaka, the extra-parliamentary opposition and certainly his own parliamentary caucus, who were given no prior notice of his intentions even though his cabinet was apprised. For the liberal parliamentary opposition, represented in the DP, the consequence of a hitherto conservative politician, in the person of De Klerk, essentially co-opting the essence of the DP election manifesto, would prove profound and politically immolating. In the next election, the DP would be reduced to a parliamentary splinter, with most of its historical voters aligning with De Klerk. The only consolation of that political wreck was that it catapulted me into the leadership, although in the early days that seemed more a curse than a blessing.

But while I and other newbie MPs were reeling from the menu on De Klerk's reform package – unbanning the ANC and other proscribed organisations that had been outlawed for 30 years or more, the imminent release of Nelson Mandela from prison and the commencement of full-blown constitutional negotiations – an even more urgent question remained.

And so, over bread rolls at La Perla, I asked Malan, who knew better than most the voters who had recently lifted De Klerk to the presidency, and some of us to Parliament, an obvious question: 'But how, Wynand, will De Klerk take his people with him?' I had in mind the recent election campaign, which had seen De Klerk speak at an election meeting in my own constituency of Houghton, decrying the mild DP leadership as 'three blind mice', whose strings were being manipulated by its alleged ANC puppet masters.

Malan, who had spent a decade, before bolting the NP, in the caucus with De Klerk, answered, 'I know my people, they will respond to strong leadership with vision.'

And, extraordinarily, De Klerk managed to keep his party united, even if the speech of 2 February provided, in the words of Heribert Adam, Frederik van Zyl Slabbert and Kogila Moodley, 'comprehensive evidence [that it was] a sellout of everything the NP had held near and dear since 1948.'[1] Slabbert himself proved an early victim of a conventional consensus. He had quit Parliament in despair just four years earlier, convinced that no NP leader would be capable of making the step changes De Klerk ushered in that morning.

As for the people De Klerk was elected to serve – the white electorate – his principal opponent, Conservative Party leader Dr Andries Treurnicht, asserted that De Klerk had no mandate and insisted that he obtain one for his unprecedented reforms. Two years later, in February 1992, having just lost a hitherto safe NP seat in a by-election in Potchefstroom, De Klerk again gazumped his opponents on the right. He called a referendum of white voters and more than two-thirds of them backed his decision to open negotiations to end apartheid.

These events proved De Klerk a master tactician, but on the strategic vision aspect suggested by Wynand Malan, he proved less convincing. In Chapter 2, I describe my meeting with Ariel Sharon of Israel, whom journalist Jonathan Freedland once described as follows:

'He could see the next hill, perhaps, but he could not and did not grasp the entire mountain range.'[2]

This is why, during the often-tortuous Codesa negotiations, De Klerk's 'bottom lines' – rotating presidencies, minority vetoes, a lengthy interim period before full-blown majority rule, permanent power-sharing – kept yielding. All of these were eventually junked and De Klerk and his changing team of negotiators gave way to the far more assured tactics of their ANC opponents. ANC president Nelson Mandela accurately suggested that 'he wished to share power, not surrender it'.

Mandela, by contrast, had an unyielding bottom line, and he also had the wind of history behind him. He too made some concessions, especially on reassurances to the white minority, during the negotiating process. One of his intimates, Mac Maharaj, would later describe travelling from the constitutional talks at Kempton Park to Mandela's Houghton home to get his sign-off on an agreement: '[Mandela's] zigzags were always leading to the same object ... When I went to see him, he would ask, "Where does it take us towards majority rule? How long will it take?" ... The Nats had no compass: in the end they became preoccupied with their selfish interests.'[3]

De Klerk, of course, had a different version of events and presented his evolution as the logical consequence of evolving NP thinking, however improbable this claim might be. But he also had to face down the diehards in his cabinet and the military who had no truck with this sophistry. Indeed, in November 1993, one of De Klerk's cabinet colleagues, Dr Tertius Delport, grabbed him by the lapels of his jacket and demanded of him, 'What have you done? You have given away South Africa.' Delport confirmed this confrontation to me years afterward.

My interactions with De Klerk evolved over time.

I observed De Klerk's presidency largely at a distance (appropriate to the chasm that separates a young opposition MP and the country's most powerful politician). After the 1994 election, until he quit Parliament in 1997, we were locked in a fight for the allegiance of his voters. My party won the contest, although there were pools of bitterness on his part at their desertion and embrace of the *liberale*.

The short stay of his hand-picked successor, Marthinus van Schalkwyk, as my deputy leader in the Democratic Alliance (formed in 2000 by an amalgamation of the NNP and the DP) led to more recriminations between us when he backed Van Schalkwyk's decision to quit the DA and align his rump party with the ANC. After the disastrous 2004 election results, which nearly wiped out the NNP, Van Schalkwyk then folded what remained of his party entirely into the ANC.

For De Klerk, this last step was the supreme betrayal. He quit the NNP and spent the rest of his life politically marooned. (By contrast, both Mandela and Buthelezi remained staunchly loyal to their parties unto death, and in the latter's case even from beyond the grave.)

For the remainder of his life, when De Klerk was politically homeless but not without some influence, we achieved a rapprochement. This was aided by the warm hospitality and thoughtfulness of his second wife, Elita. She, like Michal, was a foreigner who had arrived in South Africa after the disputes between the two parties their spouses respectively led had themselves begun to fade.

In many conversations, at social gatherings hosted by Elita, I realised that while De Klerk had embraced the tenets of the new Constitution he had helped to inaugurate, he was sceptical about the power of liberal parties to effect change. He once rather archly asked me, at a lunch party, 'How many of your liberal parties are in power in the world right now?' 'Not many,' was the correct and dispiriting answer, although, of course, most of the Western world was anchored in a liberal-democratic framework, even if purely liberal parties were often on the margins.

In one respect, though, De Klerk was correct: the *ancien régime* changes only when one of its own leads the charge.

In politics, a needle-threader is someone who can pass something through the narrow space between two often diametrically opposite impulses or ideas. US President Richard Nixon was regarded by some as a needle-threader extraordinaire. He rose to prominence as a Red-baiting California conservative. Yet, as president, he opened the path to normalising relations with 'Red' China in 1972 and pioneered détente with America's implacable Cold War enemy, the Soviet Union.

De Klerk was cut from this cloth. He was a conservative politician who rose to power on his reputation as a *verkrampte* (reactionary), a term, ironically, coined by his more enlightened brother, Wimpie. In the 1989 contest to replace PW Botha as NP leader, De Klerk beat his more liberal opponent, Barend du Plessis, by a handful of votes. Yet he then used his right-wing credentials to effect profound change – in the opposite direction of his convictions and career to that point.

But needle-threaders also risk the unstitching of their reputations. And when De Klerk died in November 2021, there was much controversy about his life and contribution. Was he a genuine reformist? Did he undergo a conversion of the soul, as he suggested once, or was he, à la Tolstoy, 'the slave of history'?

I thought the fundamental issue was impossible to reconcile: De Klerk's father, Jan, was a leading light of the NP in the Transvaal, and his uncle by marriage, JG Strijdom, was a most intransigent prime minister – in an overcrowded field. When De Klerk turned his back on this political inheritance, he was seen by many of his erstwhile supporters as a sellout. Yet the beneficiaries (although they would never so describe themselves) of his reforms, the ANC, refused in his lifetime to acknowledge his singular change-making contribution.

After his retirement, De Klerk often starred on the international stage, and it was no surprise that he forged a friendship with the last Communist leader of the Soviet Union (in fact its last president before the USSR was dissolved), Mikhail Gorbachev. Both, beyond similar hairlines (or lack thereof), dismantled the systems of privilege they had been entrusted to safeguard, and both earned the scorn of those who benefited from the change and those who lost out in the process.

In 2010, at my embassy in Buenos Aires, I hosted both De Klerk and Mac Maharaj, his one-time critic, at a conference on South Africa's democratic transition. De Klerk forcefully rebutted Maharaj's suggestion that a lot of national trauma could have been avoided if the changes De Klerk had inaugurated had been made years earlier. In De Klerk's opinion, it was only the fall of the Soviet Union – staunch ANC ally and weapons provider – that made these changes possible.

During his lifetime, there was no resolution of the question of whether events forced De Klerk to usher in a system he did not fully intend or whether he knew the game was up for white minority rule and did his best to end it in 'relatively peaceful' circumstances. (This is an apparent oxymoron given that more than 5 000 people died violently between 1990 and 1994, but far more would likely have perished had agreement between the parties not been reached in late 1993.)

Perhaps, when viewed from present times, this motivation matters only on the margins. The result does not. As two American analysts wrote: 'If De Klerk had remained committed to apartheid, the most likely outcome would have been South Africa's descent into even greater racial violence or quite possibly an all-out civil war, not much different from what is happening in Syria and Venezuela today.'[4]

After his death in November 2021, a synthesis of sorts was achieved.

At De Klerk's state funeral, on 12 December 2021, in the nave of the oldest place of Christian worship in South Africa, the Groote Kerk in downtown Cape Town, I witnessed first-hand President Cyril Ramaphosa's attempt to publicly square the circle on the thorny issue of De Klerk's legacy. He did some deft needle-threading of his own that day.

On the one hand, Ramaphosa showed up and delivered a eulogy. And, further, in stark contrast to every other speaker at the event, bar De Klerk's son Jan, he offered some thoughts in Afrikaans. Not even the Dutch Reformed Church dominee who spoke thought that a tribute to the last Afrikaner leader of South Africa might be sprinkled with some words of comfort in the late president's mother tongue.

And in contrast to his public lashings of De Klerk while he was alive, Ramaphosa found some words of praise for him in death: 'Courteous, respectful and committed ... FW de Klerk had the courage of his convictions ... the courage to steer a different course ... for his people.'

Yet, and doubtless with an anxious eye on the many detractors who questioned the wisdom of Ramaphosa's presence, and the idea of a state-sponsored tribute to the 'last apartheid president', Ramaphosa pivoted at length to the 'place FW de Klerk occupied in the hierarchy of an oppressive state'.

He carefully listed atrocities from Boipatong back to Sharpeville, although, as one guest caustically remarked, he omitted Marikana from the bill of indictment. As an observer noted to me, 'It was an impossible speech to make, but at least Ramaphosa delivered it.'

Ramaphosa's equivocations that morning once again mirrored the controversy around De Klerk's contributions and his intentions. I doubt, though, that much of it will matter in a hundred years' time. If South Africa is still studied then as an example of a country that pulled itself back from the brink of mutually assured destruction, then De Klerk will be remembered as a full, indeed essential, partner in a national success story of achievement against improbable odds, anchored by wise leadership.

Because whatever caused (or didn't) De Klerk's conversion from conservative racial nationalist to constitutional reforming democrat, in the end he gave way to the forces of change, surrendering power instead of toughing it out at hideous cost. Even if he never grasped the entire mountain range.

17

Nelson Mandela's Mask

Tuesday 16 December 1997 was a typical hot summer Highveld day in Johannesburg. Early that morning I switched on my TV to watch the commencement of Nelson Mandela's speech to the seminal 50th-anniversary conference of the ANC, convened hundreds of kilometres away in Mafikeng, North West. This was the conference where Mandela would hand the baton of the party presidency to his deputy, Thabo Mbeki, assuring him of election in two years' time as president of the country.

This conference and Mandela's presidential speech there ushered in the policy of cadre deployment, the Leninist extinguishing of a nonpartisan civil service and the promise of 'extending the power of the national liberation movement over all levers of power: the army, the police, the bureaucracy, intelligence structures, the judiciary, parastatals and agencies such as regulatory bodies, the public broadcaster, the central bank, and so on', to quote one paper which the tripartite alliance had approved before the conference.[1]

I left Mandela's oration to attend a wedding. When I returned home, hours later, after the happy nuptials and a splendid lunch, I was amazed that my TV set still showed Mandela at the podium, continuing with the same address. (The speech was in two parts, apparently, to allow the comrades to adjourn for lunch and refreshments.)

His address was not only extraordinarily long (four hours in total) but its angry rhetoric also went entirely against the grain of his presidency. Mandela's speech was, in its own fashion, unprecedented and revealing. Gone was the gentle national conciliator and the emblem of South Africa's rainbow aspirations. He gave clear notice that the heights the ANC commanded across the whole of society were insufficient for the party's appetite.

Yet, since the ANC held such a predominant position, he nonetheless had to conjure up some ghosts and phantasms to make it clear that the organisation, far from being secure, was under some kind of threat.[2] In the speech, Mandela attacked the opposition in bare-fisted fashion. Of my bête noire of that time, the NNP, Mandela menacingly suggested: 'The NP has not abandoned its strategic objective of the total destruction of our organisational movement ... and is involved in a desperate search ... to destroy its historic enemy [the ANC].' I quite enjoyed this part, but since the fast-declining NNP was then collapsing at the polls and engaged in energetic self-destruction, it was objectively an absurd remark.

But I was staggered a few lines later when he went on to attack in similar vein the rising movement I led, the Democratic Party. He accused the DP, with the NP, of being 'engaged in a desperate struggle to ... [convince] the white minority that they are the most reliable defenders of white privilege'.

Nor did 'the bulk of the mass media' – as Mandela chose to characterise what I regarded as a fawning press which generally treated Mandela as a living deity – escape his wrath. Their crime? Setting themselves up, in Mandela's words, 'as a force opposed to the ANC ... to campaign against both real change and the real agents of change as represented by our movement.'

This was the same Mandela who, just months before his speech, had offered me a seat in his own cabinet ('We must face the world with one voice, Tony,' he suggested), the Mandela who trotted me out as a sort of opposition mascot for visiting dignitaries, from Queen Elizabeth II to President Bill Clinton. Always holding my arm and affectionately advising them, 'This is the young man who gives me all my problems!'

This was the same president who, precisely one year earlier, at my 40th birthday party, had delivered a very different assessment of the DP and its leader. He lavished praise on me before the dazzled guests and my delighted parents. (One absent friend who decided to go on holiday and miss the party admonished me afterwards, saying, 'Why didn't you tell us Mandela would be there? We would have come back early if we had known!')

Now, in his Mafikeng update, I was the chief defender of 'white privilege' leading the counterrevolution! Was this cognitive dissonance on steroids? Although I forcefully and publicly pushed back against what I regarded as an essentially paranoid attack, I was mindful that Mandela's outburst needed to be weighed against so many other stellar aspects of his storied life of deep sacrifice and his inspirational presidency. And I maintain that assessment today.

So, how to synthesise the thesis of Mandela as the great guiding spirit of the country's democracy and reconciliation and the antithesis of both that was on display in this speech, which even the admiring, left-leaning UK newspaper *The Observer* labelled 'a profoundly depressing assault'?[3]

At the time, and until very recently, in puzzling over that speech's meaning and implication, I succumbed to the easier account suggested by many Mandela admirers (and some critics too). They offered an update of the biblical story of 'the voice of Jacob and the hands of Esau' as an explanation. Surely, this account went, it wasn't Mandela himself who necessarily believed the words he uttered, nor did he necessarily accept the full gamut of his party's agenda to undermine constitutional democracy via the 'national democratic revolution'.

In my book on the Mandela presidency published in 2014, months after his death, I characterised the speech as more an aberration or interruption of an otherwise remarkable presidency and person. I also found a handy figure close to Mandela to account for this. I wrote: 'Apparently Mbeki and his intellectual alter ego, Joel Netshitenzhe, wrote the speech – or were much involved in its drafting. It was clearly good politics from an internal point of view to suggest that the Mbeki age of transformation had the blessing of Mandela, and the president clearly lived up to this requirement.'[4]

Early in 2024, while writing this book, I received a jolt by way of a note that proved my assumption about the authorship of that speech to have been almost entirely incorrect. James Myburgh, arch-archival sleuth, told me that he had found, in the papers of the Nelson Mandela Foundation, the speech notes – written by Mandela in his own distinctive cursive script – the essence of which later appeared in his Mafikeng speech.

James sent me a copy of the handwritten page, on which Mandela had penned his apparent inner belief: 'The striking feature of the NP and DP towards criticism has always been a bunch of individuals who have delicate skins and frail nerves, they cannot take criticism.

'Enlightened members of both parties have deserted them and left behind an arrogant group of unscrupulous racists whose sole aim is to demonise [the ANC] movement, unashamedly to conduct a virulent campaign of disinformation ... the departure of such men as Jannie [Momberg], Dr Van Zyl Slabbert, Alec [sic] Boraine, [Jan] Van Eck ... puts the DP firmly to the right of the NP.'

He wrote of the press: 'The confused reaction of the opposition parties is also to be found in the white-controlled media.'

In those sentences lay much rage and anger and barely concealed contempt. The Mandela who had told me at numerous meetings, breakfasts and other encounters that the opposition's job was (in his precise words, at one of our first such get-togethers back in 1994) 'to hold up a mirror to the government' clearly did not like the view reflected, nor indeed the mirror-holders either.

This jeremiad clearly indicated that, contra the Jacob and Esau thesis, voice and hand in this case were one in the singular person of Mandela. Yet years later, in November 2006, the same Mandela telephoned me after I announced my retirement as party leader, purring down the phone, 'Tony, your contribution to democracy is enormous. You have far more support for all you have done than you might read about.'

Which sentiment was real? Which was fake? Or did he, in the spirit of doublethink, believe both?

Like most people, leaders of all stripes contain such paradoxes. Poet Walt Whitman, in his epic work 'Song of Myself', expressed this well: 'Do I contradict myself? / Very well then I contradict myself, / (I am large, I contain multitudes.)'

In 2010, the Nelson Mandela Foundation produced a 400-plus-page book by Nelson Mandela titled *Conversations with Myself*. It promised to 'give readers access to the Nelson Mandela behind the public figure, through his private archive'. The book omits those 1997 speech notes, although it does contain a nod to Whitman's ode when Mandela writes, 'In real life we deal, not with gods, but with ordinary human beings like ourselves; men and women who are full of contradictions, who are stable and fickle, strong and weak, famous and infamous.'[5]

At the time James Myburgh sent me the unvarnished words of Mandela, I was reading a new book by the academic and popular historian Jonny Steinberg, who suggests that there is a deeper explanation for the apparent dualism of South Africa's most important leader. Steinberg, too, mined many archives to give a rich seam of insights in his revelatory book, *Winnie & Nelson: Portrait of a Marriage*.

The book centres around the tumultuous, often tortuous, marriage of its two characters, Nelson Mandela and Winnie Madikizela-Mandela, and also chisels away at the famed images of both. Of Nelson Mandela's equally tortured relationship with FW de Klerk, for example, Steinberg writes, 'Nelson's anger at De Klerk soon curdled into loathing. A famously controlled man, he would, on occasion, set upon De Klerk savagely.'

Steinberg provides some examples of how and when Mandela's mask of general cordiality and conciliation towards his partner and rival De Klerk slipped into something far darker.

I was present at one such encounter (as was much of the country, who watched the spectacle on live television) during the commencement of the Codesa constitutional negotiations at Kempton Park in December 1991. There, as Steinberg recounts, Mandela told off the white president in unsparing terms: "'Even the head of an illegitimate, discredited minority regime, as his is", Nelson told a stunned audience ... De Klerk sitting a few feet away, "has certain moral standards to uphold." He was responding, in the heat of the moment, to an accusation De Klerk had made, but his vitriol had clearly been brewing.'[6]

After Mandela's release from prison in 1990, at the behest of De Klerk, he was one of the most famous persons on the planet, but he was also an actor playing his role on the globe and at home with a series of faces. In one instance, Steinberg observes, 'He beguiled white South Africans into the new order, throwing at them all the munificence it was in his power to perform.'[7]

That might be one explanation for the inordinate amount of face time and generous affirmation Mandela conferred on me.

And in the main, over dozens of encounters, Mafikeng notwithstanding, the masks Mandela wore were of the variety that Steinberg discerns in him just after he walked into the sunshine of freedom 35 years ago: 'Within days, that face [of Mandela] had donned an extraordinary assortment of masks: the wooden patriarch, the charming host, the delighted old man ... The more recognisable the face became, the deeper the spirit beneath it seemed to hide.

'This opacity was perhaps inevitable in a man who had ascended into myth.'[8]

There was, though, nothing opaque or hidden in one extremely hostile encounter (perhaps a unique instance) I had with Mandela, when the avuncular warmth of so many other occasions was replaced by a cold, at times hot, fury on his part. It was in its own way, I thought, very revealing.

Seated on a couch just inches away from a fuming Nelson Mandela, I shifted uncomfortably as he launched into a rare full-frontal attack and revealed an aspect of his persona I had not experienced until then.

'Well, of course, you're a young man and you want to make an impression,' the normally emollient president fumed, 'but your party is essentially a white organisation ... You head a right-wing party with a vendetta against the ANC.'

The lack of racial diversity or the ideology of the small DP of the time of course had nothing to do with Mandela's fury that morning. Rather, his anger arose from a series of questions I had asked in Parliament about the Shell House massacre of 28 March 1994, just weeks before the first democratic election. ANC guards at Shell House, then the party's Johannesburg headquarters, had shot and killed 19 Inkatha supporters, some heavily armed, who were marching on the ANC offices.

The rights and wrongs of the incident were not the subject of my parliamentary probing. Rather, it was the clear evidence, which I laid before Parliament on 29 June, that it was the ANC, instructed by Mandela himself, that had barred access to Shell House to prevent the police from conducting a forensic and ballistic investigation. The about-to-be president, in other words, had led a cover-up of a crime scene. When Mandela's newly appointed safety and security minister misled Parliament on this issue, I exposed the lie too.

Mandela did, though, tell our group in his office that he personally told the ANC guards to 'defend our headquarters as Inkatha was on its way to kill us all'. Whether this was post-event justification or a legitimate case of self-defence went unanswered, as Mandela and the party prevented a proper investigation and no ANC guard was ever held liable. (This was proven later, in 1998, at a judicial inquest and when 12 guards applied for, and received, amnesty from prosecution for their role in these events from the Truth and Reconciliation Commission.[9])

Mandela, for his part, went fully ballistic with me at that meeting (in front of my parliamentary colleagues, whom he had asked to accompany me).

A few weeks after our fractious encounter in his office, he told the Senate (today the National Council of Provinces) that he had personally given the ANC guards the order to 'shoot to kill'. Then, in the same speech, he gratuitously advised the senators that the DP had proved itself 'more right-wing than the National Party'.[10] It was the precise formulation he would provide at Mafikeng nearly three years later.

Ironically or sincerely, when Mandela inscribed my copy of his autobiography, *Long Walk to Freedom*, in the same distinctive script as he penned his Mafikeng attack notes, he wrote above his signature: 'To Tony Leon, a leader whose dynamism and capacity for analysis keep everybody on his/her toes.' The date of the inscription, 1 March 1995, was just a few weeks before our heated meeting in his office, when such 'dynamism and capacity for analysis' were very unappreciated assets in the view of the president.

In fact, it was Richard Stengel, the ghost writer of *Long Walk to Freedom*, who provided an insight into Mandela's approach to those closest to him – his family and comrades – and those objectively further from his embrace, such as me. Stengel wrote, after months of witnessing Mandela and his moods and masks and over many conversations: 'His charm is in inverse proportion to how well he knows you. He is warm with strangers and cool with intimates. That warm benign smile is bestowed on every new person who comes within his orbit. But the smile is reserved for outsiders.'[11]

The ambivalence Mandela displayed – his contradictions and various faces – did not diminish the overall effect and reach of his presidency or the height of his achievements. I could with sincerity say to him and Parliament, at the official leave-taking in 1999, as his famed presidency drew to its conclusion, 'It was a deep honour to witness from these benches the ending of apartheid and the beginning of democracy under [your] presidency. My respect and admiration for you is unconditional.'

His human essence was revealed when the mask slipped from time to time, although his inner thoughts remained elusive and opaque, often contradictory.

In his lifetime, Mandela was one of the most famous, transcendent and admired people in the world. Today, more than a decade after his death, he lives on as a spectral presence in his country and beyond it, as an almost unique example of special grace and sacrificial leadership.

In political terms, though, his legacy remains contested terrain. He is a potent example of a political Rorschach test: we can interpret his meaning in so many ways. This perhaps explains why everyone – from constitutionalists to communists, from his own partisans to his party's opponents – can claim a part of his immense whole. In fact, Mandela's paradoxes, which he mostly contained or harmonised, helped steer a deeply conflicted country to a more hopeful destination. Even if we may not conclusively determine their true meaning.

18

Mangosuthu Buthelezi's Need

Every election season, South African motorists confront the distracting hazard of election posters festooning lamp-posts and trees on the country's roads and byways. After a while, these morph into a dull backdrop, no more noticeable or ubiquitous than traffic signs.

In March 2024, driving down the M3 highway that links Cape Town's southern suburbs with the city centre, I was taken aback by one set of posters. The Inkatha Freedom Party (IFP) placards featured a photograph of the party president, which was unsurprising, since every other party's imaging had leader and party logo emblazoned in the same montage.

But the startling aspect of the IFP poster was that the leader in question, Mangosuthu Gatsha Buthelezi, had at this time been dead and buried for six months (Buthelezi died on 9 September 2023, aged 95). The slogan below his photograph hinted at his passing, together with the hashtag '#DOITFORSHENGE', although only insiders could deconstruct the meaning of it. (Shenge was his honorific clan name.)

'Ruling from the grave' is quite a well-known phenomenon across the political world, but grafting the image of a dead leader onto a party's campaign paraphernalia – suggesting he was still a living presence – was an only-in-South-Africa first.

It was also a reminder of how Buthelezi totally dominated his party – even from the afterlife, in this case.

Buthelezi founded the Inkatha movement in 1975 and remained its sole leader for 45 years until passing the baton to his hand-picked successor, Velenkosini Hlabisa, in 2019. Buthelezi chose to remain in Parliament until his death, becoming by some measure its oldest member.

Yet Buthelezi's political career stretched right back to 1954, when he assumed an office of tribal influence as traditional prime minister to the Zulu king, a post he held under three successive regents. And he comprehensively dominated the IFP (as Inkatha became) from its birth to after his own death, as its 2024 posters illustrated.

He also straddled the epochs of South African politics, from the early years of the apartheid era to full-blown democracy after 1994. Part of his straddle was successful. He used the perquisites and relative protection offered by the discredited Bantustan system (which, in line with NP ideology, set aside slivers of the country as self-ruling ethnic enclaves) to become chief minister of the KwaZulu 'homeland', in my home province of Natal. He served both to prop up the system and to mount stringent opposition within it. For example, he refused the government's offer of 'independence' for his homeland, by contrast with other Black system leaders, and campaigned for the release of Nelson Mandela from prison before this cause went global.

Yet throughout his long career Buthelezi hungered for recognition and affirmation from all sides. This would become a cardinal feature of South African politics and would at times threaten to derail the transition to democracy and the early years of the democratic era.

He was a prime local example of 'cakeism', as memorably defined by former British prime minister Boris Johnson (see Chapter 4), although this was perhaps an awkward metaphor in the case of Buthelezi, who suffered from diabetes and maintained a strict sugar-free diet. For example, he spent an inordinate amount of political and personal capital in offering a tortuous narrative, much of it lost in arcane detail, of how his decision to launch Inkatha in the 1970s enjoyed the blessing of the ANC in exile. Yet Inkatha very quickly became the most powerful internal rival to the ANC itself. A vicious fight for the allegiance of the Zulu majority in Natal and on the Witwatersrand resulted in the deaths of an estimated 20 000 people. The conflict between Inkatha and the ANC intensified after Mandela's release from prison in 1990 – ironically, a cause Buthelezi had championed.

The other aspect of his political personality was enmeshed in his personal biography: he was both a fierce Zulu nationalist and a royalist with a deep attachment to (and knowledge of) regal bloodlines and custom. On weekends at his home and headquarters in Ulundi, Zululand, he would don leopard skins and carry a rawhide shield. During the week, though – and as minister of home affairs after 1994 – he wore Jermyn Street suits and shirts with French cuffs. And he always delighted in the embrace of Western political leaders, from Margaret Thatcher to Ronald Reagan, who treated him as both an equal and a counterweight to the less ideologically congenial ANC.

Watching his funeral in mid-September 2023 in Ulundi, in the heart of rural Zululand, one marvelled that the decrepit and failing state could still muster its pomp and ceremony, and 21 guns, to lay to rest one of the more consequential figures in modern South African history.

But what legacy Buthelezi gifts to the future remains far from clear and much contested – more so, certainly, than in the cases of Mandela and De Klerk.

Once again, Cyril Ramaphosa was present to deliver the eulogy, although he was more effusive than he had been in his funereal equivocations for De Klerk. It was a reminder that the maxim of French moralist François de la Rochefoucauld still applies: 'Hypocrisy is the homage vice pays to virtue.'

To be fair, Ramaphosa's tribute to Buthelezi did not reinvent the past so much as vastly understate it. For example, he told the assembled mourners that he and Buthelezi 'at a political level ... did not always agree. We often found ourselves on opposing sides of one or another issue.'

Ramaphosa noted that their interactions were characterised by 'the spirit of camaraderie, respect, empathy and understanding', including the last-minute decision of the IFP to contest the 1994 elections. This, though, was a spectacular instance of the political condition labelled 'selective amnesia'. After all, in the fateful days preceding 27 April 1994 it was Ramaphosa, then secretary-general of the ANC, who accused Buthelezi of 'wanting to drown democracy in a sea of blood'. And another ANC leader of those times, Steve Tshwete, was far more vituperative, variously describing the IFP as 'a bandit organisation' and its leader as 'a mean-spirited gutter-mouthed politician'.

Ramaphosa also elided – except in the vaguest sense and most general terms – the vicious violence that characterised the struggle between Inkatha and the ANC/UDF (the United Democratic Front, an internal doppelganger of the ANC at the time when the latter was proscribed) in Natal and on the Witwatersrand in the 1980s and 1990s. Ramaphosa euphemistically characterised what in fact was a civil war between the two sides as merely an event which in which 'many people died'.

Two journalists I both admire and like, *City Press* editor Mondli Makhanya and international reporter John Carlin, had no truck with this soft understatement. After Buthelezi's demise, Makhanya wrote on the false hypocrisy of Ramaphosa's 'faux grief for the man who caused so much real grief'.[1] He also unearthed Ramaphosa's visit to the site of the Boipatong massacre in June 1992 (instigated by Buthelezi supporters), which upended the constitutional negotiations. He wrote: 'Ramaphosa ... visited the scene of the ... massacre in its immediate aftermath and was horrified.'

'We have never seen an incident as horrific as the one we have witnessed here', he reprised from Ramaphosa's remarks, adding that Ramaphosa was 'explicitly stating that the IFP had been used by the apartheid government'.

Carlin, for his part, was equally condemnatory. His piece about Buthelezi in *The Sunday Times* of London was headed, 'The smiling villain stained with the blood of thousands of Zulus ... a stooge of apartheid who colluded with white nationalists and whose foot soldiers carried out massacres.'[2]

Christopher Hitchens wrote of George Orwell that the great writer discredited the excuse of 'historical context' as a 'shady alibi that there was, in the circumstances, nothing else that people could have done'. But it seems to me, as an eyewitness and engaged participant from that era, that wrenching Buthelezi from the context of those times renders many of his actions both indefensible and incomprehensible.

Without engaging in the ritual of 'whataboutism', it is salutary to remember that he and Inkatha were not engaged in conflict with the Boy Scouts or Girl Guides. Harry Gwala, the Stalinist leader of the ANC in the Natal Midlands, was as bloodthirsty and as implacably immune to reason and compromise as the worst Inkatha warlord. Inkatha was inarguably armed by the apartheid security forces, but the ANC received its weapons from the Soviet Union and its satraps – not much of a choice of villains there.

One of Buthelezi's staunchest defenders is Anthea Jeffery of the Institute of Race Relations. Writing of Buthelezi's passing in Politicsweb, she noted that 'much of the violence of the people's war was directed against the IFP ... By the time [the 1994] election took place, some 400 IFP leaders and office bearers had thus been killed, often in planned attacks'.[3] While Jeffery, in her praise and defence of Buthelezi, relies on detailed research and statistics, her speculative assertion in the same appraisal that, but for this violence, the IFP 'might otherwise have won the first all-race election' is a vast overreach. No one, and I speak from first-hand electoral and campaigning experience, can for a moment doubt that the vast enthusiasm and liberating power of the ANC and its leader, Nelson Mandela, was deeply felt and widely held among South African voters.

In fact, the result achieved by the IFP after its last-minute decision to enter that 1994 election was its high-water mark electorally. It beat the ANC comprehensively in KwaZulu-Natal, although its ten per cent national total was dwarfed by the 62 per cent obtained by the

ANC. Since then, it has been a vertiginous fall. In 2024, the party recorded just 3.85 per cent of the total, although it did outpoll the fast-declining ANC in KwaZulu-Natal (18.07 per cent vs 16.99 per cent), with both parties far behind Zuma's MK Party, which won 45.35 per cent of the votes in the province.

Of course, a lot of the pre-1994 violence was fuelled by the attempts of the ANC to exclude Buthelezi from equal status with Mandela and FW de Klerk, and by Buthelezi's determined resistance to this exclusion and his fierce quest for personal acknowledgement and status and his hunger for recognition.

While the top ranks of the ANC leadership were determined to brand Buthelezi an outcast and pariah, only Jacob Zuma – surprisingly, it now seems – preferred an approach of recognition and embrace of the Inkatha leader. Little wonder that Zuma received the greatest cheer from the thronged mourners at the funeral in Ulundi.

The relationship between Mandela and Buthelezi was studded with contradictions as well. They served together in the first government of national unity, and clashed in public and in private during the former's presidency but also showered praise on each other. Normal politics, in other words.

Buthelezi's uneasy presence in the life of the Mandela presidency weighed heavily on him. When I met with Mandela in early 1994, he launched into a psychological deconstruction of the Inkatha leader. He told me that to understand Buthelezi, you had to appreciate his childhood. According to Mandela, 'Buthelezi was only the son of a chief' (so not quite royal enough). However, Buthelezi's regal mother, Princess Magogo, had a fear 'that her young son was at risk from local sorcerers and witch doctors'.

Thus, on this version, she placed young Buthelezi in the care of the royal kraal of her brother, King Solomon kaDinuzulu. In the palace, according to Mandela, Buthelezi was 'ignored and lonely'. This left him with 'a lifelong insecurity' that played out in his sharp alterations of mood and behaviour

I have little idea how much weight to accord to Mandela's psychologising. However, I do think the waspish observation of the long-suffering former wife of German chancellor Willy Brandt, that the statesman was 'a bit of saint, a bit of a sinner, a bit of a fool', is probably the best description of any politician whose long and consequential life contained, à la Whitman, large 'contradictions and multitudes'.

A few months before Buthelezi died, I was approached by kykNET, an Afrikaans-language television channel, to participate in a programme on the IFP leader. I was advised that it would be flighted after his death, as indeed it was. In my notes for this interview, I wrote of Buthelezi's achievement since 1994, referencing the role he played in politics under democracy – in both cabinet and Parliament – rather than the bloody period that birthed it:

> He was right about Aids and became the first cabinet minister to break ranks with Thabo Mbeki's denialism; he was right about floor crossing, which he denounced as 'political prostitution'; he was right about federalism but did very little to achieve it by boycotting both Codesa and the Constitutional Assembly; he was right to champion a free-enterprise economy but never explained how this tallied with the denial of tens of thousands to title to their property if they live in the lands controlled by the Zulu king via the Ingonyama Trust; he was right in resisting the ANC's monopoly of power but ambivalent on the tactics to reduce it.

Hence the contradictions embedded in his career and his achievements.

My personal relationship with Buthelezi intensified during our time together in Parliament but did not quite amount to a close friendship, since he always insisted on addressing me as 'Mr Leon'! We did, though, form a political alliance for the 2004 elections which we called the 'Coalition for Change'. It backfired with the voters and the DA lost two seats in KwaZulu-Natal, largely because of the IFP's insistence on moving the provincial capital from Pietermaritzburg, where many of our supporters lived, to Ulundi, where none of them did.

The coalition was also unpopular with some in my party in the province, and this internal opposition was led by an ambitious young Durban city councillor, one John Steenhuisen. Of course, as I ceaselessly reminded him later, after he became party leader, in the run-up to the 2024 general election, Steenhuisen himself launched his own multiparty coalition anchored by the DA and IFP.

Buthelezi was unfailingly polite in our personal interactions and extremely solicitous on matters close to my heart. Like Mandela, he attended and offered generous words on my 40th birthday (when he toasted me as 'a great son of South Africa' no less!) and later spoke at a dinner to mark my political retirement. He defended me against his bullying cabinet colleague Essop Pahad, who deliberately conflated robust opposition with unpatriotic treason. He wrote the most empathetic letter of exquisite sympathy on the death of my mother and rescued my foreign-born wife's attempts to obtain South African citizenship from the bowels of the home affairs department. It is a long list.

But Buthelezi's genuine kindness and courtesy were accompanied, in the public space, by his never-ending quest to be acknowledged and properly remembered by history. His demand for dignity weighed heavily on him and determined his actions – and, on occasion, clouded his judgement. The ANC's tactics towards him evolved over time. When contesting for support before 1994, it stigmatised him as a fomenter of violence. After that election, as his political potency waned, it flattered him with inducements, such as appointing him acting president of the country during the frequent absences of both Nelson Mandela and Thabo Mbeki.

It was during one of the joint overseas visits of Mandela and Mbeki that Buthelezi, to his pleasure, found himself again as acting president, perhaps thinking this was no less than his due, if not his birthright. Yet this time, in September 1998, it led to a serious falling-out between us, perhaps the only occasion when we sparred in public, and his ire, easily aroused, was not to be placated until many months later.

MANGOSUTHU BUTHELEZI'S NEED

It is difficult from the vantage point of today, with South Africa's military so depleted and the ruinous multibillion-rand arms deal of the 1990s so utterly unfit for purpose (we have but a single seaworthy warship, for example, and most of the ultra-expensive Gripen fighter jets have been mothballed), to recall that, in September 1998, South Africa launched a full-scale military invasion of neighbouring Lesotho.

Later in the morning of the announced invasion, all opposition leaders were summoned to the Presidency for a briefing. I found Buthelezi, who clearly had swallowed deeply the government's Kool-Aid on the topic, very unconvincing in his rationale for this incursion. (The operation was cack-handedly executed, with one armoured car driver, for example, asking a bewildered Maseru resident for directions to the government offices.) I expressed my doubts directly to Buthelezi at the meeting and suggested there were plenty of other unexplored avenues for a peaceful solution to the mountain kingdom's political turbulence, the apparent trigger for our invasion. Buthelezi fumed at my perceived impertinence and informed the meeting that South Africa's 'assistance' had been requested by the Lesotho government and mandated by the Southern African Development Community, the regional body to which both countries belonged. He chose to studiously ignore my point.

Ironically, while South Africa's government, to which Buthelezi belonged, chose never to even remonstrate with the pillaging of democracy in another neighbouring state, Zimbabwe, it also some years later joined the international condemnation of George W Bush's pre-emptive invasion of Iraq 'to restore democracy' via Operation Iraqi Freedom in 2003. The Lesotho fracas was described by a hawkish DA provincial legislator, Jack Bloom, as 'pure Bush doctrine, three years before Bush himself enunciated it'.

It perhaps suited both Mandela and Mbeki to be absent from the country when the decision to invade Lesotho was executed. Buthelezi could then be the scapegoat for any fallout from pesky opposition figures such as me. My relations with Buthelezi went into cold storage for a few months, but we soon after resumed our opposition to the

ANC, as the 2004 Coalition for Change testifies.

A number of the DA and IFP meetings we held were convened in Ulundi, the place of lost votes for the DA and today Buthelezi's final resting place. It was far removed, geographically and politically, from the urban centres where most of my political business was conducted. But I journeyed there knowing the special place it held for Buthelezi and his party at the heart of Zulu history. Often, to save time and in the interests of efficiency, I would fly there from Durban.

On one occasion, when I was due to speak with Buthelezi at a joint rally, I arrived in Ulundi at the Prince Mangosuthu Buthelezi Airport. I then was driven along the Mangosuthu Buthelezi highway and arrived, for the event, at the Prince Mangosuthu Buthelezi stadium (the venue for his state funeral).

So, in the furthest reaches of northern KwaZulu-Natal, he will not be forgotten. In his lifetime he insisted on no less. But in the wider republic, his place in history and the success of his party, which remains so wrapped in his huge presence in life, are in flux.

VII
THE *NOSTOS*

*'We all come into the world with baggage
which, in the end, we have no
hope of reclaiming.'*

– Robert Hughes, art critic and writer

19

'Nostalgia Isn't What it Used to Be'

We often use familiar words without thinking about their origins.

A decade or so ago, in the appropriately retro confines of the elderly Labia Theatre in Cape Town, I received an update on the overused word 'nostalgia'. It was a warm Saturday in March 2015, with Cape Town buffeted by gentle winds. There was a lot of interest inside from the arty crowd (plus me) when my old university friend Matthew Kentridge set about softly interrogating his famous brother, the internationally acclaimed artist William Kentridge.

The event centred on the hefty (and high-priced) book Matthew had curated on his brother's animated films.[1] One of these was a short feature titled *Tide Table*, in which the central figure, Soho Eckstein, is inspired by a photograph of the Kentridge grandfather Morris (a lawyer and parliamentarian), incongruously dressed in a pinstriped suit, seated on a deck chair on Muizenberg Beach more than 60 years earlier.

Pain of the past

William explained his cross-generational theme, etched across the movies, as deriving from the Greek word *nostos*, which means 'return home'. Yet, in the narration to the films the nostalgia image is laced by pain, since 'what is far more painful is to look back through the eyes of experience and to reflect the path down which we have come, the blunders, the wrong turnings'.

It is instructive to look back at some of the key near misses, lost opportunities and grasped moments of the past that inform the present and even the future, although I pause to remind myself and the reader how distorting the dangers of nostalgia, or a misremembered and suffocating looking back, can be. *New Yorker* editor David Remnick once flagged this as the 'common malady' of 'nostalgia without memory'.[2]

Most politicians, for example, retreat into falsehoods about the past. You can roll them up into a long line. In 2016, Brexit offered the UK a return to freedom from the shackles of Europe, 'a new golden age', according to boosterish Boris Johnson. It has since inflicted much economic harm on the island nation. Vladimir Putin's lament that the fall of the Soviet Union, which released millions of Eastern Europeans from tyranny and worse, 'was the major geo-strategic disaster of the [20th] century' led directly to his decision to attempt to recreate the old Soviet empire by invading Ukraine in 2022, to reverse this 'disaster'.

Dead communists return

During the Soviet era, millions perished on the whim of Joseph Stalin. More latterly, internal critics of Valdimir Putin have been brutally targeted. As I listened to Kentridge's thoughtful remarks, I was struck by the ahistorical gibberish offered by a local politician.

Nathi Mthethwa, a keen supporter of Jacob Zuma, achieved infamy as the police minister who presided over the massacre of striking miners at Marikana in 2012. By 2015, he had been 'demoted' to minister of arts and culture. (He was removed from this post in 2023 and rewarded with the plum post of ambassador to France. Go figure, as they say.) In March 2015, Mthethwa pontificated at a ceremony to mark the return, from Russia, of the last remains of struggle veterans and staunch communists JB Marks and Moses Kotane, who had been buried in the Soviet Union in 1971 and 1978, respectively. Unlike many others, they were fortunate to die of natural causes in Moscow, not in the frozen wastes of a Gulag prison colony, or with a bullet in the back of the neck.

The historically selective Mthethwa advised that the comrades' journey to the USSR in the 1930s placed them in 'one of the most desirable destinations for knowledge and information' where SACP luminaries were able 'to study the science of socialism'. The extraordinary time frame he referenced was precisely when Stalin was bloodily purging, torturing and murdering his intellectual and party opponents and kulak peasants and much of society that did not meet his capricious, changing definitions of socialist orthodoxy. Holidays in hell, if the political tourists had looked properly.

The ANC's predecessor, the NP, did the opposite: it was expert at pathologising communism, and the fear of its arrival here, as a club to silence and stigmatise its opponents and rile up its voters. The return of the two dead and now-lionised communists completed the circle. It was a baleful reminder of the repetition of history, first as tragedy and then as farce.

Misremembering the past

This cartoonish view of history and the elision of real facts, panel-beating them for modern purposes, has far more influential and effective advocates than a hapless ANC apparatchik like Mthethwa. But what unites the political class in offering a misremembered past is the equivalent of a Kentridge sketch: painting over the truth.

For example, Donald Trump, first in 2016–2020 and then after his triumphant return to power in late 2024, embraced nostalgia with his winning slogan (borrowed from Ronald Reagan's campaign of 1980) 'Make America Great Again', widely known by the acronym MAGA. Trump turned MAGA into a personality cult, of broad though uncertain meaning. However, he never had, and likely doesn't have, any intention of returning America to a sepia-tinged update of a mid-century Norman Rockwell painting, to some paradise of middle-class prelapsarian amity and contentment. His rocket fuel is rage and resentment, with an agenda to match.

Thomas Mallon, a US novelist and essayist, has written: 'Trump promised to make America great again, but he never said that greatness would look like it had before. His would be a new greatness, a gold-plated authoritarian spectacle; no more barbershop harmonies coming from the village band shell but, rather, a single voice blaring from the stadium speaker.'[3]

He also noted ruefully that, whatever sleight of hand Trump performed on the past – and Trump is the most successful and performative politician of this or any other era – 'Trump added to nostalgia's terrible civic reputation'.

The US and the world await the full meaning and consequence of the second coming of Trump. He has vowed to bury the 'deep state', avenge his enemies, deport millions and close the borders. And to be a 'dictator – but only on day one'. That is quite a list, and a lot of it is unprecedented.

But in one key respect his proposal to protect American workers and industries by imposing a wall of tariffs on cheap imports threatens to ignite a new version of the 'beggar-thy-neighbour' trade wars of the 1930s. Real history suggests that these do much harm. Globalisation, for all its faults and imperfections, is better at allowing goods, ideas and technologies to flow across and improve the world.

Another Trump favourite is his disdain for the international multilateral instruments of continental peace and integrated commerce (from NATO and the World Bank to the World Trade Organization) that have anchored the post-1945 era. As a minimum, the world will now be unmoored. A new version of the isolationism of 'America First' (another of his borrowed slogans, also from the 1930s), now sits at the apex of the world in Washington, DC.

Of course it is entirely possible, like prognosticating on the survival of South Africa's current government, that the immolation might not happen in the manner suggested. Perhaps, with a nod to the fervent

Bible-bashers who venerate Trump, it will be like the story of Moses on Mount Horeb: the bush (read the world) will be aflame but will not be consumed.

'Decisive moments'

One of my favourite historians, Niall Ferguson, offers real insights, not misplaced comparisons à la Nathi Mthethwa. We became friends when I audited his hugely popular lectures (it helps that he looks more like a film star than an academic) on the history of money and finance at Harvard in 2007. We have remained in touch since then, especially as South Africa is a place of interest, and occasional holidays, for the British-American intellectual polymath. (He sent me a warm note of congratulations after the GNU was formed in 2024.)

A few years back, in 2017, Niall observed that the top-of-mind book for the leadership of the all-powerful Chinese Communist Party was Stefan Zweig's almost entirely forgotten *Decisive Moments in History* (1927). The book was recommended reading for the standing committee of the Politburo, making that body, in Ferguson's wry words, 'the world's most influential book club.'[4]

Zweig notes that, very occasionally, 'a critical moment occurs in the world [that] is decisive for decades and centuries ... a single moment that determines and decides everything: a single yes, a single no, a too early or a too late makes that hour irrevocable for a hundred generations.'[5] It is easy to be swept along by Zweig's vivid phrasing, although much cold water has been poured on monocausal explanations for historical events.

Still, Ferguson drew attention to one of the more striking items on the idiosyncratic list compiled by Zweig. The fall of Constantinople to the Ottomans in 1453 marked the end of the Byzantine Empire and the arrival of Islam. One of the reasons for the city's fall was a fatal breach in the walls, the result of a humble gate left open. A forgotten gate decided world history, in the writer's view.

Until Niall wrote his account of Zweig's appeal to the Chinese leadership, I was unaware of *Decisive Moments in History*. I was witness to quite a few such moments on the home front and reflect in these pages on the hinge of history, and on some 'what ifs' and 'what if nots' that shaped (or didn't) today's South Africa.

20

A Personal Pentimento: Fresh Paint on Old Signs

Highlighting my list of moments seized and tantalising wrong turns taken, and finding some meaning from fragments of witnessing history, is like a pentimento, a form of art in which one paints over a picture but the original seeps through anyway. What I know now didn't always apply at the time events happened. But lessons from the past offer something for present and future times too, especially if you apply a new lick of paint to them. What follows are six of the many signposts, gathered over the past six decades, that have guided or misdirected my journey in life, politics and the wider world.

1. Twenty Votes

'Can't you take a pill or something to calm down?' growled Harry Schwarz, veteran MP for Yeoville. It was around 10 pm on Wednesday 26 February 1986 inside the dilapidated Masonic Hall in Hunter Street, Bellevue, in northeastern Johannesburg. It is, at this writing, nearly 40 years ago, but every frame from that evening is seared in memory.

I was the young and unknown Progressive Federal Party (PFP) candidate in a municipal by-election, my first electoral contest. Schwarz was the local MP. We were locked in a fierce vote count against the better-known, better-funded NP candidate. Every headwind had been against me and our campaign: the desertion of party leader Van Zyl Slabbert from his post as leader of the parliamentary opposition, just ten days earlier, made it gale force. A vast propaganda campaign against us was captured by a full-page anti-PFP advert in the local rag, the *North Eastern Tribune* (back in those days read by everyone), stating, 'Tony Leon is a young Turk radical leftist who will bedevil your future.' (Not a label that my ANC opponents would later apply to me.)

My deep anxiety, which so irritated Schwarz, was due to the closeness of the vote in the agonisingly slow count (just 2 000 white residents voted), where the piles for both candidates were evenly matched. I have always – across many endeavours – subscribed to novelist Ian McEwan's description of the 'irreducible urge to win, as biological as thirst'. Yet at that moment it seemed as though my long-held dream of a political career would stumble at the first hurdle.

Back then, ballots for each candidate were placed in bundles of 50 papers. I had, at the moment of Schwarz's remark, 17 bundles and my opponent 18. It appeared, despite my back-breaking efforts (I knew by name or by sight practically every voter who pitched), I was about to lose by so little.

Then, as though delivered by some gracious god, but in fact deposited more earthily by my hawk-eyed election agent, Alan Gadd, a pile of my votes was found hidden under my opponent's stack. The returning officer, duly alerted, then inspected each bundle. Like a magical croupier who stops the wheel and lets the ball bounce from the number you haven't backed to the zero you've staked the house on, he lifted 50 votes from the NP pile and placed them on mine. I was victorious by a margin of just 39 votes. I had just won my first election (of seven I would contest as candidate, locally and nationally). None later would be remotely as close, nor any future win as sweet. At the time I felt, in the heady exhilaration of victory, that I had climbed a personal political Everest. It was, in fact, no more than a foothill, but I was now on my way as a politician.

A PERSONAL PENTIMENTO

There was a lingering after-effect from that night, beyond the relief of winning, and it came in the form of a dream, which recurs even years later: instead of a 39-vote margin, just 20 Bellevue residents voted the other way, and I lost. This deep anxiety is set alongside many others that arrive sometimes in restless sleep – of sitting for an exam at Wits University without having done the revision or, worse, being unable to find the exam venue, and so on.

The 1998 movie *Sliding Doors* is about how a person's life irrevocably changes in parallel universes. Helen, played by Gwyneth Paltrow, sees her life take two diametrically opposite paths: in one, she catches her train and comes home to find her boyfriend in bed with another woman; in the other scenario, she misses the train and returns home after the woman has left. In the first version she dumps the boyfriend and finds a new partner and has a happy life; in the second, she stays with the boyfriend and lives a miserable life. It is a romantic version of Stefan Zweig's 'forgotten gate which changed history' mentioned above. My late mother used to say, 'It all can change in just a moment.' Doesn't it just?

In my own case, if just 20 voters had decided against me in February 1986, it would likely have been a career- and life-changing moment. Perhaps I would have spent the next decades practising (with more riches but little enthusiasm) as an attorney. I would likely have never gone to Parliament in 1989. And if not an MP, I wouldn't have gone on the political mission to Israel in 1991 where I first met the woman who would become my wife. I would have watched, but only on television, the dramatic events which transformed South Africa. I certainly would not have been ringside, either, for the momentous formation of the 2024 coalition government. I think and dream about those alternative scenarios often.

My 'just-made-it brand of victory', as the *Weekly Mail* headlined my 1986 Bellevue win, has also meant that any voting day since then has induced in me a deep feeling of unease.

Wednesday 29 May 2024 was general election day in South Africa. I had left Parliament and the party leadership some 15 years earlier and was no longer the front man leading the party, or a candidate who had a direct and personal stake in the poll outcome.

But I remained invested in my team and decided that, although I had no role in this election (beyond hosting a fundraiser for provincial premier Alan Winde), I couldn't just sit at home on voting day. I decided to volunteer to help the DA side at our local polling station.

Just after 7 am, when I rocked up at the Alphen Centre, Constantia, I was very impressed to see a long line of voters already queuing to cast their ballots in what was, correctly, seen as a hinge election. But like many first impressions, it was off the mark.

Three hours later, the line had barely budged. The queue had little to do with voter enthusiasm or its lack, but everything to do with the vast inefficiencies of the Independent Electoral Commission (IEC), charged with organising the election. There were about as many voters registered at this Constantia polling place in 2024 as there were in Bellevue in 1986. But there it took about three minutes to process each voter; here, decades later, it took around two hours! There were many reasons for the systems failure and many excuses offered by the hapless and essentially hopeless IEC officials.

In the previous election, in 2019, the IEC had shown similar form; five years on, the problems had multiplied, with worse results. Helen Zille's 2019 description of the IEC as combining 'ineffable smugness with incompetence' applied with a vengeance in 2024.

The historic low poll of 58 per cent in 2024, down from 89 per cent in 1999, was attributed to voter apathy. However, my eyewitness account of just one polling station, multiplied across 23 000 others – many apparently far worse – suggested that the IEC could also take a deep bow.

Yet the same self-congratulatory remarks made by the IEC and President Cyril Ramaphosa in 2019 were parroted again in 2024 – 'a world-class peaceful election despite the challenges', blah, blah. It reminded me of a wonderful sermon I heard at Harvard in December 2007. In the Memorial Church there, the preacher, Professor Peter Gomes, railed against what he called 'the mendacity of mediocrity'. It had universal application and many local calling cards.

In 2019, South Africa was still recovering from the norms of 'Zumafication'. Five years on, with Ramaphosa at the helm, Zuma was gone from office (though not away), but the pathologies continued. Often, there was scarcely a nod towards consequences for malfunction, and the hollowing-out of institutions was hard to reverse. The will to do so – beyond calling in the business sector to rescue the state – often faltered.

The IEC's excuse, to the extent that it offered one, was that it had been subject to severe budget cuts – mainly because the government had blown its budget on bribing civil servants with huge pay hikes and R500 billion had been squandered on propping up failing state-owned companies. But, then again, decent performance does not depend on money alone, or at all.

There are indeed islands of commitment and competence amid the sea of dysfunctionality in the sprawling state machine, but in the vital matter of administering a competent election in 2024, the IEC was not among their number.

2. Durban Days

Cape Town – the country's legislative capital – was my place of work for most of my life. My political career, as you have just read, began in Johannesburg, the country's commercial capital. It was, though, in South Africa's third city, Durban (capital of nothing), that my life began.

In the luminous early-morning light of 6 February 1970, residents of Lambert Road, in Durban's Morningside suburb, beheld an unusual sight. A long column of schoolboys from Clifton Preparatory School, dressed in their beige short safari suits, snaked out of the entrance gate with the large, puce-faced, white-haired headmaster, Tim Sutcliffe, striding purposefully at the front, holding a stout staff.

He was leading the whole school on a march a few kilometres down the hill to Durban's Kingsmead cricket ground, site of the first day of South Africa's epic second Test against Bill Lawry's visiting Australian team.

It wasn't just that the cricket Springboks (as today's Proteas were then called) were like all sports stars of the time – the objects of hero worship by the boys, their achievements keenly followed and deeply venerated. The long march to Kingsmead was occasioned by the presence in the team of batsman Barry Richards, playing his second Test for South Africa. He was then (perhaps still is) the most illustrious old boy of the school.

I was in the march that day, in my final year of primary school. I remember it well, though little of the match we witnessed from the grassy banks on the side of Kingsmead, except that Richards nearly scored a century before lunch and went on to bat 'for three magical hours', as radio commentator Charles Fortune described it, before being dismissed for a total of 140.

When the sun set that day on Richards and his even bigger hitting partner, Graeme Pollock, it would also herald the beginning of the end of international cricket Tests for South Africa: after routing the Aussies 4–0 in the series, neither Richards nor his teammates would ever play for South Africa again. By late 1970, the country's apartheid policy saw it ejected from international competition. (The ban was finally lifted 21 years later, in 1991.)

The livin' is easy – except ...

Durban in 1970 was a magical place for a young white boy of the middle classes. In the words of George Gershwin's 'Summertime', 'the livin' was easy' – and cheap. You could, as we did, go to the beach by bus for ten cents, buy a hamburger, Coke and chips (from the famous roadhouse cafes on North Beach, the Nest or the Cuban Hat) for about 35 cents and then, if the mood took you, go into town to catch an afternoon movie. (Cheap seats in the front two rows of the Playhouse went for 12 cents each.) After the show, you could catch the bus home to our hillside suburb of Berea, which overlooked Durban Bay, and still have change from one rand. (Even adjusted for inflation, that modest one rand would today be worth around R97, suggesting that Durban prices then were a bargain.)

A PERSONAL PENTIMENTO

In 1970, your one rand would have bought you around $1.40 (versus about five cents today). But that was just a statistic, since few people travelled overseas (though if you did so venture, the guidebook *Europe on $5 a Day* did not lie). Durban was our town and our world; an exciting visit to Johannesburg for a taste of more sophisticated city life was a big adventure.

Ranged against this halcyon idyll, there was, of course, a very dark side. It was well described by Leslie Myers, the father of a friend of mine. Leslie had emigrated to sunny South Africa from cold, war-ravaged London in the early 1950s. I once asked him about life in the Golden City in those years. 'Johannesburg was a paradise, provided you had a white skin and no conscience,' was his thoughtful response.

The city of Durban, where I grew up amid sweltering humidity and no air conditioning in the 1960s and early 1970s, was just so. There was, though, the Natal exception: the province had an English-speaking majority in its white minority group. This led to its voters rejecting the NP, which held sway in the rest of the country. Helen Suzman, the sole Progressive Party MP of that time, once waspishly observed of Natal's English that 'their fear of Blacks is only exceeded by their dislike of Afrikaners'. ('Natal stay free' was the winning slogan in provincial elections for the United Party.)

Fervent support for Rhodesia, which had declared unilateral independence from Britain in 1965 to avoid majority rule, was another item on right-wing Durban's political menu. And we had plenty of Rhodesian neighbours carrying the flag for 'good old Smithy' (Ian Smith, hardline prime minister of the renegade country).

Matters of the British Empire – even in my childhood more a relic than a reality – had fond expression in Anglophile Durban: the rugby stadium, Kings Park, was named in honour of King Edward VII; the Victoria Embankment, near the city's yacht clubs (one still enjoys the prefix 'Royal'), was named after his mother, the Queen Empress. The nearby Durban Club was a wannabe replica of a London original, complete with oil paintings of dead royals on its staircase. It was built in 1904, aptly in the Edwardian style. Its membership at the time of its founding, and for decades after, was confined to white Christian men only – women guests allowed just once a month.

Peculiar and prejudiced

My liberal mother went against the easy prejudices and peculiarities of middle-class white Durban. Her political conscientising of her young sons meant we were exposed to the ravages of racism, and we were taken to political meetings and served as election-day helpers for losing campaigns for the Progressive Party. The latter lit the fuse in me that would burn for many years, even decades. But I must not overegg this: in the arch phrase of journalist Rowan Philp, we also 'enjoyed the unasked for, but unearned, apartheid dividend'.[1]

In any event, politics was, as the route of the Clifton march suggested, far removed from the everyday realities and interests of my schoolfriends – however much it intrigued me. Far more immediate concerns and excitements were beach, cricket, rugby, socialising on Saturday afternoon at the Durban ice rink – these topped the list for young schoolboys. Queen's immortal song 'Radio Ga Ga' came many years later, but it gives a clue about our radio nights in those days. We had no audio-visual distractions bar the occasional home movie. Springbok Radio serials, from *No Place to Hide* to *Squad Cars*, filled the gap and were the staples that fed preteen imaginations. (Appropriately, our headmaster, with his dramatic baritone voice, and his wife, Yolande d'Hotman, were stars on the station.)

Long before I ever read Judith Rich Harris's book *The Nurture Assumption*,[2] which argues that children identify with their classmates rather than with their parents, I intuited its meaning at school. I sometimes went along to get along to gain entry to the elect among the boys ('the main okes') who made the social weather.

But whether you were a member of the in-group or outside this magic circle, one common fear factor at school was the unwelcome summons to the headmaster's office. This was not to sit down for a cup of tea. Mr Sutcliffe (only ever referred to as 'Sir') did not want to know about your 12-year-old angst or share your emotional pain.

Rather, he wanted to inflict punishment on your tender backside with 'six of the best', a flogging he regularly administered with ferocious intensity and much enthusiasm. And with deep and humiliating results for the recipient: you left the office clutching your trousers, desperately fighting back the tears which, if flowing, couldn't ever be shown, although the welts and bruises from this one-sided battle were shown off and often admired by your peers. Canings were only for very major offences, of course: not completing your homework, being late for class and 'being untidy' or 'giving cheek' – the latter two being my special, fairly frequent, calling cards.

Overall, though, I was happy at Clifton and loved my Durban childhood. But my dread of the cane and 'getting cuts' was going to get a whole lot worse as I exited that school and arrived at another.

3. Hit Parade Nights

Kearsney College is situated in rambling grounds atop Botha's Hill (in Natal it was always deliberately mispronounced 'Both are's Hill' to anglicise it), midway between Durban and Pietermaritzburg, with sweeping views over the dramatic Valley of a Thousand Hills. I was a boarder there from 1971 to 1974.

On any given Thursday night, at around 8.30 pm, a line of nervous young schoolboys would queue outside the entrance to the 'junior common room'. I found myself, alas, too often among their number. This was the weekly school ritual, administered at the same time every week during term, in each of the four boarding houses. It was macabrely called 'hit parade' and owed its name not to pop music but to punishment.

If you committed an infraction – and here the range exceeded the Clifton list – such as leaving your socks outside the laundry locker or, my repeat offence, talking in the dormitory after lights-out, your name was recorded by a prefect (called a 'mark'). Sometimes six days would pass between recording the offence and the punishment for it – a lifetime of nervous anticipation for a 13-year-old. On Thursday night, offenders lined up to receive a flogging (called 'flaps' in schoolboy argot).

The condemned boy went into the common room, bent down and placed his head under a desk. At the opposite end of the room, the head boy awaited you. His inclinations could range from severe to savage. He seemed – and, given the prevalence of rugby stars in the head prefect cohort, usually was – about twice your size.

At this moment, the head boy strode across the room, at quickening pace, and belted your exposed backside with what was euphemistically called a 'flogging slipper' – thick pieces of floppy leather joined to a hard handle. The more sadistic of the head boys would hold the soft leather side and administer the beating with the handle.

The pain was mind-numbing, and the humiliation extreme. The big test, keenly watched by fellow boarders waiting – like Madame Defarge – outside the common room, was whether you could emerge with your dignity intact, walking out and not running, shaken perhaps but never 'drizzing' (crying). I sometimes failed that test.

Where were the adults?

Of course, vesting such powers of pain and punishment in the hands of 16- or 17-year-old boys, as the matriculant prefects were, has an inbuilt risk of abuse, especially since the flogging ritual extended down the line to all house prefects as well.

Where, the reader of today might ask, were the adults in all this? The answer, in those times, was that they enabled it. Indeed, from 'hit parade' lists to less ritualised beatings, headmaster and housemaster gave the green light and also stood, for more serious offences, at the top of the caning chain. They made it 'kosher' – not a word much used at my staunchly Methodist school.

These events are unimaginable for today's 'snowflake' generation. The school, and indeed national law, has changed to render flogging illegal, a bygone relic from a different age.

Was there a plus side to this weekly horror show (and a great deal of institutional bullying that was also in the school toolbox), as I now view it? Many years later, when as DA leader I was dealing with a huge political crisis, it was suggested to me that there was.

One of our provincial leaders had just deserted his party post at the height of a battle (ironically, one triggered by the same leader). My close confidant and the party executive chairman, James Selfe (who from the age of six had been placed in boarding schools), turned to me and said: 'His problem is that unlike you and me he never went to boarding school, was never thrashed and never had cold showers.'

Boarding school certainly toughened you up, as James suggested and as he, with typical stoicism, had experienced. And even a Dickensian place, which Kearsney somewhat mimicked in the 1970s, had added benefits that continue 50 years after I left it: lifelong friends based on shared experiences and the occasional empathetic, even profoundly influential, teacher whom I remember with admiration to this day. And I did finally learn to put my socks away.

For me, at least, despite my flat feet making me a duffer at sports (the highest form of school recognition), there was affirmation and accolades for extracurricular achievement of all sorts. In my case, it was public speaking and debating. Kearsney had a 'school parliament' and I was elected in 1974 as its Leader of the Official Opposition. It was a useful dress rehearsal for the real thing, which happened in 1999, when I became Leader of the Official Opposition in South Africa's Parliament.

The Escape Artist

One of my most enjoyable pro bono activities these days is serving on the board of the Franschhoek Literary Festival (FLF). It fell on its face during the Covid lockdown, and Michal roped me and a group of friends and old FLF hands in to revive it.

At the 2023 festival, I interviewed Jonathan Freedland, the *Guardian* columnist, on his extraordinary book *The Escape Artist*. It is a remarkable tale, expertly told, concerning the only two Jews ever to escape from Auschwitz. Its key character, then 19-year-old Rudi Vrba, is a true, almost entirely unknown, hero of the 20th century. He emerges as ranking alongside Anne Frank and Primo Levi as 'those who define history's darkest chapter'.

My conversation with the hugely erudite Freedland – via a video link – covered many of the themes in this fine book. One of these themes particularly resonated with me. It concerned the question that Vrba kept asking and that Freedland partly answers: why was there not more of a fightback by the victims in the concentration camps or even before arriving there? Objectively, this was nigh impossible to answer, but Vrba had a very specific view on it: 'Rudi had an answer ... Jews did not need to organise a formal resistance to thwart or slow the Nazi operation: even a ... panicked refusal to go [on the transport trains] would have been enough. It would have forced the Nazis to hunt deer rather than sheep.'[3]

Throwing sand in the machine of death at Auschwitz was nearly impossible, although Vrba later reconsidered that view. But the question of deference to authority and grimly acquiescing to it has reference far beyond that story, in much lesser places than the fearful setting described in the book.

For instance, on the trivial matter of boarding school and its institutionalised violence, I now ask myself: why didn't we rebel against some of the petty rules and minor tyrannies inflicted on us? Why did we go along to get along? Of course, that question suggests its own answer: the herd leads, not the renegade. My school, which was no worse and in many instances much better than others, reflected the spirit of its age: the culture of obedience and deference to authority hard-wired into the South African psyche and across its institutions.

Recently, I received a jarring reminder of another inducement to conform to the rules, however arcane or indeed arbitrary these are. Or worse than that, as a documentary series revealed.

In 2024, the four-part series *School Ties* was screened on local television. It captured, in harrowing detail, the grooming and sexual abuse of schoolboy water polo players at four of South Africa's leading schools. Happily, Kearsney was not among them. (I was unaware of any acts of paedophilia at the school and doubt there were any.)

However, there was one line in *School Ties* that chimed with our acquiescence, decades back, to the ritualised physical violence meted out to us. A schoolboy whistleblower who had drawn attention to the abuse of water polo players by the teacher in charge was shunned and mocked by his seniors, and even by the old boys' network. He was also warned, 'Snitches are bitches who get stitches.'

Back to school

I made a brief return to Botha's Hill in 2024 for the founders' dinner and my matric class's 50th reunion. A far more liberal ethos and a multiracial school and teacher body now held the ring. This would have been unimaginable from the perspective of the entrenched conservatism, ingrained racism and support for the political status quo of my era (when even, for example, support for the moderate Progressive Party was regarded as bizarrely eccentric, almost an apostasy).

That night, the new headmaster, Patrick Lees, gave an address of enlightened empathy, a clarion call for a new way of doing things and for advantaging the most disadvantaged. This was a reminder that in some cases – and contra the cynical adage – things can change and for the better.

The evening evoked some ghosts from my past life. Some years before, I had observed how distorting and damaging it can be to see life through the rear-view mirror. Especially when *nostos* afflicts an entire country. Moisés Naím, an exiled Venezuelan intellectual, has popularised the term 'ideological necrophilia', or the blind fixation with dead ideas. I was to get first-hand experience of this, aptly, in South America.

4. Pampas Years

In late 2012, I returned home after three years abroad in Buenos Aires as South African ambassador to Argentina (and Uruguay and Paraguay). I learnt many lessons from a place where 'vote for a better yesterday' was a winning political formula.

In a recent podcast, Donald Trump, according to songwriter Tim Rice, described the musical *Evita* (which Rice wrote with Andrew

Lloyd Webber) as his all-time favourite. 'Trump watched it six times,' Rice said.[4]

This was not surprising: Trump has successfully torqued the image of the strongman, or *caudillo* in Spanish, and coupled it with political nostalgia ('Make America Great Again'). The power couple at the heart of *Evita* – Juan Domingo Perón, thrice elected president of Argentina, and his glamorous second wife, Maria Eva Duarte 'Evita' Perón – in turn wrote the script for modern populism. Like Trump would do later, the Peróns converted fame before entering politics (he as a military officer, she as a radio star) into potent political currency.

As for ideology, strictly speaking, there wasn't one. But the Peróns gave their name to an entire movement, Peronism, which was the dominant force in Argentine politics long after their deaths and during my three-year residence there.

The *caudillo* returns with a corpse

Peronism is an elastic concept, the political equivalent of the biblical injunction that 'in my father's house there are many mansions'. It is more about power than ideas, and its platform, in many iterations and under different leaders, amounts to a gaseous mishmash: 'Nationalism, European fascism, socialism and [Spanish] falangism with Argentine paternalism, authoritarianism and sentiment', in the acute description of a modern historian.[5]

Evita died of cancer in 1952, aged just 33, while first lady of Argentina. Her husband, the archetypal military officer-turned-authoritarian-*caudillo*, first served as president from 1946 to 1955, then was ousted in a coup and fled into exile. With its hankering for past perceived glories, a restive nation called him home after 18 years' enforced absence, in 1973. Ailing and enfeebled, he again assumed the reins of the presidency. He died after just one year in office, and was succeeded by his third wife, Isabel, a former nightclub dancer, whose formal education ended in the fifth grade. Her disastrous 20 months in office paved the way for full-blown military rule (the fifth coup in the country's history), one of the worst chapters of human rights violations in modern history.

In an only-in-Argentina true story, the plane that brought Juan and Isabel Perón home in triumph from Spanish exile in 1973 (interrupted by a massacre at the airport when warring Peronist factions turned their guns on each other) also had on board the embalmed corpse of Evita.

During our tenancy of the high-rise triplex penthouse in upmarket Palermo, Buenos Aires, the official residence of 'HE Ambassador Extraordinary and Plenipotentiary of the Republic of South Africa' (to give my full and pompous title), we entertained dozens of visitors. There was no shortage of guests seeking good lodgings in this captivating city. Michal and I would urge each to visit the long list of essential sights, from antique markets to football matches and, of course, the obligatory tango show.

High on the list was the most visited spot in the bustling capital city. Eerily, though, this was a cemetery, Recoleta, situated in the middle of the plush suburb of the same name. On any day, amid the tombs and headstones, you could easily spot the mausoleum of Evita. There was always a crowd of mourners, bouquets of flowers placed around it – a veritable shrine to 'Santa Evita', as she was known. (An entire book was written about the bizarre journey, complete with suggestions of necrophilia, of her embalmed corpse over the decades until it reached its final resting place here.[6])

While Evita had been dead for nearly 60 years when I arrived in Argentina, she remained a living presence in the life and politics of her people. Why this was so has several explanations.

Cristina channels Evita

I presented my ambassadorial credentials to Cristina Fernández de Kirchner, then president of Argentina, at the Casa Rosada (Pink House), the presidential palace. (It is from the balcony of the Casa Rosada that Madonna belts out her songs in the 1996 movie version of *Evita*.) Kirchner too was a hard-charging leader of the Peronist movement, and had succeeded her late husband, Nestór, as president.

Kirchner's fiery public persona was not in evidence that evening. Rather, I noted that she cut an alluring and demure figure. She had Titianesque hair, her lilac shirt offset by a string of pearls, which showed off her perfectly unlined face to full advantage. Given her age – on the day of the ceremony she was 56 – she, like many of her compatriots, doubtless enjoyed the benefits of cosmetic enhancement, not least her 'Angelina Jolie' lips, which I noticed on handing over my 'letters' to her outstretched hand. (Argentina boasts, along with psychotherapists, one of the highest concentrations of cosmetic surgeons in the world.) Her exquisitely opulent appearance was a study in contrast with her working-class supporters in whose names and with whose votes she governed.

Yet Kirchner was also attempting to Botox her failing political image at the time, in a country beset by rampant inflation, extreme protectionism, deep corruption, ransacked institutions and a medley of financial crises caused by her government. To do this, she conjured up the imagery and tactics of the long-dead Evita. 'Santa Evita' was often mentioned by Kirchner, and a vast profile of Evita was silhouetted on a government building in South America's widest and longest street, Avenida 9 de Julio.

Hate as hope

Novelist VS Naipaul visited Buenos Aires in 1974, when the country had returned briefly again to the rule of Juan Perón. He noted that the politics of destructive but redemptive victimhood championed by Evita (and her movement) chimed with the national sentiment. He called it the 'hate as hope' brand of Peronist populism. Although Eva Perón was only the wife of the president, the real power and drive came from her support for the downtrodden (the *descamisados*, or 'shirtless ones', as she called them). Her bond with them was real enough, even if she enjoyed 'High flying, adored', and the spoils of presidential plunder.

When I read Naipaul's essay 'The Return of Eva Perón', I had the uncomfortable thought that it could easily have been penned about elements of the political discourse in South Africa, then and even today. Naipaul observed:

Eva Perón devoted her short political life to mocking the rich, the four hundred families who among them owned most of what was valuable in the million square miles of Argentina. She mocked and wounded them as they had wounded her [she was the illegitimate daughter of a rich landowner and was shunned by his family]; and her later unofficial sainthood gave a touch of religion to her destructive cause.[7]

Of course, the Peróns and their political successors had a basic ingredient for their winning recipe: the deep inequalities, class- rather than race-based, that disfigured Argentina. These they were determined to change, which they did, even if it meant bankrupting the country in the process, as they also did.

There was a personal edge for Evita. As she wrote in her autobiography, *La razón de mi vida*, of her impoverished childhood, 'and the strange thing is that the existence of the poor did not cause me as much pain as the knowledge that at the same time there were people who were rich.'[8] Class envy, Argentina-style. The ANC/EFF/MK attacks on white monopoly capital and the Stellenbosch Mafia were almost exact local versions of this – minus any conferred sainthood.

My guests in Buenos Aires included veteran newspaper editors Tim du Plessis, Peter Bruce and Mondli Makhanya. We fed them the obligatory football-size steaks, washed down with copious glasses of Argentina's famed Malbec nectar. Reflecting on that visit, Tim drew a direct line between the Peronists and the ANC. He wrote: 'Argentina's current political leaders are just like the ANC: inherently corrupt, instinctive power abusers, with hardly any respect for democratic institutions ... And nothing is ever their fault. They are the masters of the art of handing out blame and finding excuses. Just like the ANC.'[9]

Ouch. And he was on the money, except for the fact that, in the 19th century, Argentina essentially imported its majority white population from Europe and decimated its indigenous people.

Cristina Kirchner revved up the engines of hatred against her opponents and widened her enemies list to include the press, the International Monetary Fund, the opposition and one Jorge Bergoglio, the Cardinal Archbishop of Buenos Aires. On occasion he attended our embassy functions, an admired local figure of impressive humility. When he criticised her conflictual politics, though, she vowed never to set foot in his cathedral again. She was as good as her word until 2013, when he was elected by the papal conclave in the Vatican as Pope Francis. Cristina immediately flew to Rome to kiss his ring.

'As rich as an Argentine'

There are vast riches in Argentina, from the most fertile farmlands in the world (the Pampas) to untapped critical mineral deposits down south and the famous Mendoza vineyards. From footballer Lionel Messi to writer Jorge Luis Borges, Argentina has produced many global talents. Little wonder that, a century ago, it was one of the ten richest countries in the world, and 'as rich as an Argentine' was a refrain heard from London to New York. Yet Argentina's very bad politics and eccentric – or worse – governance, largely at the hands of successive Peronist administrations, led to its vertiginous descent downwards to an economy smaller than South Africa's. It also holds the unenviable record for the highest number of sovereign debt defaults in world economic history.

On my last day in Buenos Aires, I took a farewell stroll down the tree-lined Avenida Alvear, a high-end shopping street. I noticed the empty display windows in one of its upmarket emporiums. The fashion retailer Louis Vuitton, a favourite of Cristina Kirchner – who, like Margaret Thatcher, enjoyed wielding a handbag – had just announced it was closing its doors. Its exit from the country followed that of other international luxury brands fleeing what was termed the 'crisis of Cristinanomics': draconian currency controls, import-suppression measures, forced nationalisations and the manipulation of economic data.

Cristina (both as president and later as vice president) and her brand of crisis economics continued to hold the fort in Argentina – with one brief interruption – until November 2023.

Furious and fed up with their impoverishment caused by rampant inflation and state corruption, Argentina elected by a landslide a libertarian economist, Javier Milei. He sported Elvis-style sideburns, cloned his dogs, campaigned with a chainsaw and, in the most Catholic of countries, studied the Hebrew Torah. He described himself as an 'anarcho-capitalist'. He too had his enemies list, topped by leftists and wokeists in the world and Peronists at home. Milei detested Kirchner and her party and promised to dismantle their economic and political agenda. Unlike the Peronists, he loved America and loathed Cuba.

Spinning in her tomb

Milei had some early successes, most notably in slashing the state bureaucracy, trimming the budget, taming inflation and ramping up the economic growth rate. He faced stiff headwinds, though, since Peronists still controlled many provinces and much of Congress. And dismantling the vast number of subsidies gifted by his predecessors, on everything from bus fares to gas prices, enraged many poorer Argentinians.

To close the circle with Donald Trump, who so loved the musical *Evita*, Milei was the first foreign leader to visit the recently re-elected US president in November 2024 at his Mar-a-Lago compound. 'Make Argentina Great Again,' Trump joked with Milei. 'You know, MAGA, he's a MAGA person.'[10] Doubtless, the real Evita was spinning in her mausoleum in Recoleta cemetery.

5. On Da Nang Beach

Da Nang in Vietnam is on the other side of the world from South Africa and even further away from Argentina. It offers, beyond its warm sparkling waters, a spot to contemplate how one place and country was not imprisoned by its past, à la Argentina and South Africa, but has totally transcended it.

Sitting on its sandy beach a few years back, my view of the lapping South China Sea was obscured by a photo session featuring a grinning

Korean family (father, mother and son, each clad in identical tailored pyjama outfits). I was thinking more about what happened there decades before. In 1965, the first batch of US troops landed on the same beach.

My musings were aided by a fat book I was reading. Max Hastings's *Vietnam: An Epic Tragedy* retold how the nearby Da Nang airport had served as the major base for the US Air Force during that enervating conflict. At the height of the war, it recorded more aviation traffic than any other place in the world.[11]

The US dropped more than 7.5 million tons of bombs on North Vietnam (more than three times the total ordnance dropped in World War II). In 1965, as the war escalated dramatically, US Air Force Chief of Staff General Curtis LeMay commented of the North Vietnamese: '[T]hey've got to draw in their horns and stop their aggression, or we're going to bomb them back into the Stone Age.' It didn't happen, although an unimaginable two million Vietnamese perished (alongside 58 126 US troops) during the years of the Vietnam War.

My sightings in and beyond Da Nang that day revealed the opposite of the Stone Age: Vietnam has emerged from the embers of more than 50 years of conflict to fire up a powerhouse economy whose seven per cent growth rate in 2018, the year before my visit, drew a gushing review from the World Economic Forum. Its pre-Davos paper on Vietnam was headlined 'The Story of Viet Nam's Economic Miracle'.

I had another revelation that day: how do certain countries overcome the burden of their history while others do not?

And, even more incautiously, given the heresy of commenting on colonialism in South East Asia, in contrast to colonialism in South Africa, I wondered: how did Vietnam overcome not one or two doses of the colonial yoke, but four different and fairly brutal occupations? China for nearly a millennium, French rule for 75 years, Japanese occupation in World War II and the reduction of the southern half of Vietnam to a US vassal state after 1965?

Certainly, the wounds of this legacy appeared in the war museums dotting the major cities, especially in Hanoi and Ho Chi Minh City (the former Saigon) – cathedrals to anti-American propaganda and heroic in their depiction of the virtuous struggle waged by the Viet Minh and Viet Cong.

But, to signal how today's Vietnam has shed the weight of its past, a guide we engaged in Da Nang proudly showed us a Samsung factory that employs a staggering 65 000 people and produces more mobile phones than any other such facility on Earth.

After sharing these impressive metrics of what is dubbed 'South East Asia's Silicon City', he then waved in the direction of the newish five-star Sheraton Grand Resort, replete with private beach – in a communist country! 'It was opened in November 2017,' he boasted, 'just in time for President Trump to stay there for the Asian Pacific Economic Summit'. Now my interest was pricked. Having seen *Trump: The Art of the Deal* on display, in both Vietnamese and English editions, in a Hanoi bookshop, I cautiously enquired about the controversial 45th President's standing in still-socialist Vietnam. 'We love Trump,' he answered, and before I could ask further, he offered, 'he stands up to China.'

Of course, for an outward-looking, export-led country like Vietnam, having China, the second-largest economy in the world, on your doorstep is a huge advantage. This is one reason why Vietnam, its leaders dubbed 'ardently capitalist communists' by *The Economist*, exports more than 100 per cent of its GDP in goods and services. By comparison, South Africa struggles to reach 30 per cent.

But with China aggressively pushing its claims in the South China Sea, our guide's approval of the United States was understandable.

Still, on my return to our hotel, I sought to verify this anecdote. But here is where the command and control of the Communist Party kicks in. While Vietnam might practise a form of 'market Leninism', it certainly is unrelenting in limiting access to the political internet. However, on my return home the journal *Politico* offered confirmation: according to the nonpartisan Pew Research Center, Vietnam was then, and likely still is, among seven out of 37 countries surveyed where most of the population says they like Trump.[12] The same survey recorded that 84 per cent of Vietnamese view America favourably, the highest figure for any country surveyed. Talk about shrugging off your history.

Return to Saigon

The most revelatory aspect of this visit was my return, after 24 years, to Saigon (as Ho Chi Minh City is still commonly known). When I was last there, in 1994, on a political visit to South East Asia with colleague Mike Ellis, the city was in the tight grip of an unsmiling and heavy military presence. There was one modern tourist hotel, the Saigon Century, and all the brandings associated with international tourism were totally absent. Little surprise, for Vietnam had been freed from a total US trade embargo only a few months earlier. The best mode of transport was the ubiquitous bicycle, and the one international restaurant (La Bibliothèque) was famous for having hosted one of the very few Western leaders to visit, French President François Mitterrand. Dinner for the two of us there in 1994 cost just $10.

By the time of my second visit, 25 years later, Saigon was a different universe: choking car and moped traffic, the gleaming spires of modern finance capitalism, top-dollar restaurants and the endless energy of an entrepreneurial people, where nearly a third of its residents own their own business.

The depressing aspect of that return visit to this modern Asian megacity was to be reminded where both our countries stood in the first year of South African democracy, and before the so-called Doi Moi pro-market economic reforms were implemented in Vietnam.

Back in 1994, Vietnam's exports, as a measure of GDP, were the same as South Africa's, at around 30 per cent. By time of my next visit, they outpaced us threefold. And while official statistics from this repressive state need to be treated with caution, Vietnam's unemployment rate was below five per cent, while ours was six times higher, at least. Foreign direct investment, or FDI, which is objectively measurable, barely existed when I was first in Vietnam. But in 2016, the country recorded a $16 billion spurt in FDI, while South Africa had to make do with a paltry $2.23 billion, one-eighth the amount.

Vietnam has embraced the world. It has welcomed investors and unleashed its entrepreneurs, while we have gone in the opposite direction.

It took around 30 years, following the collapse of South Vietnam and the departure of the last American troops in 1975, for the victorious communists to embrace capitalism with decidedly authoritarian characteristics. Imposing an unworkable communism on an entrepreneurial people such as the hugely industrious Vietnamese proved an impoverishing example of ideological overreach. Yet Vietnam's overlords had the pragmatism to abandon it.

The ANC was allied to the North Vietnamese during the communist struggle for ascendancy in Vietnam and learnt from their ally the uses of violence to promote a 'people's war' during the end days of apartheid.

Afterwards, though, the ANC embraced democracy – by contrast to Vietnam's rulers. But never, in the higher reaches of the new South Africa, did the party shrug off the communist ideology of state control and disdain for business (unless it came to the rescue of the ailing state or lined the pockets of its senior cadres). The ANC retained deep faith in dogma, and sometimes their technocrats offered a blur of statistics to defend policies and ideas (for example, NHI or industry 'master plans') that flew in the face of basic common sense. This too had an echo from the Vietnam War.

Before my second visit to Vietnam, I spent many hours watching the brilliant ten-part Netflix series *The Vietnam War* by Ken Burns and Lynn Novick. One episode focused on former US Defense Secretary Robert McNamara, one of the 'best and the brightest' (as the stars of the Kennedy and Johnson administrations were dubbed, not without irony). McNamara was a technocrat and former business executive who placed inordinate faith in hard data analysis. The episode concentrated on 1967, when the Vietnam War, far from being won, had reached a bloody stalemate. McNamara then ordered the Pentagon to perform an extraordinary task. Its mainframe computer (one of the very few anywhere in the world at the time) occupied the entire basement of the building. An army advisor recalls how over one weekend they put in 'everything you could quantify' – statistics on ships, ammunition, planes, the entire US military toolkit.

'Then they put it in the hopper and said, "When will we win the war in Vietnam?" They went away on Friday and the thing ground away all weekend. They came back on Monday and there was one card in the output tray. And it read, "You won in 1965."'

6. A Bar in Berlin, A Garden in Kanazawa

Germany

My mother's third and last husband was Paul Ferdinand Wilhelm Schulz, of whom she said, 'A German joke is no laughing matter.'

One night in June 2005, her view was confirmed when I spoke to a crowd of young Germans at a bar in a suburb of Berlin. I had been invited to offer words of encouragement to campaign workers gathered in support of the federal election efforts of the Free Democratic Party (FDP), the liberal movement and a sister party of the DA. The Free Democrats had been the junior partner in many of the Federal Republic's governments since 1949, the year of Germany's democratic restoration.

Yet most of the young audience gathered that evening seemed rather sombre, even glum. This did not extend to my host, party leader Guido Westerwelle, who was, at the age of just 44, on the cusp of achieving an electoral breakthrough. By contrast to most of his earnest volunteers, he was upbeat and cheery. (In time, he would become foreign minister, although his life and career were tragically cut short by leukaemia just ten years later.)

In my brief remarks that night, I reflected on the economic powerhouse that Germany had become over the decades and its deeply entrenched democracy. I offered – as a foreigner – my sense of awe at what the country, the aggressor nation by far in the two devastating world wars that engulfed 20th-century Europe, had achieved since 1945.

A PERSONAL PENTIMENTO

My view of Germany's achievement was deeply influenced by a play I had just seen in London, appropriately titled *Democracy*. British playwright Michael Frayn's award-winning drama achieved both critical and commercial success despite its seemingly dull premise: German politics in the 1970s.

I watched the performance utterly mesmerised as the play toggled between two themes. First was the highly charged political drama – the fall of left-wing West German Chancellor Willy Brandt and the complexity of coalition politics and high treason in the chancellor's office. The second theme examined the interplay between the political and the personal, specifically the contradictions of Brandt's character and personality and his role as a key resurrector of German democracy after 1945, and the role of his chief aide, Günter Guillaume, who was revealed to be an East German spy.

In his programme notes, Frayn revealed what attracted him to write the drama. I read an extract to the young FDP activists:

> The only part of German history that seemed to arouse much interest in the British is the Nazi period. Yet [what's striking] is the amazing recovery of Germany after the Second World War ... Almost every city was in ruins, and the country was morally shattered. The Nazis had invaded every aspect of German social life, every political and religious institution. The judicial system was totally corrupted. Yet somehow Germany managed to reconstruct a very, moderate, stable society.

This achievement, against such a fraught backdrop, is the political heart of Frayn's play. *Democracy* proved to be every bit as dramatic as the resignation of Brandt – the first left-wing chancellor of West Germany – in May 1974.

Maybe such successful stability and achievement were taken for granted in modern Germany 60 years after the fall of the Third Reich. I thought it worth reminding the FDP crowd how impressive an outsider like me found this to be. I did not mention to them (utterly unremarkable in the Germany of 2005) that I was Jewish – and that the genocidal mass murder of six million Jews was central to the Nazi programme. Nor that their leader, my host Guido, was the first openly gay political leader in German history – a status which in the 1940s could have condemned him to death or to imprisonment in a concentration camp.

My observations were received with dutiful applause, although I doubted whether complimenting a country on its moderation and balance was particularly stirring, not that modern German politics offered any rewards, or applause, for messianic speechifying. That had disappeared under the rubble of Hitler's bunker.

Kaput?

This of course would change two decades later with the rise of the far-right AfD party, which used incendiary rhetoric against immigrants to vote-winning effect and was nonchalant, at best, about the country's Nazi past. But by 2024 Germany's economic ascendancy had stalled, even reversed. Its once-heralded model of social and political progress was kaput, as the title of a new book proclaimed. Wolfgang Munchau, the author of *Kaput*, subtitled his bestseller 'The End of the German Miracle'.[13] Still, I would not bet against German strength (economic, rather than military) and resilience, as its democratic and economic resurrection on the stoniest soil has proven.

After my attempt to rouse some enthusiasm among the FDP campaigners, I returned to my modern hotel in the heart of Berlin, now a united city at the very crossroads of Europe. In 2005, Berlin's unity and modernity were taken as utterly normal. Yet, reflecting on my first visit there, in late October 1989, as a freshly elected South African MP, this too was a contemplation of deep contrast, in fact of two halves.

Back then, Berlin offered so many grim examples, post Hitler and the birth of the Cold War pitting East against West, of blockades and division. Most infamous was the wall erected to seal East Berlin, part of the Soviet-backed German Democratic Republic (GDR), from the free Western enclave, controlled by the Federal Republic of Germany. Some Berliners called it the 'wall of shame'; in the East it was officially the 'antifascist barrier', although, as my German-born political boss Harry Schwarz caustically noted, 'No one in its history was shot trying to escape from West to East.'

My visit to divided Berlin in 1989 allowed me a chance to spend a day in East Berlin. One crossed via the Friedrichstrasse U-Bahn station where, in exchange for some Deutschmarks, a day visa for the cash-starved GDR was obtainable for foreigners. My host, a West Berlin MP, told me to look closely at the (threadbare) shops, the (depressed) shoppers, the (grim) restaurant fare and the (many) uniformed soldiers. 'This,' he informed me, 'is the showpiece city, of the showpiece republic of the entire Soviet bloc. It won't last.' I doubted this prediction.

He was right. Within weeks of my departure from the city, its infamous wall would be breached and the map of Europe changed irreversibly, as it seemed at the time.

I wrote after that visit, succumbing to the smug 'end of history' thesis, that the Cold War was won 'decisively and irrevocably by the West'. As predictions go, this too has not aged that well. In 1989, Vladimir Putin was just a KGB officer in the GDR. On 24 February 2022, as Russian president, he invaded Ukraine, unleashing the greatest land war in Europe since 1945. The passage of time had not dimmed the Soviet sense of euphemism, though. Putin insisted, on pain of imprisonment for any Russian who termed it otherwise, that the invasion was just a 'special military operation'.

Japan: Fall, rise, and fall

No shortage of clichés attach to the other great loser of World War II, Japan. On a recent visit there I found many of these to be entirely true. And embedded within them were some winning lessons – and a warning to boot.

We had just arrived in the city of Kanazawa, a coastal enclave on the Sea of Japan, nestled under the Japanese Alps. Robert Louis

Stevenson's old saw 'to travel hopefully is a better thing than to arrive' proved half true as we sped there from Tokyo by Shinkansen (bullet train), which raced through the 470 km distance in just two and a half hours. Our departure was precisely as advertised on the Japan Railways ticket – 8.33 am, to the millisecond. As the train pulled in, a British tourist sitting next to me said, 'And doubtless if it were late the Chairman of Japan Railways would resign.' 'Or commit hari-kari,' I offered in response.

The faultlessly polite staff and the ultra-cleanliness of the carriage impressed us. But when Michal left her phone on the train, the exceptional honesty of the public came to the fore. After frantic phone calls, we learnt that it had been handed in at the station.

That journey told us a lot about today's Chrysanthemum Kingdom. Kanazawa added to the mystique of how this island nation melds antiquity with modernity and seems, at first blush, at ease with both.

Kenroku-en garden, in the heart of the city, was constructed during the Edo period, in the 1620s. It has been maintained by generations of gardeners who preserve and enhance the 'Garden of the Six Attributes' – 'landscape, seclusion, artifice, spaciousness, waterways and panoramas'. Even a horticultural philistine like me was awed by its hectares of manicured perfection.

One of the reasons for the perfect preservation of the garden and other relics of Japanese antiquity spread across the city was that Kanazawa, like the larger city of Kyoto, was spared the raids by US bombers that incinerated so many of Japan's urban centres in the final stages of World War II.

While I watched the hands of the gardeners tend and cultivate the exquisite floral splendour of Kenroku-en, I couldn't help thinking of their forebears, who in the 1940s enslaved thousands of Allied prisoners of war – Australians, English and Americans most prominently – whom they, like the Nazis, viewed as subhuman. I also thought directly back to a trip some years earlier to the River Kwai in Thailand. There, thousands of graves in the Kanchanaburi military cemetery, as immaculately tended as this majestic garden, bore silent witness to the horrors of Japanese cruelty, its inhabitants killed through starvation, disease and torture while building such pharaonic infrastructure for Imperial Japan as the Burma 'death railway'.

Before such morbid thoughts overwhelmed, we crossed the road to discover the other Japan. We strolled into Kanazawa's 21st Century Museum of Contemporary Art and literally advanced 500 years from the antique garden nearby. And of World War II there was no sign either. One of the museum exhibitions involved a humanoid robot, or Asimo (advanced step in innovative mobility). This version of the future, dressed appropriately in a space suit, but built by Honda in the 2000s, can walk, skip, jump, sing and talk. It was a sci-fi comic book of my childhood come to life.

That night back in antiquity, or rather in our *ryokan* (traditional inn), lying on our futon on the tatami floor – there was no other furniture in the room, which was enclosed by sliding doors – we watched an episode of the TV series *Tokyo Vice* on Michal's computer. This was a portal into another Japan, one not on public display to tourists. The series explores the world ruled by the Yakuza criminal bosses, portrayed as ruthless gangsters whose reach extends into the very heart of Japan's government. *Tokyo Vice* is based on the memoir of an American journalist, Jake Adelstein, a *gaijin* (foreigner) who became the very first foreigner to work as a staff writer on a major Tokyo newspaper, writing copy entirely in Japanese, in which he was proficient.

The occupation

Here was another irony on constant display in Japan: the deep linkages between this conquered nation, on which the US dropped the only two atomic bombs ever used in war, and the conqueror. It was the American occupation of Japan after 1945 that birthed Japan's modern democracy and economy, a broad replica of the evolution of post-war Germany. There are more active-duty US troops stationed in Japan and Germany than in any other country in the world. Signs of American influence, from 7-Eleven convenience stores to KFC, are ubiquitous.

It is also salutary, or perhaps a matter of history and culture, that the imposition of democracy in both places by the same occupying power sustains itself generations after US military government ended. By contrast, a similar attempt dismally failed when America tried to impose democracy on Iraq during Operation Iraqi Freedom in 2003.

But, as in Germany today, much ails the Japanese economy. Thirty years ago, Japan was reckoned to be on the cusp of overtaking the US economy, before its economy flatlined. One distinctive feature of Japan's decline is its devastating demographics.

If Africa faces the challenge of feeding its teeming millions of teenagers and finding work for an ever-bulging youthful population, Japan's problem is the reverse. Its population is in the deepest decline. One recent report noted that Japan's 'native population' is falling at a rate of nearly 100 people an hour, and it lost 857 000 people through death in just 12 months in 2023, the year of our visit.[14] Births are now at their lowest level in centuries.

The adjective 'native' in the report is significant. *Gaijin*s are welcome to visit Japan, but not to immigrate there. Long before the US, and increasingly Europe and even South Africa, embraced xenophobia as policy, Japan led the way. This contains another lesson from the Land of the Rising Sun as it contemplates a future where the old die at a far greater rate than new babies are born. In Japan, sales of adult nappies, unsurprisingly, outpace, by some margin, infant diapers.[15]

VIII
THE RETURN

'What convinces is conviction. You simply have to believe in the argument you are advancing: if you don't, you're as good as dead. The other person will sense that something isn't there.'

– Robert Caro, biographer of Lyndon Johnson

21

Return to Parliament

This book was not written for politicians, but many of the stories in it are, given the course of my life, from the political world. I was once reminded by my stepson Etai that if you confine your gaze just to politics and its borders, the state of government can induce despair and depression. 'But if you look beyond that into wider society, you'll see a lot of good, sometimes great things happening,' he said. Wise words.

I would hazard a guess, though, that some of my readers are involved in politics, and some who are not might consider a political career at some stage.

In many ways, we inhabit – in the true sense – a leaderless world. Mostly, our leaders are either pedestrian placeholders or titanic ego-driven populists who use high office as an engine for self-enrichment or as an instrument of revenge against enemies, real or perceived. The Peronists in Argentina, the Zumas in South Africa, the Trumps in America and the Netanyahus in Israel – all are political grifters who set one section of society against the other. They weaponise differences and grievances, ride roughshod over rules and respect for others, and hijack public institutions for personal ends.

The other, mediocre sorts of leaders simply seek public office and (in Helen Zille's apt phrase) 'fall into the comforting pillows of the state'. Their agenda is to enjoy the perquisites and privileges of power and bide their time there to prop up the system, which delivers riches that their own modest talents could not bestow on them elsewhere.

Let me add a big 'BUT' here. Not every political life and career need be so remembered.

I was reminded of this on my very sad return to Parliament in May 2016, seven years after I exited its precincts on my retirement as an MP.

Incidentally, like much else in life, knowing when to bow out and leave the stage is an important but underrated political skill. It is also far better to jump off than to be pushed out. So, I stood down as party leader in 2007 and as an MP two years later, having achieved all that could be reasonably done when it came to consolidating the opposition and winning back power in the City of Cape Town in 2006 – two key goals. The party had also advanced from seven MPs to fifty under my leadership. But, having once been considered, on my debut in 1994, as indispensable to the party's growth, 13 years later I was seen by some of my one-time admirers as an obstacle to its prospects. I could read the runes!

Both for me and for the party I led, any longer at the top would, in all senses, have been a case of diminishing returns. I was much impressed by the remark of Morné du Plessis, the great rugby captain, who said, when he retired from the helm of the Springboks, 'I would rather people ask why I was no longer on the field than ask why I was still on it.' Good advice to today's political class. I was also both bored and exhausted by the high dramas and low intrigues that are the staples of political leadership. I wanted to explore some other things to do with my life after nearly 25 years in the public realm.

My brief return to Parliament in May 2016 was occasioned by the sudden passing, at the age of just 68, of a friend and colleague, Dene Smuts. There was something fitting that her commemoration was held in the Old Assembly Chamber of Parliament.

It was in the furthest reaches of the back benches there, in September 1989, that Dene and I first met as two newly elected MPs to the last tricameral parliament of this country.

RETURN TO PARLIAMENT

And it was there that Dene, as the MP for Groote Schuur, Cape Town, found her political voice and shared her singular views as South Africa went about dismantling the old order of 350 years and planted on our stony southern soil of past conflict and entrenched racism the hopeful flag of a new non-racial democracy.

In my eulogy, I suggested that new MPs would do well to look upon Dene and learn from her career. I denoted two types of politician (and perhaps some who inhabit the muddle in the middle):

> You can either be a weathervane or a signpost. If you are the former, you will twist in the wind, depend for your key advisor on the last person you spoke to or the last opinion poll you consulted. You will suck up to those in power and trim your sails to the prevailing winds of political correctness. That is the easy path of least resistance, but it usually leads, over time, downhill. Or you can be that rarer bird in the political aviary, a signpost which does not bend to the vagaries of the moment but stands for a cause greater than personal advancement or temporary vote winning, for an enduring set of principles and beliefs. Beyond argument, Dene belongs to the second category. That, incidentally, did not make her the easiest or most agreeable of colleagues, but over time she served this party and its causes with unusual distinction.

Paradoxically, Dene was the most loyal of colleagues, yet this never silenced her adamant views, which she was never afraid to express, and against all comers – the good, the great, the less than good and the downright useless. She called things as she saw them and dug in her heels whenever necessary. Too many of her colleagues, then and long after, 'go along to get along', hence the dumbing down and deterioration of our civic space.

At the dawn of democracy in 1994, the DP was reduced to very few MPs. (One wag said we held our caucus meetings in the parliamentary elevator.) I, along with a handful of colleagues and even fewer resources, had to juggle myriad tasks and a hundred commitments. This was a time, ironically, of both political survival and national renewal.

I had been elected leader of the party in May 1994. One of the early decisions of our young strategist Ryan Coetzee, who makes many appearances in this book, was that most of our available resources should be placed in the leader's office. Dene was mightily unimpressed. She told our small caucus that one 'could hear the sucking sound of our resources being pulled into the west wing', as she ironically termed the rather modest offices reserved for the DP leader on the fifth floor of the Marks Building. The tag 'west wing', after a famous TV series, stuck fast.

Dene's close involvement in writing the Constitution of South Africa also pointed to an apparent anomaly: high intelligence and hard graft sometimes trump formal qualifications. My brother Peter, a lawyer, much involved in the DP constitutional preparations, remarked to me once that Dene and the late Colin Eglin were the 'finest constitutional lawyers in the room, though in truth the one is a journalist and the other a quantity surveyor'.

Somehow, through all the occasional peaks and more often the valleys that marked the political landscape for our party in those challenging times, Dene and I forged a durable friendship, sometimes a rarity in the snake pit of politics. I once told her that we were like an old married couple – a lot of quarrels, much affection and an occasional diplomatic loss of hearing!

On the hard-graft side, Dene also practised the 'mathematics of legislating', as she once described it. This is the line-by-line work, in hours of committee proceedings, required to improve so many bills, about everything from the Truth and Reconciliation Commission to the right to public information, on which she laboured and which defined the age of a new democracy. There were so many fine moments and so many finest hours.

One of them has application here and now, decades after its occurrence.

In the heady early days of democracy in Parliament, around 1995,

RETURN TO PARLIAMENT

Dene Smuts looked quizzically as another apparatchik arrived before the portfolio committee on which she served, which interrogated the so-called Chapter 9 state institutions 'supporting constitutional democracy'. The hapless IEC was among their number, although it was the head of another, the Commission for Gender Equality, who demanded of the committee more money to effect its work (with little sign of achievement then or now). She incurred a vintage Dene Smuts smackdown.

Dene advised the commission head, 'You don't need a larger budget but what you do need to be effective is a good brain between your ears and a sturdy pen in your hand.' No doubt today she would have been 'cancelled' for such a comment – not that Dene would mind. And her truth lives on as ever more cadre-filled wagons are hitched to an overburdened gravy train.

I recall also a glorious Cape Town summer afternoon on 26 March 1998. Parliament that day, in the radiant presence of President Nelson Mandela, hosted the first (and to date, only) address from a serving US President, Bill Clinton, then in his second term of office. He was on a long trip to Africa in the aftermath of the Monica Lewinsky scandal.

The speaker, Frene Ginwala, chose Dene to deliver the vote of thanks after Clinton's stirring speech. She appeared in a shimmering white outfit and delivered a speech of grace and concision. Afterwards, when Mandela introduced me to Clinton, he remarked to me, 'That lady is from your party? Damn fine speech she made just now.'

In her remarks that day, Dene reminded President Clinton of a speech delivered by another famous US politician in Cape Town on 6 June 1966. It was the Day of Affirmation speech of Senator Robert F Kennedy at the University of Cape Town. The words she chose from the speech also appear on Kennedy's memorial in Arlington National Cemetery:

> Few will have the greatness to bend history; but each of us can work to change a small portion of the events, and in the total of all these acts will be written the history of this generation ... Each time a man stands up for an ideal,

or acts to improve the lot of others, or strikes out against injustice, he sends forth a tiny ripple of hope, and crossing each other from a million different centres of energy and daring those ripples build a current which can sweep down the mightiest walls of oppression and resistance.

This book is dedicated to the memory of Dene Smuts and to two other liberal colleagues and staunch friends of that era, James Selfe and Greg Krumbock, who also died long before their time.

James served two decades as party executive chair – 'cleaning out the lavatories', as Douglas Gibson called this essential and unglamorous job. Greg was first party CEO and for many years afterwards its national campaign manager, a post he held when he died in 2024.

They both, often outside the public gaze, built an organisation and helped transform a marginal political party on the edge of oblivion into the second-largest political force in the country, which today helps govern South Africa. I also had the sad duty to give the eulogy at their respective memorial services.

These three builders of democracy, and countless others across time and in different places, stood fast for an ideal and struck out against injustice. In politics and beyond, myriad acts large and small send forth tiny ripples of hope and much more.

The final lines of *Middlemarch* make it clear that these works do not always require acts of public visibility. George Eliot wrote of her heroine, Dorothea Brooke, 'Her full nature, like that river of which Cyrus broke the strength, spent itself in channels which had no great name on the earth ... for the growing good of the world is partly dependent on unhistoric acts.'

I do hope that any reader of this book, in whatever field of endeavour, will convert ripples of hope into waves of purpose that crash through the barriers of cynicism, prejudice and ignorance.

And that each, in their own way, will either perform 'unhistoric acts ... for the growing good of the world' or help write the history of their generation.

Acknowledgements

My sincere thanks to Alfred LeMaitre for his editing, and to Jeremy Boraine, Eugene Ashton and the team at Jonathan Ball Publishers for their professionalism. Grateful appreciation to Paul Boughey and the team at Resolve Communications for providing me time away from the office to complete this book. Finally, to Michal, my indomitable wife, as ever my indispensable muse, thanks.

Notes

Introduction
1. Roger Cohen, *An Affirming Flame: Meditations on Life and Politics* (Knopf, 2023), p 7.

Chapter 1   Lunch with Arafat
1. Staff Writer, 'The cost of South Africa's misguided AIDS policies', Harvard TH Chan School of Public Health, 15 May 2009, https://hsph.harvard.edu/news/spr09aids/.
2. 'Mbeki, Leon in "snake-oil" row', SAPA, 11 August 2000.
3. Thomas L Friedman, *From Beirut to Jerusalem* (Farrar, Straus and Giroux, 1989), pp 125–126.
4. Howard Jacobson, 'Who dares to "hijack" the Holocaust?', *The New Statesman*, 12 March 2024, https://www.newstatesman.com/comment/2024/03/jonathan-glazer-zone-of-interest-oscars-speech

Chapter 2   Counting Jews with Sharon
1. David Baddiel, *Jews Don't Count* (HarperCollins, 2021), p 93.
2. Abba Eban, *Diplomacy for the Next Century* (Yale University Press, 1998), pp 50–59.
3. Daniel Finkelstein, 'Why the left has a problem with antisemitism', *The Times*, 13 February 2024.
4. Ibid.

Chapter 3   Winning Lessons from 'Loser' Peres
1. Dan Senor and Saul Singer, *Start-Up Nation: The Story of Israel's Economic Miracle* (Twelve, 2009), p xiii.
2. Ibid, p xi.
3. *The New York Times*, 30 September 2016.
4. *The New York Times*, 27 September 2016.

Chapter 4   Leadership Matters
1. Henry Kissinger *Leadership: Six Studies in World Strategy* (Allen Lane, 2022), p 414.
2. Martin Wolf, 'Global elites must heed the warning of populist rage', *Financial Times*, 19 July 2016.
3. Nick Cohen, 'Cakeism is Boris Johnson's true legacy', *The Spectator*, 12 July 2022.
4. Jason Felix, '"Mathematical hooliganism": Motsoaledi rubbishes estimation NHI will cost R1.3 trillion', News24, 9 September 2024.

Chapter 5   The Art of the Ask
1. Fitzgerald's short story 'The Rich Boy' appeared in the magazine *Red Book* in 1926.
2. Tony Leon, *On the Contrary: Leading the Opposition in a Democratic South Africa* (Jonathan Ball Publishers, 2008).
3. Donwald Pressly, 'Mbeki: Stop bad-mouthing SA', News24, 10 September 2004.

NOTES

Chapter 6   The Patrician and the Boytjie
1. Michael Cardo, *Harry Oppenheimer: Diamonds, Gold and Dynasty* (Jonathan Ball Publishers, 2023).
2. Matt Taibbi, 'The Great American Bubble Machine', *Rolling Stone*, 5 April 2010.
3. Alex Ross, 'How American racism influenced Hitler', *The New Yorker*, 23 April 2018, https://www.newyorker.com/magazine/2018/04/30/how-american-racism-influenced-hitler.
4. Alec Russell, 'South Africa's "lost leader" faces the end game', *Financial Times*, 18–19 May 2024.
5. Hilary Joffe, 'Failure narrative is strong but reforms can lead to success', *Business Day*, 24 May 2024.
6. Ann Bernstein, 'ANC's paltry jobs offer is an insult', *Sunday Times*, 7 April 2024.
7. Russell, 'South Africa's "lost leader"'.
8. 'Worse than a warzone, and the blood is on Cele's hands – Action Society on Crime Stats Q1 23/24', Action Society, 18 August 2023, https://actionsociety.co.za/worse-than-a-warzone-and-the-blood-is-on-celes-hands-action-society-on-crime-stats-q1-23-24/.

Chapter 7   Ronnie to the Rescue
1. South African Institute of Race Relations, *1992/93 Survey* (SAIRR, 1993), p 440.
2. *A Righteous Man: Nelson Mandela and the Jews of South Africa* [film], directed by Ingrid Gavshon (2000).
3. Greg Mills, 'Ronnie Kasrils' grotesque commentary on Hamas' attack reveals his lack of a moral compass', Brenthurst Foundation, 11 December 2023.

Chapter 8   Creation
1. Peggy Noonan, 'Biden can't spin his way out of this', *The Wall Street Journal*, 3 July 2024.
2. 'Fikile the Clown fails to fix, instead he struts', editorial, *Mail & Guardian*, 10 March 2022.
3. Timothy Snyder, *On Tyranny: Twenty Lessons from the Twentieth Century* (Tim Duggan Books, 2017), p 9.
4. On the details of this timeline, see Helen Zille, 'A cracked cellphone screen, chaotic document control, and the making of a new SA', News 24, 18 June 2024.

Chapter 9   Endgame
1. Pieter du Toit, 'Ramaphosa will need to get the ANC on-side, otherwise the DA could walk away', News24, 20 June 2024.
2. Hajra Omarjee, 'Tensions rise in the GNU as DA states demands', *Business Day*, 24 June 2024.
3. Peter Bruce, 'DA holds its nose as Cyril frets over cosying up to it', *Business Day*, 27 June 2024.
4. Tony Leon, 'The ANC faces its own "Sophie's Choice"', News24, 28 June 2024.
5. Peter Bruce, 'The president's prerogative? Not so much …', *Sunday Times*, 30 June 2024.

Chapter 10   Aftermath
1. 'South Africa's rand hits 13-month high on economy optimism', Bloomberg/*Daily Maverick*, 30 August 2024.

2 'Moseneke calls for review of presidential powers', News 24/*City Press*, 12 November 2014.
3 Amanda Khoza, 'Super Presidency: Meet President Ramaphosa's new eyes and ears', News24, 9 July 2024.
4 Speech by Deputy President FW de Klerk, 3 June 1996, quoted in 'FW de Klerk: the ultimate "joiner"', Inside Politics, 7 March 2013, https://inside-politics.org/2013/03/08/fw-de-klerk-the-ultimate-joiner/.
5 News24, 10 May 2024.
6 Daily Investor, 26 February 2024.
7 'Brain drain or brain gain: The NHI will either prove to be a blessing or a curse', Mancosa press release, 21 March 2024, https://www.mancosa.co.za/press-release/brain-drain-or-brain-gain-the-nhi-will-either-prove-to-be-a-blessing-or-a-curse/.
8 Victoria O'Regan, 'Ramaphosa signs Bela Bill into law, but presses pause on two controversial clauses for three months', *Daily Maverick*, 13 September 2024.
9 See, for example, Natasha Marrian, 'An X-word trigger that fires a blank', *Financial Mail*, 30 January 2025.
10 'Addressing Egregious Actions of The Republic of South Africa', Presidential Actions, executive order, 7 February 2025, https://www.whitehouse.gov/presidential-actions/2025/02/addressing-egregious-actions-of-the-republic-of-south-africa/.

Chapter 11   Fractures and Finesses
1 Adriaan Basson, 'Cabinet's rogues' gallery grows as Ramaphosa declines to act', News24, 21 January 2025.
2 Jason Felix, 'Opposition parties want Ramaphosa to act against Ntshavheni after R2.5m tender fraud charges', News24, 20 January 2025.
3 Natasha Marrian, 'Penny has yet to drop for failing ANC as it runs out of voter currency', *Business Day*, 30 August 2024.
4 Zimasa Matiwane, '"These outbursts are shocking": SACP, ANC leaders clash over GNU', *Sunday Times*, 1 September 2024.
5 'Roman Dutch law forced down our throats with genocidal force – John Hlophe', speech to Parliament by John Hlophe, 19 July 2024, Politicsweb, 5 August 2024, https://www.politicsweb.co.za/documents/roman-dutch-law-forced-down-our-throats-with-genoc.
6 'State capture architects sworn in as MPs an insult – George Michalakis', Politicsweb, 28 August 2024, https://www.politicsweb.co.za/documents/state-capture-architects-sworn-in-as-mps-an-insult.
7 Denene Erasmus, 'Number of unemployed people rises to 8.4-million record high', *Business Day*, 14 August 2024.
8 Fred McMahon, *The Road to Growth: How Lagging Economies Become Prosperous* (Atlantic Institute for Market Studies, 2000).
9 'An interview with Paul Romer on economic growth', econlib.org, 5 November 2007, https://www.econlib.org/library/Columns/y2007/Romergrowth.html.

Chapter 13   The Interview
1 James de Villiers, 'Saturday Profile: Former DA leader Tony Leon: "Checking your privilege is absolute garbage"', News24, 3 April 2021.

NOTES

2 Tony Leon, *Future Tense: Reflections on My Troubled Land* (Jonathan Ball Publishers, 2021), p 28.

Chapter 14 Two Weeks Hate
1 James Myburgh, 'The Two Weeks Hate and Tony Leon', Politicsweb, 12 April 2021, https://www.politicsweb.co.za/opinion/the-two-weeks-hate-and-tony-leon.
2 Mark Mazower, '*How Democracy Ends* by David Runciman review – what Trump and Corbyn have in common', *The Guardian*, 21 June 2018.

Chapter 15 What If?
1 Thomas Carlyle, *On Heroes, Hero-worship, & the Heroic in History* (James Fraser, 1841), p 1.
2 Tony Leon, *Opposite Mandela: Encounters with South Africa's Icon* (Jonathan Ball Publishers, 2014).
3 Leon, *Future Tense*.
4 Amos Elon, *The Pity of it All: A History of Jews in Germany, 1743–1933* (Metropolitan Books, 2002), p 11.

Chapter 16 FW de Klerk's Needle-threading
1 Heribert Adam, Frederik van Zyl Slabbert and Kogila Moodley, *Comrades in Business: Post-Liberation Politics in South Africa* (Tafelberg Publishers, 1998), p 53.
2 Jonathan Freedland, 'The Enigma of Ariel Sharon', *New York Review of Books*, 21 December 2006.
3 Anthony Sampson, *Mandela: The Authorised Biography* (HarperCollins, 1999), pp 464–465.
4 Daniel Byman and Kenneth M Pollack, 'Beyond Great Forces: How Individuals Still Shape History', *Foreign Affairs*, November/December 2019.

Chapter 17 Nelson Mandela's Mask
1 'The State, Property Relations and Social Transformation', *Umrabulo* (third quarter, 1998); quoted by James Myburgh, *The Last Jacobins of Africa: Thabo Mbeki and the Making of the New South Africa* (unpublished manuscript, 2007), p 117.
2 Leon, *On the Contrary*, pp 279–280.
3 Sampson, *Mandela: The Authorised Biography*, p 352.
4 Leon, *Opposite Mandela*, p 188.
5 Nelson Mandela, *Conversations with Myself* (Pan Macmillan, 2010), p xvi.
6 Jonny Steinberg, *Winnie & Nelson: Portrait of a Marriage* (Jonathan Ball Publishers, 2023), p 438.
7 Ibid, p 460.
8 Ibid, p 409.
9 'Shell House Massacre March 28 1994: The inquest findings', Politicsweb, 28 March 2014, https://www.politicsweb.co.za/documents/shell-house-massacre-march-28-1994-the-inquest-fin.
10 *Cape Times*, 2 June 1995.
11 Richard Stengel, *Mandela's Way: Fifteen Lessons on Life, Love, and Courage* (Crown Publishers, 2010), pp 5–7.

Chapter 18   Mangosuthu Buthelezi's Need
1   Mondli Makhanya, 'Fake grief from Ramaphosa and others is not being loyal to the truth', *City Press*, 17 September 2023.
2   John Carlin, 'Mangosuthu Buthelezi: The smiling villain stained with the blood of thousands of Zulus', *The Sunday Times*, 10 September 2023.
3   Anthea Jeffery, 'Mangosuthu Gatsha Buthelezi (1928–2023)', Politicsweb, 10 September 2023, https://www.politicsweb.co.za/opinion/mangosuthu-gatsha-buthelezi-19282023.

Chapter 19   'Nostalgia Isn't What it Used to Be'
1   Matthew Kentridge, *The Soho Chronicles: 10 Films by William Kentridge* (Seagull Books, 2015).
2   David Remnick, 'Danse macabre', *The New Yorker*, 13 March 2013.
3   Thomas Mallon, 'What if nostalgia isn't what it used to be?', *The New Yorker*, 20 November 2023.
4   Niall Ferguson, 'For Trump it's a stellar moment – or epic fail', *The Times*, 13 August 2017, https://www.thetimes.com/article/for-trump-its-a-stellar-moment-or-epic-fail-f8gp9h9ml?region=global.
5   Stefan Zweig, *Decisive Moments in History: Twelve Historical Miniatures* (Ariadne Press, 2007).

Chapter 20   A Personal Pentimento: Fresh Paint on Old Signs
1   *Sunday Times*, 19 December 2004.
2   Judith Rich Harris, *The Nurture Assumption: Why Children Turn Out the Way They Do* (The Free Press, 1998).
3   Jonathan Freedland, *The Escape Artist* (John Murray, 2022), p 306.
4   'The Great Political Fictions: Tim Rice on *Evita*', episode of podcast *Past Present Future*, 4 August 2024.
5   Jill Hedges, *Argentina: A Modern History* (IB Tauris, 2011), p 109.
6   Tomás Eloy Martínez, *Santa Evita* (Seix Barral, 1995).
7   VS Naipaul, *The Return of Eva Perón with The Killings in Trinidad* (Knopf, 1980), p 166.
8   Ibid.
9   Tim du Plessis, 'South Africa and Argentina' [translation], *Beeld*, 16 April 2010.
10 Ryan Dube, 'Milei looks for Trump to help "Make Argentina Great Again"', *The Wall Street Journal*, 18 November 2024.
11 Max Hastings, *Vietnam: An Epic Tragedy, 1945–1975* (HarperCollins, 2018).
12 Kristen Bialik, 'Asian countries on Trump's trip have largely positive views of US but disagree on policy', Pew Research Center, 3 November 2017, https://www.pewresearch.org/short-reads/2017/11/03/opinions-in-asian-countries-on-trump-trip/.
13 Wolfgang Munchau, *Kaput: The End of the German Miracle* (Swift Press, 2024).
14 Leo Lewis, 'Japan's native population declines at record rate as births plunge', *Financial Times*, 13–14 April 2024.
15 Sasha Rogelberg, 'Japan's population is getting so old that a diaper manufacturer is only making products for adults, not babies', *Fortune*, 28 March 2024.

Index

A
Ackerman, Dirk 56
ActionSA 151–152
Adelstein, Jake 241
AfD *see* Alternative für Deutschland
African National Congress (ANC) 5, 11, 25–26, 45, 48, 53, 56, 58–62, 67–81, 83–100, 102–122, 124–131, 136–137, 149–141, 143–144, 147–154, 156–158, 163, 167, 171, 179, 182–183, 186–187, 189, 192, 197–203, 209, 229–230, 235
  see also national working committee (NWC); national executive committee (NEC)
AfriForum 144–146
Afrikaans mother-tongue education 91, 143–147
Afrikaners 148, 179, 184, 219
  see also Basic Education Laws Amendment Act (BELA)
Al Jama-ah 112
Allen, Woody 4, 66
Alternative für Deutschland (AfD) 172, 238
ANC *see* African National Congress
Anglo American plc 45, 48, 51–52, 106
apartheid 18, 46, 49, 60, 155, 162–163, 175, 180, 184–185, 193, 196, 198–199, 218, 220, 235
Arafat, Yasser 9–10, 12–20, 22, 26–27
Argentina 4, 87, 225–232, 245
authoritarianism 157, 162, 176, 210, 226, 235

B
Baddiel, David 22–23
Basic Education Laws Amendment Act (BELA) 91, 143–146
Basson, Adriaan 149
BEE *see* black economic empowerment
BELA *see* Basic Education Laws Amendment Act
Ben Gurion, David 31–32, 34
Berlin 4, 15, 236, 238–240
Bernstein, Ann 55, 157

Bill of Rights 81
Bishop, Michael 97
black economic empowerment (BEE) 79, 119
Blair, Tony 16, 34
Bloom, Jack 203
Bosasa 150
Botha, Andries 77
Botha, Dominique 77–79, 93–94, 109
Botha, PW 175, 179, 183
Botha, Sandra 77–78, 109
Brandt, Willy 201, 237
Brexit 37, 164, 208
Brink, Cilliers 151–152
Broers, Alec 43
Bruce, Peter 120, 126, 229
Buenos Aires 183, 225, 227–230
Bush, George HW 65
Bush, George W 15, 129, 203
Business Day 54, 116, 121
Business Unity South Africa 141
Buthelezi, Mangosuthu 69, 176–177, 182, 195–204
Buthelezi, Thulasizwe 93

C
Cabanac, Roman 133–134
cabinet 13, 26, 35, 50, 59, 61–62, 66, 69, 74–75, 77, 86, 90–91, 93, 96, 97–99, 102–103, 106–110, 112–113, 116–117, 119–127, 129, 131–140, 142, 145, 149–150, 152, 154, 179, 181, 187, 201–202
  see also government of national unity (GNU)
cabinet clusters 136–137
cadre deployment (ANC) 56, 111, 186, 248
cakeism 36, 38–39, 196
Camp David 14, 16, 26
'cancel culture' 4, 249
Cape Town 5, 11–12, 20, 22, 35, 60, 80, 88, 94–95, 98, 103, 111, 130, 152, 184, 195, 207, 217, 246–247, 249
capitalism 4, 26, 37, 234–235
Cardo, Michael 50

Carlin, John 198
Carlyle, Thomas 36, 175
Castro, Fidel 25
censorship 162
Centre for Risk Analysis 150
Chávez, Hugo 25, 77, 156
China 153, 183, 232
Chinese Communist Party 211
Churchill, Winston 10, 31, 74
City Press 198
Clifton Preparatory School 217–218, 221
Clinton, Bill 14–15, 30, 35, 188, 249
'Coalition for Change' 201–204
coalition government 5, 72, 75, 91–92, 215
  see also government of national unity (GNU)
Codesa *see* Convention for a Democratic South Africa
Coetzee, Johann 88
Coetzee, Ryan 11, 70–72, 74, 82, 88–89, 105–107, 109–110, 115, 118, 124, 135, 167, 248
Cohen, Nick 39
Cohen, Roger 5–6
Cold War 25, 138, 183, 219, 238
colonialism 11, 233
Commission for Gender Equality 249
Commission on Growth and Development 157–158
communism 59, 183, 1984, 208–209, 211, 233–235
concentration camps 224, 238
'confidence and supply' 72–75, 86, 92, 135
Conservative Party 180
Conservative Party (UK) 38–39, 171
Constitution of South Africa 56, 69, 73, 81–82, 95, 124, 134, 138, 147, 154–155, 182, 248
Convention for a Democratic South Africa (Codesa) 59, 66, 76, 86, 90, 181, 191, 201
cooperative governance 86
corporal punishment 221–224
corruption 14, 55, 67–68, 72, 81, 85, 115, 124, 137, 149–151, 164, 228–229, 231, 238
Congress of South African Trade Unions (Cosatu) 94, 104, 154

Covid-19 55, 223
Creecy, Barbara 122
Cuba 25, 231

D
DA *see* Democratic Alliance
Da Nang 231–233
Davis, Dennis 76
Davis, Mick 127
De Beer, Zach 49–50
De Klerk, Elita 182
De Klerk, FW 3, 30, 32, 34, 66, 77, 91, 138, 175–185, 190–191, 197, 200
De Klerk, Jan (father of FW) 183
De Klerk, Jan (son of FW) 184
De Klerk, Wimpie 183
De Lille, Patricia 119
Delport, Tertius 181
democracy 46, 56, 66–67, 106, 133, 139, 157, 172, 175–178, 188–189, 193, 196, 198, 201, 203, 234–235, 237–238, 242, 247–250
Democracy (play) 237–238
Democratic Alliance (DA) F5, 11, 43, 45, 51, 61–62, 65–66, 68–69, 71–74, 76–77, 80–81, 84–86, 88–89, 90–94, 96–100, 103–110, 112–123, 124–140, 142–155, 157, 166–168, 182, 201–202, 204, 216, 236
Democratic Party (DP) 44, 49–51, 56, 66, 71, 179–180, 182, 187–189, 192–193, 247–248
De Villiers, James 165
Dickinson, Joshua 103
Didiza, Thoko 100
Dlamini, Marshall 124
DP *see* Democratic Party
Du Plessis, Barend 183
Du Plessis, Morné 246
Du Plessis, Tim 229–230
Durban 9, 50–51, 59, 83, 87, 100, 106, 161, 168, 202, 204, 217–221
Du Toit, Pieter 104
Du Toit, Steve 83

E
Eban, Abba 7, 16, 23
Economic Freedom Fighters (EFF) 68–69, 72, 74, 76–77, 80–83, 86–88, 92–93, 96, 111, 118, 120, 122, 124–125, 128, 130, 145, 151–156, 163, 229

INDEX

Eglin, Colin 49, 153, 178, 248
election, general 66–67, 69, 215–217
Ellis, Mike 234
Enthoven, Adi 77–78, 84, 90, 94–95
Erekat, Saeb 15–16
Eskapa, Shirley 58
EU *see* European Union
European Commission 38
European Union (EU) 38–39
Evita 225–229, 231
Expropriation Act (also Bill) 146, 147, 148

F
'fake news' 80, 110
FDP *see* Free Democratic Party
Ferguson, Niall i, 211
Financial Times 14, 36, 48, 54
Finkelstein, Daniel 25–26
Fortune, Charles 218
France 37, 208, 232
Frank, Anne 223
Franschhoek Literary Festival (FLF) 223
Frayn, Michael 237
Free Democratic Party (FDP) 236–238
Freedland, Jonathan 180, 223–224
Freedom Front Plus 88, 112, 124
Friedman, Thomas 17–18, 27
fundraising 43–46

G
Gadd, Alan 214
Garrun, Cliff 114
Garrun, Kim 114
Gauteng 84, 88, 102, 111, 127, 145, 149, 151–152
Gaza 10, 14, 18, 22, 24, 26
GDP *see* gross domestic product
genocide 24, 62
George, Dion 126, 136
Germany 4, 115, 172, 176, 236–239, 241
Gibson, Douglas 44, 46, 101, 250
Ginwala, Frene 249
GNU *see* government of national unity
Godongwana, Enoch 80, 84, 90–91, 127
Godsell, Bobby 106
Goldberg, Denis 60
Goldstone Commission 60
Gomes, Peter 216
Good Party 112
Gorbachev, Mikhail 30, 183

Gordhan, Pravin 76
government of national unity (GNU) (1994–1996) 71, 82, 91, 133, 137–140, 200
government of national unity (GNU) (2024–2025) 5, 72, 77, 85, 88–92, 96, 98–100, 102–105, 107–110, 116, 120–121, 124–125, 129–133, 136–140, 144–145, 147, 150, 153–154, 156, 165, 211, 215
Graham, Philip 70
gross domestic product (GDP) 55, 81, 233, 235
Gumede, William 137
Gupta family 68
Gwala, Harry 199
Gwarube, Siviwe 70, 72–73, 75, 85, 97, 107, 115, 126, 143–144, 146

H
Hamas 10, 13, 18, 22, 24–26, 62, 153
Harris, Cyril 60
Harris, Judith Rich 220
Harvard University 129, 211, 216
Hastings, Max 232
Healey, Denis 35
Herman, 'Chookie' 49
Hill-Lewis, Geordin 80, 100, 119
Hitchens, Christopher 199
Hitler, Adolf 238–239
HIV/Aids 11, 201
Hlabisa, Velokosini 196
Hlophe, John 155
Holman, Michael 14
human rights 62, 227

I
IEC *see* Independent Electoral Commission
IFP *see* Inkatha Freedom Party
Independent Electoral Commission (IEC) 69, 216–217
Independent Media 76, 109, 163
inflation 38, 218, 228, 231
Inkatha Freedom Party (IFP) 69, 72–73, 87, 93, 96–97, 102, 136, 192, 195–196, 198–199, 201
International Court of Justice 24
Iran 25, 37, 153
Iraq 16, 129, 203, 242

Israel 9–26, 28–34, 36, 40, 61–62, 75, 79, 172, 180, 215, 245
Israel Forum 10, 29

J
Jacobson, Howard 19
Jaffe, Abe 58–59, 61–62
Jaffe, Hilary 58–59, 61–62
Japan, Japanese 4, 233, 239–241
Jeffery, Anthea 199
Jerusalem 10, 12, 14, 17–18, 22, 29
Jews 17–18, 20–21, 23–25, 27, 37, 49, 60–62, 223–224, 238
Joffe, Hilary 54
Johannesburg 29, 45, 50, 52, 54–55, 59, 65–66, 70, 72–73, 78, 83–84, 88–89, 94–95, 101, 111, 114, 124, 163, 165, 186, 192, 213, 217, 219
Johnson, Boris 38, 196, 208
Johnson, Paul 34–35
Jonker, Elzanne 97
Juncker, Jean-Claude 38–39

K
Kadima (Going Forward) 22
kaDinuzulu, Solomon 200
Kahn, Meyer 52–53, 55–57
Kanazawa 236, 239–241
Kasrils, Ronnie 58–62
Katz, Michael 101
Kearsney College 83, 221, 225
Keating, Paul 29
Kekana, Nkenke 72, 79, 84, 95
Kennedy, Robert F 249
Kentridge, Matthew 207
Kentridge, William 207–209
Kern Affair 21
Kern, Cyril 20–22
Kingsmead 217–218
Kirchner, Cristina Fernández de 227–228, 229–230
Kirchner, Nestór 227
Kissinger, Henry 35–36, 46, 75
Kok, Marizanne 87
Kotane, Moses 209
Krumbock, Greg 250
KwaZulu-Natal 68–69, 73, 78, 84, 88, 92–93, 102, 111, 156, 199–201, 204

L
Labour Party (Israel) 30
Lamola, Ronald 84, 86, 105, 127, 136

Larsen, Annika 131
Lawry, Bill 217
le Carré, John 10–12
Lees, Patrick 225
Leon, Jacqueline 50
Leon, Michal Even (Zahav) 10, 20, 22, 29, 79, 100, 109, 121, 123, 162, 182, 202, 215, 223, 227, 240–241, 251
Leon, Peter 165–166, 248
Leon, Ray 9, 18, 50, 161–164, 168
Leon, Sheila 9, 162, 202, 220, 236
Leon, Tony
  ambassador 4, 87, 183, 225–227, 229, 232
  books 165–168, 176–177, 188–189
  Clifton Preparatory School 217–221
  on FW de Klerk 182–187
  Kearsney College 83, 221–225
  on Mangosuthu Buthelezi 195–204
  MP 176, 180–181, 189–190, 215, 246–250
  municipal councillor 213–214
  on Nelson Mandela 187–194, 200
  offered cabinet position 66, 91, 187
Le Roux, Michiel 167
Lesotho 203
Lesufi, Panyaza 88, 102, 127, 145, 147, 151–152
Liberal Democratic Party 136
Liberal International 18
Liebenberg, Chris 56
Likud Party 21–22, 30
Lloyd Webber, Andrew 225–226
load shedding 26, 54, 67
Lotriet, Annelie 100

M
Mackay, Graham 52
Macpherson, Dean 87, 126, 147–148, 153, 165
Madikizela-Mandela, Winnie 168, 190
Mafikeng 186, 188–189, 191, 193
MAGA *see* 'Make America Great Again'
Magwenya, Vincent 105
Maharaj, Mac 181, 183, 184
Mail & Guardian 78, 163
Maimane, Mmusi 166–171
'Make America Great Again' (MAGA) 209–210, 226
Makhanya, Mondli 198, 229

INDEX

Makhura, David 84, 88, 90, 92, 95–96, 105
Malan, Wynand 179–180
Malatsi, Solly 127
Malema, Julius 68, 156
Mallon, Thomas 210
Mandela, Nelson 3, 32, 34, 44, 54, 56, 60, 66, 91, 101, 133, 140, 147, 168, 175–177, 179–182, 186–194, 196–197, 199–200, 202–203, 249
Mantashe, Gwede 72, 80, 84–87, 119, 150, 154
Manuel, Trevor 157
Mapaila, Solly 154–155
Marikana massacre 185, 208
Marks, JB 209
Marrian, Natasha 150
Marxism, Marxists 61, 175
Mashaba, Herman 151
Mashatile, Paul 72, 74, 79–80, 84, 119, 149
Masondo, David 154
Mazower, Mark 171–172
Mbalula, Fikile 13, 72, 75, 78–80, 84, 103, 105, 108, 110–111, 113, 124
Mbeki, Thabo 11, 23, 45–46, 59, 147, 166, 186, 188–189, 201–203
McKenzie, Gayton 72, 88
media, press 21, 79, 81, 90–91, 99, 114, 116, 150, 165, 171, 189, 230
medical aid funds 141–143
 see also National Health Insurance (NHI)
Meyer, Ivan 70, 72, 75, 85, 99, 122
Meyer, Roelf 76, 81, 133
Middle East 4, 10, 12, 17, 23, 27, 32, 36, 40
Milei, Javier 231
Millen, Sarah Gertrude 94
mining 45, 48, 51, 106, 118
MK *see* Umkhonto we Sizwe
MKP *see* Umkhonto we Sizwe Party
Mokonyane, Nomvula 72, 85
Moseneke, Dikgang 133
mother-tongue education 91, 144, 146
 see also Basic Education Laws Amendment Act (BELA)
Motsoaledi, Aaron 140–144
Mpofu, Dali 156
Msimang, Mendi 50

Mthethwa, Nathi 208–209, 211
Munchau, Wolfgang 238
Myburgh, James 169–170, 189–190
Myers, Leslie 219

N

Naím, Moisés 225
Naipaul, VS 228–229
National Assembly (Parliament) 89–90, 98, 100, 108, 131–132, 138, 145, 153
National Council of Provinces 192
'national democratic revolution' 74, 138, 158, 188
national executive committee (NEC) 72, 76, 83, 90, 104, 109, 149–150
National Freedom Party (NFP) 73, 93
National Health Insurance Act 140–141
National Health Insurance (NHI) 39, 69, 140–143, 145–147, 235
nationalism 37, 156, 226
National Party (NP) 49, 51, 53, 76, 119, 175, 179–181, 183, 187, 189, 193, 196, 209, 214, 219
 see also New National Party (NNP)
National Prosecuting Authority (NPA) 85, 134
National Treasury 86, 153
national working committee (NWC) 80–82
NATO 38, 210
Nazis 172, 176, 224, 237–238, 241
NEC *see* national executive committee
Nel, Andries 84, 99
Nelson Mandela Foundation 189–190
Netanyahu, Benjamin 26, 28, 34, 172, 245
Netshitenzhe, Joel 188–189
New National Party (NNP) 44–45, 51, 66, 71, 138, 182, 187
 see also National Party (NP)
News24 94, 104, 121, 149, 165–167
New York Times, The 5, 17
NFP *see* National Freedom Party
NHI *see* National Health Insurance
Nixon, Richard 75, 182
NNP *see* New National Party
Noonan, Peggy 65–66
North Vietnam 232, 235
nostalgia 207–208
NP *see* National Party
NPA *see* National Prosecuting Authority

Ntshavheni, Khumbudzo 150
Ntuli, Thami 102
NWC *see* national working committee
Nzimande, Blade 154

O

Observer, The 188
Operation Vulindlela 81
Oppenheimer, Bridget 50–51
Oppenheimer, Ernest 49–50, 52
Oppenheimer, Harry 35, 49–52
Oslo Accords 32–33
O'Sullivan, Meghan 129
Oz, Amos 19

P

PA *see* Patriotic Alliance
PAC *see* Pan Africanist Congress
Pahad, Essop 202
Palestine, Palestinians 10–12, 14, 16, 18–19, 23, 32, 62, 79
Palestinian Authority 10, 13–14
Pan Africanist Congress (PAC) 112
Pandor, Naledi 25, 127
Parliament 49–51, 59, 66, 68, 72–73, 75, 77, 79, 82, 84, 94, 96–99, 102, 110, 122, 128, 133, 135–137, 139, 142, 148, 151, 153, 155–156, 166–167, 171, 178–180, 182, 192–193, 196, 201, 215, 223, 245–248
Parris, Matthew 171
Passenger Rail Agency of South Africa (Prasa) 155
Patel, Ebrahim 112
Patriotic Alliance (PA) 72, 88, 112
Peres, Shimon 27–34, 36
Perón, Evita 4, 226, 228–229
Perón, Isabel 226
Perónist movement 227–231, 245
Perón, Juan Domingo 226–229
Pew Research Center 233
PFP *see* Progressive Federal Party
Philp, Rowan 220
Pietermaritzburg 83, 201, 221
Politicsweb 169, 199
Pollak, Joel 22
populism 4, 36–37, 53, 68–69, 87–88, 130, 145, 147, 156–157, 172, 226, 228, 245
Potchefstroom 128, 180

Potgieter, Fébé 84, 86, 88, 90, 94, 99, 114, 131–132
Powell, Enoch 171
Prasa *see* Passenger Rail Agency of South Africa
Presidency 44, 53–55, 59, 68–69, 72, 98, 103, 114, 122, 134–137, 146–148, 150, 153, 155, 180–181, 186–188, 193, 200, 203, 226
presidential prerogatives 131–132
Pretoria 12, 20, 52, 81, 103–104, 121, 144, 151
Progressive Federal Party (PFP) 213–214
Progressive Party 49, 168, 219–220, 225
property rights 81, 148, 155, 201
  see also Expropriation Act
proportionality 93, 96–97, 99, 108, 113, 116–117, 119
protectionism 37–38, 112, 228
public service 81, 103, 113
Putin, Vladimir 78, 153, 208, 239

Q

Qatar 25–26

R

Rabin, Yitzhak 15, 27, 30
racism 37, 76, 170, 189, 220, 225, 247
'radical economic transformation' 76
Ramallah 10, 12–13, 17–18
Ramaphosa, Cyril 13, 34, 54–55, 68–69, 72–73, 76, 80–82, 84, 86, 89–91, 95, 97–100, 102–104, 106–109, 111, 113, 115–122, 123–127, 132–135, 137, 140–148, 150, 152–153, 156–158, 184–185, 197–198, 216–217
Ramokgopa, Gwen 85
Ramokgopa, Maropene 135
Reagan, Ronald 34, 65, 197, 209
Remnick, David 208
Resolve Communications 111, 251
Rhodesia 219
  see also Zimbabwe
Rice, Tim 225
Richards, Barry 218
Rivlin, Ruvi 30
Rodgers, Francois 93
Romer, Paul 158
Rubinstein, Amnon 18
rule of law 82, 124
Russell, Alec 54–55

INDEX

Russell, Audrey Hamilton 109
Russia 25, 28, 68, 78, 93, 153, 208, 239–240

S

SAB *see* South African Breweries
Sachs, Albie 60
SACP *see* South African Communist Party
SAPS *see* South African Police Service
Sartre, Jean-Paul 147
Sarupen, Ashor 153
Schmidt, Helmut 32
School Ties 224–225
Schreiber, Leon 75, 99, 103, 115, 126, 153
Schultz, Paul 9, 236
Schwarz, Harry 213–214, 239
Segev, Tom 33
Seitlholo, Sello 128
Selfe, James 101, 105–106, 223, 250
Sharon, Ariel 15–17, 20–27, 30–31, 34, 180
Sharon, Gilad 21
Shivambu, Floyd 80, 100, 156
Simelane, Thembi 150
Sisulu, Lindiwe 80
Slabbert, Frederik van Zyl 45, 55, 180, 189, 214
Slack, Sandy 44
Slovo, Joe 60, 86
Smith, Mervyn 60–61
Smuts, Dene 101, 246, 248–250
Smuts, Jan 51, 53
Snyder, Timothy 91
social grants 39, 142
socialism 209, 226, 233
social media 76, 80, 113–114, 162, 164, 169, 172
Solidarity 144–146
South African Breweries (SAB) 52–53, 55–56
South African Communist Party (SACP) 59, 94, 104, 154, 209
South African Institute of Race Relations 199
South African Jewish Board of Deputies 60
South African Jewish Museum 60
South African Medical Association 142
South African Police Service (SAPS) 56–57

South African Reserve Bank 81, 134, 156
Southern African Development Community 203
Soviet Union (USSR) 115, 172, 183–184, 199, 208–209
Sowetan 170
Special Investigating Unit 150
Spectator, The 38–39
Spence, Michael 157
Spier Initiative 23
Springbok Radio 220
Springboks 218, 246
Stalin, Joseph 208–209
Starmer, Keir 34
statement of intent, GNU 96–97, 101, 104–105, 113, 116–117, 122, 124, 132, 145–146
state-owned enterprises (companies) 55, 136, 141, 217
Steenhuisen, John 65, 70–71, 75, 82, 86, 95, 96–100, 103–104, 106–107, 109, 111–116, 118, 119–126, 133, 137, 142, 144, 202
Steenhuisen, Olivia 121
Steenhuisen, Terry 121
Steinberg, Jonny 190–191
'Stellenbosch Mafia' 44, 229
Stengel, Richard 193
Strijdom, JG 183
'sufficient consensus' 90, 96–99, 131–132, 145
Sunday Times 87, 125
Sunday Times, The (UK) 58, 198
Sunday World 87, 109
Survé, Iqbal 76, 109, 163
Sutcliffe, Tim 217, 220–221
Suzman, Helen 49, 219

T

tariffs 38, 210
Tau, Parks 72, 84, 86, 88, 90, 92, 127
taxation 26, 39, 135, 141–142
 see also National Health Insurance (NHI)
Tel Aviv 18, 30
tenders 111, 119, 149
Thatcher, Margaret 34, 197, 230
Theron, SDJ 163
Times, The (London) 25
Tokyo 240–241

263

trade unions 35, 85, 94, 126, 144, 154
  see also Cosatu; Solidarity
trade wars 38, 210
Trahar, Tony 45–46, 48
Transnet 120, 155
Treurnicht, Andries 180
Trump, Donald 4, 34–37, 148, 153, 164, 172, 209–211, 225, 231, 233, 245
Truss, Liz 34
Tshwane 151–152
Tshwete, Steve 198
Turok, Ben 60
Twitter (now X) 80, 104, 161, 163, 168–169, 171
two-state solution 14, 23, 32–33
Tyson, Mike 84, 89

U
UDF *see* United Democratic Front
Ukraine 35, 57, 78, 208, 239
USSR *see* Soviet Union
Ulundi 197, 200–201, 204
Umkhonto we Sizwe (MK) 59
Umkhonto we Sizwe Party (MKP, or MK) 68–69, 72, 74, 76, 80–83, 88, 92–93, 96, 118–120, 122, 129–130, 145, 153, 155, 156, 200, 229
unemployment 54, 67, 157, 235
United Democratic Front (UDF) 198
United Democratic Movement 112
United Kingdom (UK, Britain) 24, 34, 38, 136, 219
United Party 51, 219
United States of America (USA) 4, 26, 37, 58, 75, 104, 107, 115, 151, 170, 172, 183, 209–210, 232–235, 242
University of Cape Town 249
University of Natal 162
University of the Witwatersrand 54, 137, 215

V
Van Schalkwyk, Marthinus 182
Venezuela 25, 156–157, 184, 225
Venter, Rina 91
veto right 38, 131–132
Vietnam 4, 233–236
Vietnam War 232, 235–236
Vrba, Rudi 223

W
Wall Street Journal, The 66
Washington Post, The 70
Weekly Mail 215
West Bank 10, 12, 14, 18, 32–33
Westerwelle, Guido 236–237
white minority 155, 178, 181, 184, 187, 219
'white monopoly capital' 37, 229
Whitfield, Andrew 135
Winde, Alan 70, 72, 80, 82, 106, 115–116, 122, 216
wokeism 37, 123, 231
Wolf, Martin 36–38
World Bank 38, 158, 210
World Economic Forum 232
World War I 49, 167
World War II 15, 38, 232–233, 237, 239–241

X
X (formerly Twitter) 80
xenophobia 242

Y
Yom Kippur War 21, 75
Young Progressives 106

Z
Zikalala, Sihle 148
Zille, Helen 69–76, 79, 85, 88–89, 91, 93, 94–96, 98–99, 103, 105, 110–111, 113–115, 117–118, 121, 131, 144, 168, 216, 245
Zimbabwe 157, 203
  see also Rhodesia
Zionism 9, 17, 20–22
Zondo, Andrew 163
Zondo Commission 72, 85, 118, 150, 155
Zondo, Raymond 100
Zulus 68, 196–198, 204
Zuma, Jacob 4, 45, 53–55, 67–68, 78, 105, 118–119, 134, 147, 155–156, 200, 208, 217, 245
Zweig, Stefan 211–212, 215